WALKING THE JULIAN ALPS OF SLOVENIA

MOUNTAIN WALKS AND SHORT TREKS

by Roberto Lombardo

JUNIPER HOUSE, MURLEY MOSS,
OXENHOLME ROAD, KENDAL, CUMBRIA LA9 7RL
www.cicerone.co.uk

Third edition 2025
ISBN: 978 1 78631 215 0
eISBN: 978 1 78765 214 9
First edition 2005
Second edition 2015

MIX
Paper | Supporting responsible forestry
FSC® C004791
FSC www.fsc.org

Printed in Singapore by KHL Printing on responsibly sourced paper.
A catalogue record for this book is available from the British Library.
All photographs are by the author unless otherwise stated.

Route mapping by Lovell Johns www.lovelljohns.com

Cicerone's EU representative for GPSR compliance is Easy Access System Europe, Mustamäe tee 50, 10621 Tallinn, Estonia. Email gpsr.requests@easproject.com.

Updates to this guide

While every effort is made by our authors to ensure the accuracy of guidebooks as they go to print, changes can occur during the lifetime of an edition. Any updates that we know of for this guide will be on the Cicerone website (www.cicerone.co.uk/1215/updates), so please check before planning your trip. We also advise that you check information about such things as transport, accommodation and shops locally. Even rights of way can be altered over time.

The route maps in this guide are derived from publicly available data, databases and crowd-sourced data. As such they have not been through the detailed checking procedures that would generally be applied to a published map from an official mapping agency, although naturally we have reviewed them closely in the light of local knowledge as part of the preparation of this guide.

We are always grateful for information about any discrepancies between a guidebook and the facts on the ground, sent by email to updates@cicerone.co.uk.

Register your book: To sign up to receive free updates, special offers and GPX files where available, create a Cicerone account and register your purchase via the 'My Account' tab at www.cicerone.co.uk.

Front cover: The location of the Pogačnikov dom is truly spectacular (Walk 28)

CONTENTS

PREFACE

As I present this new edition of Hiking in the Julian Alps of Slovenia under the expert guidance of Roberto Lombardo, I wish to express my profound gratitude to Roy Clark and Justi Carey, whose dedication to these mountains has been the cornerstone of Cicerone Press's Julian Alps guides since 2005.

For nearly two decades, Roy and Justi's intimate knowledge – born of their years living amidst these magnificent peaks – has introduced countless walkers to Slovenia's alpine treasures. Their meticulous research, passion for the region, and commitment to providing reliable guidance has established an exceptional foundation upon which this new edition builds.

As Roberto takes the helm, he inherits not merely a guidebook but a legacy of careful stewardship. I thank Roy and Justi for their outstanding contribution to our understanding of this remarkable landscape, and for the spirit of adventure they have inspired in all who have followed their paths through the Julian Alps. I look forward to Roberto continuing this tradition and introducing even more visitors to this spectacular area in the years to come.

Joe Williams, Cicerone Publishing Director, May 2025

Signposts on the grassy shoulder of Križ (Walk 29)

Mountain safety

Every mountain walk has its dangers, and those described in this guidebook are no exception. All who walk or climb in the mountains should recognise this and take responsibility for themselves and their companions along the way. The author and publisher have made every effort to ensure that the information contained in this guide was correct when it went to press, but, except for any liability that cannot be excluded by law, they cannot accept responsibility for any loss, injury or inconvenience sustained by any person using this book.

International distress signal *(emergency only)*
Six blasts on a whistle (and flashes with a torch after dark) spaced evenly for one minute, followed by a minute's pause. Repeat until an answer is received. The response is three signals per minute followed by a minute's pause.

Helicopter rescue
The following signals are used to communicate with a helicopter:

Help needed: raise both arms above head to form a 'Y'

Help not needed: raise one arm above head, extend other arm downward

Emergency telephone numbers
The emergency services number is 112. Dial 113 for the police. The international prefix for Slovenia is 386.

Unusually for the Alps, mountain rescue is still free in Slovenia unless you are shown to have been ill-prepared or unduly negligent, in which case the charges can be fearsome. It is always strongly recommended that you take out adequate travel insurance, including cover for mountain activities.

Mountain rescue can be very expensive – be adequately insured.

Symbols used on route maps

Symbol	Meaning
	route
	alternative route
S	start point
F	finish point
SF	start/finish point
	route direction
	glacier
	woodland
	urban areas
	international border
	pass
	station/railway
	tunnel
	bus stop/station
	bridge/footbridge
	peak
	building
	cave
	manned/unmanned refuge
	water feature
	viewpoint
	cable car
	cemetary
	campsite
	hotel
	church
	castle/fort
	museum
	tourist info
P	parking
	groceries
	refreshments
	tunnel

Relief
in metres

2800–3000
2600–2800
2400–2600
2200–2400
2000–2200
1800–2000
1600–1800
1400–1600
1200–1400
1000–1200
800–1000
600–800
400–600
200–400
0–200

SCALE: 1:50,000

0 kilometres 0.5 1

0 miles 0.5

Contour lines are drawn at 25m intervals and highlighted at 100m intervals.

GPX files for all routes can be downloaded free at www.cicerone.co.uk/1215/GPX.

ROUTE SUMMARY TABLE

Walk	Name	Start/Finish	Time
Section 1 Kranjska Gora			
1	Zelenci	Kranjska Gora	3hr 45min
2	Peč (Tromeja)	Rateče	3hr 30min
3	Slap Martuljek (Martuljek waterfall)	Gozd Martuljek	3hr 15min
4	Vitranc and Ciprnik	Kranjska Gora	6hr 30min
5	Slemenova špica	Vršič pass	2hr 30min; 5hr 15min via Slatnica saddle
6	Tamar and Planica	Kranjska Gora	5–6hr
7	Mala Mojstrovka	Vršič pass	3hr 30min
8	Vrata valley	Mojstrana	5hr 45min
9	Jerebikovec	Mojstrana	4–5hr
10	Prisank	Vršič pass	6hr
11	Jalovec	Vršič pass	2 days
12	Špik	Kranjska Gora	10–11hr
Section 2 Bohinj			
13	Tour of Lake Bohinj	Ribčev Laz	3hr 45min; 5hr 45min via Savica waterfall
14	Korita Mostnice	Stara Fužina	3hr 30min
15	Pršivec	Stara Fužina	7–8hr
16	Vogel	Vogel	4–5hr
17	Črna prst	Bohinjska Bistrica	6hr
18	Spodnje Bohinjske Gore	Vogel/Polje	9hr
19	Bogatin and Mahavšček	Koča pri Savici	9hr
20	Triglav Lakes valley and Veliko Špičje	Koča pri Savici	2 days
21	Triglav – the southern approach	Stara Fužina	2 days
22	Kanjavec	Dom Planika pod Triglavom/ Koča na Doliču	5hr
Section 3 Bovec			
23	Kluže	Bovec	4hr 30min
24	Svinjak	Kal-Koritnica	5hr
25	Izvir Glijuna and Slap Virje	Bovec	2hr 15min

Distance	Grade	Ascent	Descent
14.5km	1	260m	260m
8.7km	2	660m	660m
7.6km	2	500m	500m
15.7km	2/3	1005m	1005m
4.9km; 15.9km via Slatnica saddle	2; 3 via Slatnica saddle	410m; 410m via Slatnica saddle	410m; 1200m via Slatnica saddle
21km	1	370m	370m
4.1km	3	700m	700m
19.9km	2	370m	370m
9.3km	2/3	1000m	1000m
8.3km	4	950m	950m
17.6km	4	1585m	1585m
19.1km	4	1615m	1615m
11.6km; 19.2km via Savica waterfall	1; 1/2 via Savica waterfall	205m; 530m via Savica waterfall	205m; 530m via Savica waterfall
11.3km	2	305m	305m
18.1km	3	1350m	1350m
10.4km	3	720m	720m
14.8km	3	1375m	1375m
17.3km	3	595m	1740m
22.7km	3	1455m	1455m
24.4km	4	1955m	1955m
33.5km	4	2560m	2560m
6.1km	4	475m	710m
12.3km	2	530m	530m
7.3km	3	1210m	1210m
6.6km	1	160m	160m

Walk	Name	Start/Finish	Time
26	Visoki Kanin	Kanin ski gondola	5hr
27	Soča Trail	Trenta/Bovec	6hr 30min
28	Pogačnikov dom and Kriški podi	Trenta	7hr 30min
29	Križ, Stenar and Bovški Gamsovec	Pogačnikov dom na Kriških podih	5hr 30min
30	Krn	Dom dr. Klementa Juga	9–10hr
31	Mangart	Mangartsko sedlo	5hr
Section 4 Bled			
32	Tour of Lake Bled and Osojnica	Bled	3hr 30min
33	Vintgar gorge	Bled	3hr
34	Galetovec	Bohinjska Bela	4hr 45min
35	Debela peč, Brda and Lipanski vrh	Pokljuka plateau	6hr 15min
36	Viševnik	Pokljuka plateau	3hr 45min
Section 5 Kobarid			
37	Drežniški kot	Kobarid	4hr
38	Krasji vrh	Drežniške Ravne	5hr
39	Stol	Kobarid	9–10hr
40	Matajur	Avsa village	5hr

Acknowledgements

Thank you, Martina, and thank you, my little Gaja; the time I have given to this guide I have taken from you. With your constant affection and support, you have sustained me on the trails, even more than the trekking poles and boots.

A special dedication also goes to my parents, who were always in my thoughts during my travels. They were the first to show me the way, both in life and in the mountains.

Finally, my thanks go to Justi Carey and Roy Clark, authors of the first editions of the guide and the true souls of this book, and to Joe and all the staff at Cicerone for giving me the opportunity to edit this new edition.

Distance	Grade	Ascent	Descent
6.7km	4	470m	470m
21.7km	2	220m	390m
16.8km	3	1550m	1550m
6.6km	4	815m	815m
19.8km	3	1710m	1710m
7km	4	840m	840m
9.1km	2	390m	390m
9.7km	1/2	300m	300m
12.7km	3	845m	845m
18.4km	3	1145m	1145m
6.3km	3	695m	695m
13.7km	2	545m	545m
11.4km	3	1120m	1120m
23.9km	3	1505m	1505m
12.4km	3	845m	845m

Looking down from the summit of Triglav (Walk 21)

The Soča river – one of the most beautiful rivers in the Alps (Walk 27)

INTRODUCTION

Triglav showing its classic three-headed profile, which is featured on the Slovenian flag (Walk 21)

[The Julian Alps] have become for me, after forty years' devotion to mountain scenery, the most desirable of all mountains...I believe this feeling is greatly due to their surprising quality of mystery...Triglav reigns over a dreamworld, sundered from time, full of unbelievable hidden nooks, of unsuspected passages, of sudden visions of cliffs which cannot be real. Surely there is no other mountain land like this.

T Longstaff, in a letter to Julius Kugy

Thus wrote Tom Longstaff, former president of the Alpine Club, of this mountain range at the south-eastern end of the Alpine chain that stretches across Europe. The Julian Alps are not as high as their western relations – the highest peak, Triglav, is 2864m – but they are no less imposing. The limestone scenery here is outstanding – steep rock faces plunge into forests and flower meadows, while waterfalls and rivers cascade from the cliffs only to mysteriously disappear into the bedrock and re-emerge elsewhere. Beautiful open pastures nestle beneath crags and are scattered through the forests that abound as far as the eye can see. The flowers, painted an amazing rainbow of colours, change with height and situation but always retain the same great variety of hue. The mountain walker can return here again and again and always delight in the changing landscape and seasons.

A lovely path through meadows and flowers

The main bulk of the Julian Alps lies within the borders of Slovenia, in the north-west corner of the country, with a small part of the range extending into Italy. The name was known in Roman times and is thought to be linked to the imperial Roman family of Julian. Slovenia has been called 'Europe in miniature' because this tiny country, only about half the size of Switzerland, really does have a bit of everything – coast, caves, plains and rivers – as well as some truly magnificent mountain scenery, which is the focus of this book. Although only 11% of the land area is covered by high mountains, 90% is higher than 300m above sea level, and Slovenia still proudly considers itself an Alpine country. It is hard to overestimate the place of Triglav in Slovenes' hearts; it is considered the soul of the nation and essential for all true Slovenes to climb the mountain at least once in their lives.

Triglav National Park, which contains most of the Julian Alps range, is Slovenia's only national park. Development is kept to an absolute minimum – this is an area where the walker, not the motorist, reigns supreme. The footpaths and protected routes on the mountains are well maintained and signed, and the many mountain huts are strategically placed for refreshments and overnight accommodation – so it is possible to wander for days or even weeks without descending to the valley at all. The abundant wildlife – chamois, ibex, marmots, choughs and even eagles – seem comfortable with the walkers who share their landscape, making for excellent wildlife spotting and birdwatching, and plenty of photo opportunities.

In spite of its modern cities and excellent transport networks, Slovenia still has an air of the past, when the pace of life was slower. Slovenes keep in close contact with their families and their land; in many cases, families have worked the same land for hundreds of years. Much of the population still lives in villages, where almost every house has its own vegetable patch; even in the cities, allotments are common. The country, independent since 1991, has a total population of about 2.1 million, centred on Ljubljana, the capital city. There are only a handful of other large towns, the most important being Maribor, Celje, Kranj and Koper. Mountains have shaped the country and its culture, and it is common to see whole families out walking together, such is the Slovenes' enthusiasm for the outdoors.

However, the mountains provide more than enough room for all walkers – even in the summer season of July, August and September – to find places where they can be alone on the hill, where there is a surprise in the form of a new vista around every corner and where the limestone scenery is as unspoilt as it was when the glaciers first receded. This is a country to enjoy and return to over and over again.

GEOLOGY AND LANDSCAPE

At the heart of the Julian Alps stands Triglav, which, at 2864m, is over 100m higher than its nearest contender, Škrlatica. The area around Triglav is an upland of peaks and ridges bounded to the north by the Upper Sava valley and to the south by Bohinj. Komna and the Lower Bohinj mountains form the southern boundary of the national park, and to the north-west, close to the Italian border, lie the Kanin range and the peaks of Mangart and Jalovec.

The Julian Alps are mostly composed of limestone, primarily from the Triassic geological period. Its main characteristic, which has a dramatic effect on the topography of the range, is its porous nature, which means that water sinks directly into the rock. The term 'karst', derived from the Slovene word *kras*, is used all over the world to describe the characteristic landscape of areas like the Julian Alps where the rock is readily dissolved by water. Karst features include deep, steep-sided gorges and dry valleys; sinkholes; springs; water-dissolved caves and tunnels underground; and water-eroded surface rocks that result in the formation of limestone pavements.

The porosity of the rock in the Julian Alps means that, compared to other European Alpine ranges, there is little surface water. Many riverbeds in the national park are dry for most of the year. Those streams and lakes that exist on the surface are linked below ground level by complex systems of caves and channels, many of which are still not fully explored. Several cave systems are known to be well over 1000m deep.

As throughout the Alps, glaciation has played a major part in forming the landscape, and there are many textbook examples of U-shaped valleys, glacial moraines and erratic boulders.

The Julian Alps also contain areas of high mountain karst, typified by the Kaninski podi in the Kanin range. High mountain karst is formed from limestone plateaus situated above the treeline, with little vegetation cover, in areas of high precipitation. Here snow and water remain at the surface for more than half the year, so water erosion is greatly increased, resulting in diverse rock formations that are of great interest to geologists and cavers.

TRIGLAV NATIONAL PARK

The idea to protect the area around Triglav was first conceived in 1908, although it was not until 1961 that Triglav National Park (Triglavski narodni park) was established. Nowadays it covers over 84,000 hectares – around 4% of the territory of Slovenia.

The park includes most of the Julian Alps within Slovenia and is divided into two areas. The highland area, including all the main mountain ranges, has the strictest protection, while the valley areas have slightly more relaxed regulations in order to accommodate the communities that live and work there, and to acknowledge the fact that the lowland landscape has, to some extent, been shaped by humans.

The park has a number of regulations which aim to protect, and encourage the respectful treatment of this fragile environment. For more information on the park and its Code of Conduct, visit www.tnp.si.

LONG-DISTANCE ROUTES

Several long-distance routes weave their way across the Julian Alps:

The Slovenian Mountain Trail (SMT)

Opened in 1953, the SMT (www.slovenska-planinska-pot.si) is the oldest and longest long-distance mountain trail in Slovenia. It starts in Maribor, in the north-east of the country, and wanders across various mountain ranges of Slovenia – Pohorje, the Kamniško-Savinjske Alpe, the Karavanke and the Julian Alps – to finally arrive, after several weeks, at the coast. It's marked with the Knafelc blaze (a white dot inside a red ring), which is accompanied by the number 1.

The Via Alpina

The Via Alpina (www.via-alpina.org) is a long-distance trail that crosses the Alps from the Adriatic Sea to the

Ligurian Sea through eight European countries. The trail starts in Trieste and heads north to eventually reach the Dolič hut below Triglav – here it goes down to Trenta and on to Kranjska Gora before heading into Austria. You will often see the distinctive logo on routes in this guide.

The Alpe Adria Trail

This long-distance path leads from the Grossglockner in Austria to the Adriatic Sea, and again you will see the signs on many of our routes. The website, www.alpe-adria-trail.com, is in German, Italian, Slovene and English.

Pot miru, the Walk of Peace

This walk links outdoor museums and other monuments along the line of the Soča (Isonzo) Front of World War 1, which resulted in over a million casualties in the greatest mountain battle in history. Several walks around Bovec and Kobarid meet the Walk of Peace winding past old trenches and military buildings. For more information, visit www.thewalkofpeace.com.

The Juliana Trail

Opened in 2019, this new circular, long-distance trail mostly covers the valleys of the Julian Alps. The basic

Walking towards Krn (Walk 30)

circuit is divided into 16 stages with a total length of 270km, but in recent years the trail has been extended with four access stages (60km) from the Goriška Brda wine region and three extra stages (42km) to the Breginjski kot area (see *Hiking Slovenia's Juliana Trail*, 2023, by Rudolf Abraham).

THE WALKING TERRAIN

The Julian Alps are everything a mountain walker could wish for, but they can be a bit daunting for first-time visitors. The nature of limestone means that the Julian Alps are very steep and the rock is generally loose. Once you're out of the valleys, the going can be rough over rocks and tree roots, even at a relatively low level, and higher up there is loose rock, scree, stone fall, steep cliffs and exposure. The many protected sections, which give a sense of security when via ferrata equipment is used appropriately, are interspersed with steep loose paths that offer no security at all.

Make sure you are fit, have a good head for heights and the right equipment, and are a competent scrambler before attempting any of the higher, longer routes. Also, always check the weather forecast and know how long it is likely to take you to get to safe ground if you need to.

Limestone mountains are generally dry, and there are not many springs in the high mountains; this means almost every drop of water must be carried from the valley or bought in the huts at premium prices. Food is not a problem – there are mountain huts on most of the

Autumn colours on Lake Bohinj (Walk 13)

walks which provide food as well as accommodation.

A fragile environment

The Alps are a fragile and endangered environment, under pressure from climate change, noise, traffic and pollution, and not least from the erosion caused by the walking boots of those who love them. As a visitor to the area, it is your responsibility to minimise your environmental impact by sticking to the footpaths and taking all your litter away with you. Remember, too, that this is a working landscape – leave gates as you find them, keep dogs on a lead and do not disturb livestock.

CLIMATE AND WEATHER

Slovenia's position in Central Europe means that, in spite of its small size, it has three distinct climatic zones: a Mediterranean climate by the coast, with warm sunny weather throughout much of the year along with mild winters; a Continental climate in Eastern Slovenia, with hot summers and cold winters; and an alpine climate in the north-west, with warm summers, cold winters and abundant precipitation. Most of the area covered by this guide is in the alpine area, although as you go further south the Julian Alps are increasingly influenced by the Mediterranean.

Trends over past decades suggest that the effects of global warming are now being felt. Temperatures are rising, resulting in less snow in winter (the Triglav glacier marked on older maps is now reduced to a large snow patch), and summers are hotter. Wind patterns are also changing, and long periods of drought have been followed by extensive flooding, which can be devastating in an area of steep-sided valleys and mountains.

In any mountain area, the weather is notoriously difficult to forecast. Snow can occur at any time of year and can render a summer walking trip a disaster for those not adequately prepared. In summer, snow does not tend to lie for long, but the peaks and high-altitude paths can be snowbound from October to May in some years. April and November see the maximum rainfall. Thunderstorms are common in July and August and can obviously be particularly dangerous on ridges and high-altitude routes; they can spring up out of clear air within half an hour, perhaps not leaving enough time for you to reach to safer ground. Thunderstorms are most common in the afternoon and evening, so it's often advisable to make an early start so you have a chance of achieving your objective before a storm occurs.

For reliable weather forecasts for Slovenia, visit https://vreme.arso.gov.si: to access the mountain forecasts, click on the word 'Gore' (mountains). Forecasts can also be obtained from local people and the staff of the hut where you are staying.

Floods are common after heavy rainfall, and these have the greatest effect on lower valleys, as the water can bring down tons of boulders and rubble from the loose limestone. They can have a profound impact on paths, completely re-routing them in some cases, and bridges may be washed away.

Limestone is usually pale and can be extremely bright when the sun shines on it. Sunglasses are therefore recommended, even on a cloudy day.

In the summer of 2023, severe storms with high winds and heavy rainfall caused the worst natural disaster in Slovenia's history. Heavy flooding hit the north and centre of the country, resulting in severe damage to infrastructure and casualties among the population. The Julian Alps were not the hardest hit, but in some valleys strong winds brought down trees and damaged paths. Most of the paths have been cleared, but some were still closed at the time of writing. Information on the current status of the paths can be found on the maPZS app (https://mapzs.pzs.si), which shows all the mountain paths in Slovenia managed by the Alpine Clubs and the Alpine Association of Slovenia.

WILDLIFE AND FLOWERS

Over 5500 species of plants and wildlife have been identified in Triglav National Park, some of which are unique to the area. This section describes only some of the key species that can be observed.

Partly because they are lower than other Alpine ranges, the Julian Alps, from lush valley to rocky summit, are a botanist's delight. The thin soil does not allow any one species to dominate, with the result that an astonishing variety of plant life flourishes here, even among the rocks of the highest peaks. Some of the best places to see high-alpine plants are the Lower Bohinj mountains (Walks 16, 17 and 18), the Triglav Lakes valley (Walk 20) and Debela peč (Walk 35), but all routes described in this book are studded with flowers. The white stars of edelweiss are common, along with the deep blue of various gentians, but there are two flowers in particular that the Slovenes have made their own: the pink cushions of the Triglav rose (*Potentilla nitida*) are supposed to have sprung from drops of blood of the Zlatorog, the golden-horned ibex, and Zois' bellflower (*Campanula zoysii*) is related to the harebell; it has grown in the rock crevices of this area since the last ice age.

About half of Slovenia is covered with trees, and almost all the walks pass through sections of beautiful woodland. Spruce, beech, pine and larch are interspersed with other species in true mixed forest which gradually changes its nature with height. The highest of all is the dwarf pine before the trees give out altogether, leaving only short grass sprinkled with flowers among the rocks. If you visit in late June, notice the pendulous yellow flowers of alpine laburnum, which

Butterflies abound in the Julian Alps (top), while Zois' bellflower (bottom left) and edelweiss (bottom right) brighten cracks among the rocks (photo: Roy Clark)

can be seen as splashes of yellow in a band across the hillsides at an altitude of roughly 800–1200m. Particularly good forest walks are Pršivec (Walk 15) and Debela peč (Walk 35), as well as most of the valley walks.

The wonderful, lush growth of the alpine hay meadows needs no introduction here. Regular cutting of the plants, two or three times a year, means that the hardier species do not get the chance to dominate the more delicate ones. Yellow, blue, purple and white are the predominant colours, and they are reflected in the many species of butterflies. The valley walks around Kranjska Gora (Walks 1 and 6) provide many excellent examples of hay meadows.

The chamois (*Rupicapra rupicapra*) is perhaps the most typical of the alpine mammals and a common sight on the high-level walks. They are smaller and have shorter horns than the ibex (*Capra ibex*), which became extinct in Slovenia in the 17th century but after being successfully reintroduced in the 1960s, it is now thriving. Marmots (*Marmota marmota*) were also introduced here in the 1960s and have multiplied across large areas of Triglav National Park.

Alpine choughs, ravens and golden eagles can all be seen in the high mountains; choughs in particular are more than happy to eat your sandwiches on the summits! In the forests listen out for the capercaillie (*Tetrao urogallus*), a large game bird whose call, when disturbed, is reminiscent of the gobbling sound of a turkey – you are more likely to hear them than see them. A common amphibian which can often be seen in the beech forests, especially on damp days, is the strange black-and-yellow fire salamander (*Salamandra salamandra*). The rarer black alpine salamander (*Salamandra atra*) can sometimes even be seen on the ridges in rainy weather; interestingly, they do not spawn in water but give birth to two live young.

The fire salamander is sometimes seen in the lower forests, usually during rain

Most wildlife is protected within the boundaries of the national park. Identifying animals and plants is a pleasure for all – but take care to disturb them as little as possible.

WHEN TO GO

The main walking season is from mid June to the end of September, when most of the routes are snow-free and the weather is generally stable. Most of the high-mountain huts are open from July to September, but each has its own opening times; for more information, visit the website of the Alpine Association of Slovenia: www.pzs.si.

During May, the spring flowers are wonderful on the lower-level routes, and in autumn the colours are fabulous; however, the weather can be unsettled at this time of year, and there is less choice of accommodation. In winter, it is skiing and the resorts that draw the crowds, but many high-level huts have an unmanned 'winter room' supplied with blankets for ski-tourers and winter mountaineers.

One of the appeals of the Julian Alps for walkers is that there are no glaciers and therefore no crevasses to worry about, but snow and ice can still be a factor throughout the summer if the previous winter has seen heavy snowfall. Snow patches can lie all year in the high gullies and on north faces, and an ice axe is sometimes (although rarely) necessary on high routes, even in July.

GETTING THERE

With excellent road and rail links, Slovenia is an easily accessible destination. Frequent flights are also possible from many European cities.

Visas

Citizens of the European Union (EU) do not need a visa to enter Slovenia and, at present, there is a visa-free agreement with several third countries, including the UK, for stays of no more than 90 days. For more information on entry requirements, visit www.gov.si.

By train

Bled and Bohinj (Bohinjska Bistrica) lie on the main rail link between Northern and Southern Europe, between Munich and Trieste, and so are easy to get to by rail. Kranjska Gora can be reached from the international rail link at Jesenice via a regular bus connection. The nearest railway station to Kobarid and Bovec is at Most na Soči, on the Jesenice–Bled–Bohinj–Nova Gorica line; the link is then by bus.

By bus

The FlixBus service, which connects Slovenia with other European cities, is becoming increasingly popular (www.flixbus.co.uk).

By air

Slovenia's main international airport is at Brnik (LJU), 23km north of Ljubljana and 1–2hr by car from the walking centres around which this guide is based. The airport is served by low-cost, full-service airlines with flights to major European destinations as well as non-European destinations, such as Istanbul and Dubai. Airports in neighbouring countries, such as the well-served airports in Venice and Zagreb, or the smaller airports in Trieste and Klagenfurt, are alternative options.

GETTING AROUND

Public transport

Slovenia has an efficient, modern public bus system, and during the summer and winter seasons, tourist offices at various destinations in the Julian Alps increase the number of services and add extra routes, making the walking trails even more accessible. For regular-bus timetables see www.arriva.si and www.nomago.si; the schedules of the seasonal services and shuttle buses can be found on the websites of the various tourist offices.

Travelling around Slovenia by train is a rewarding experience, although journey times are generally longer than by bus. The most interesting line is the one between Nova Gorica and Jesenice, also known as the Bohinj railway. Built at the time of the Austro-Hungarian Empire, this line, which runs through the Soča valley to the Julian Alps, is considered one of the most beautiful in Europe. For train timetables, see http://potniski.sz.si.

Regular buses run from Brnik Airport (Letališče Brnik) to the main bus and train station in Ljubljana and to Bled. Buses leave from outside the train station.

For private and shared shuttle transfers from/to the airports and train stations, check www.goopti.com.

By car

Slovenia has a good road transport network, with motorways linking all the major centres. To drive on the motorways, it is mandatory you purchase a vignette, which is available online (http://evinjeta.dars.si) or at the border. Especially in the low tourist season, some of the routes are difficult to access by public transport, and a car makes life a lot easier in the rural areas described here; cars can be hired at the airports and in reasonably sized towns.

The Julian Alps Card

Several destinations within the Julian Alps offer visitors benefits cards, which provide free or reduced-price access to transport and free parking. Other benefits include discounts and free admission to sites, attractions and museums. Julian Alps Cards can be purchased at tourist information centres and at certain accommodation providers in Bled, Bohinj, Soča valley and Radovljica. Check local tourist office websites for more information.

AREAS AND BASES

This guide is divided into five regional sections, each centred around a base: Kranjska Gora, Bohinj, Bovec, Bled and Kobarid. The bases make a rough circle around the main Julian Alps massif. They were chosen for ease of access by public transport, for tourist infrastructure and for the variety and appeal of the walks in the area. Due to the compact nature of the range, many of the mountains can be reached by several different approaches; where this is the case, the most practical routes for people without their own transport have been selected. However, car parking and alternative starts for those with their own transport are also mentioned.

Kranjska Gora is a winter ski resort and a superb base from which to explore the full range of alpine walking in the summer. The area includes beautiful easy valley treks as well as some of the most demanding peaks in the Julian Alps.

Lake Bohinj, and its surrounding area, is one of the gems of Slovenia, and several villages near the lake (there is no town called Bohinj) provide access to a variety of walks, from valley waterfalls to long mountain ridges.

The upbeat, sporty town of Bovec is close to the river Soča, a mecca for canoeists. Within easy reach of the town are several interesting walks which investigate some of the history of the area, particularly from the World War 1 era, and there is also no shortage of beautiful high-mountain trails.

Lake Jasna (Walks 4 and 12)

Blejska koča na Lipanci (Walk 35)

Bled, with its lake island, is probably Slovenia's most visited resort, and its unique setting provides the backdrop for some lovely walks with excellent viewpoints.

The little Italianesque town of Kobarid, to the south of the main peaks of the Julian Alps, has some fascinating World War 1 sites, as well as long mountain ridges with views all the way to the Adriatic Sea.

Note that the bases are relatively close together; Kranjska Gora and Bohinj are about an hour's drive from each other, with Bled in between, and Kobarid is only 20min from Bovec. It's about an hour's drive from Kranjska Gora to Bovec (via Italy and the Predel pass; going via the Vršič pass takes longer, especially in the busy summer season). This means that staying at one base does not limit you to the walks only in that area, especially if you have your own transport.

ACCOMMODATION

Slovenia offers a full range of accommodation, from five-star hotels to campsites and bivouac huts. Generally, prices are reasonable compared with other European countries. A tourist tax is payable for each night, and proprietors of all types of accommodation will need to see your passport. Especially in high season, from July to mid September, it is recommended you book in advance; information and booking facilities can be found in the local tourist information office or directly online.

All the towns used as bases in this guide have a range of hotels and pensions, with varying facilities and prices: *sobe* (private rooms) offer a bed for the night and some offer breakfast as well; *apartmaji* (apartments) are also common; youth hostels and backpackers' hostels have become popular in recent years and several can be found at all bases; *turistične kmetije* (tourist farmhouses) offer comfortable rooms and excellent home-grown, home-cooked food.

Slovene campsites are clean and the facilities are of a high standard. Most cater for tents, caravans and motorhomes, and some offer cabin-type accommodation. All of the bases used in this guide have campsites within a kilometre or so. Campingaz and other screw-type gas cartridges can be bought in sports shops. Note that wild camping is illegal throughout Slovenia.

Mountain huts

Mountain huts, called *dom* or *koča* in Slovenian, are ubiquitous in Slovenia and are part of the country's culture. They are all manned and divided into categories according to their accessibility, which determines the price of food and accommodation. Sleeping accommodation is in *skupna ležišča* (dormitories) or *sobe* (rooms), with rooms being more expensive. Blankets and pillows are provided, but you will need a sleeping bag liner – these can be rented in huts for an additional fee. Prices (for accommodation but not food) are cheaper if you are a member of the Alpine Association of Slovenia (Planinska zveza Slovenije – PZS) and there are reciprocal agreements with the Alpine Clubs of some other countries.

The lower huts usually have running water, with shared bathrooms and often coin-operated showers, but the higher huts have no water except rainwater, which means washing facilities are limited. You will need to buy drinking water too; make use of any springs you find en route for replenishing your water supply – they are mentioned in the text. In Slovenian, drinking water is *pitna voda*, while *voda ni pitna* means the water is undrinkable.

Most huts use solar panels to generate electricity and it is not always possible to charge mobile phones. Power sockets are also sometimes scarce, so it is a good idea to take a charged power bank with you.

For a complete and up-to-date list of all the huts and their telephone numbers, visit the PZS website (www.pzs.si). The website also provides information on the months when the huts are open and their opening times (check the 'hut status' to find out which days of the week the hut is open). The high-level huts are almost all closed during the winter but most have a *zimska soba* (winter room) with open access to basic facilities when the hut is unmanned.

The high huts will be busy in good weather in July and August, and you should book beforehand. However, you will never be turned away in bad weather, even if you have to sleep on the floor. For several huts in the Julian Alps, it is now possible to book your overnight stay online on the PZS website. Reservations can be made via links to the mountain huts and can be modified or cancelled free of charge one to two days before arrival (depending on the mountain hut).

All huts serve basic, reasonably priced meals, even if you are not staying overnight. Generally, there is no problem with eating food you have brought with you in the huts (e.g. sandwiches), but there are no facilities for self-catering. The food in the huts is filling so *klobase* (sausages) and thick soups and stews with hunks of bread prevail. Vegetarians will manage, but vegans will struggle. Some huts, especially the lower ones, which are frequented by locals, will serve local specialities. Sweets include *palačinke* (pancakes), *štruklji* (a kind of dumpling, often with cream cheese) and *zavitek* (strudel).

FOOD AND DRINK

Slovenes love to eat, and food is generally fresh and well prepared. Prices are reasonable and portions large – there seems to be an almost pathological fear that you might go home hungry! It is difficult to define typical Slovene food, as it is heavily influenced by the different countries and culinary traditions that surround

Dormitories in mountain huts

it. From Italy come pastas and pizzas, from Austria sausages and schnitzel, from Hungary goulash and from the former Yugoslavia treats like *čevapčiči*, a grilled dish of minced meat, and *burek*, a puff-pastry roll filled with meat or cheese. Generally, Slovenes dislike spicy food. Ethnic restaurants, such as Chinese and Indian, are rare; however, this does not mean there is a lack of culinary choice. Large towns and villages will have a variety of eating places, called *gostilna* or *okrepčevalnica*, which provide excellent home-cooked food. Many hotels and pensions also have restaurants that are open to non-residents.

Food is freshly prepared and served (look out for signs saying *domača kuhinja*, meaning 'home-made'). In some cases, the ingredients are even freshly gathered, as there is a great tradition in Slovenia of eating food from the land. For example, dandelion leaves are made into delicious salads with eggs and potatoes in the early spring, and in many areas wild herbs are collected for teas and medicines. Slovenes are enthusiastic mushroom collectors in the late summer and autumn.

Slovene *juha* (soup) is excellent. Try mushroom soup for a hearty snack – you will often find it made with several different varieties of locally gathered mushrooms. Soups sometimes arrive in a 'bowl' made of bread, which you can eat as well.

In the mountain huts, thick soups and stews with hunks of bread prevail

Particular specialities include trout from the Soča river, Adriatic fish, dishes made with buckwheat and sweet or savoury *štruklji* (dumplings). Slovene cakes and pastries are delicious, for example, *gibanica*, a layered cake with fruit and poppy seeds, or *potica*, a nut-filled sponge roll traditionally made for special occasions – every Slovene family seems to have its own recipe!

The Slovene diet is generally a meaty one, and vegetarianism is not very common. However, most restaurants will offer meat-free options.

Where to eat

All the bases mentioned in this book offer a range of places to eat, with Bled and Kranjska Gora being particularly well served. Many hotels and pensions also have restaurants that are open to non-residents.

Slovenes take their main meal in the middle of the day, although they will eat out in the evenings on special occasions. This means that a full meal can be obtained easily at almost any time of day, but it may be difficult to find lunchtime snacks (some supermarkets sell ready-made sandwiches or will prepare them for you).

Drinks

Slovenia produces several beers, of which the most popular are Union and Laško. Laško's Zlatorog is a lager-type beer that holds up its head, as it were, with the best beers in Europe. Slovenia's climate also provides the raw materials for some excellent wines – the white wines are particularly good.

All bars and mountain huts serve not only alcoholic drinks but also tea, coffee and hot chocolate. If you ask for *čaj* (tea), you will get a fruit tea without milk; for English-style tea, ask for *angleški čaj* or *črni čaj z mlekom* (black tea with milk), although not all places stock it, and mountain huts usually don't – there you can ask for *vroča voda* (hot water) and bring your own teabags. *Kava* (coffee) is usually served black unless you ask for *z mlekom* (with milk) – *bela kava* is coffee made with milk. Note that most huts serve Turkish-style coffee; only a few huts have espresso machines. *Vroča čokolada* (hot chocolate) is served in some places.

MONEY AND SHOPPING

The currency in Slovenia is the euro. All five base towns in this guide have ATMs, and in most shops, hotels and restaurants you will be able to pay by card. However, smaller B&Bs and tourist farmhouses may only accept cash.

Take plenty of cash with you for payments at mountain huts. Although many huts now also accept credit cards (but not all!), a secure connection is not always guaranteed. Allow around €75 per person per day for accommodation, food and drink in the huts (more if you like a few beers).

Opening hours

Shop opening hours are long in Slovenia, from early in the morning until 7 or 8pm, with no break for lunch. On Saturdays, some shops close a bit earlier, although they may be open for longer during the main tourist seasons. On Sundays and public holidays, most shops are closed, but certain essentials are available at the main petrol stations. Post offices usually keep shop hours during the week.

COMMUNICATIONS

Slovenia has extensive mobile coverage, which is high even in mountain areas, but you may lose signal in dense forest or in certain locations. Internet access is generally available in hotels and cafés. Located in the CET zone (Central European Time), Slovenia is 1hr ahead of GMT.

HEALTH AND HAZARDS

Slovenia is generally a healthy place to be. Tap water is safe and good to drink throughout the country – help to reduce your environmental impact by bringing a water bottle and filling it from the tap, rather than buying water in plastic bottles.

For EU citizens, the European Health Insurance Card (EHIC) gives access to medically necessary, state-provided healthcare during a temporary stay in Slovenia. If you are a UK citizen, make sure you carry the Global Health Insurance Card (GHIC), which allows you to receive necessary public health care in EU countries in the same way as a resident of that country. Visitors from outside Europe will need medical insurance; wherever you are from, you should check to see if your travel insurance covers you for mountain activities.

Medical services

Small towns have a medical centre where GPs and dentists are based, while larger centres have a hospital. A pharmacy (*lekarna*) is identified by a green cross. You will need to ask for what you require rather than helping yourself from the shelf, but pharmacists usually speak at least some English and are very helpful.

Approaching the Mangart saddle (Walk 31)

Hazards

There are few hazards in Slovenia, but one to mention here is the tick. In Slovenia they can carry not only Lyme disease, a nasty infectious illness, but also encephalitis, an inflammation of the brain which can be very serious indeed. Ticks thrive in grassy areas and meadows on the edge of forests – fortunately, they are less common the higher you go. If you find one attached, use tweezers or a tick tool to pull it out from as close to the skin as possible, to make sure you remove the head as well as the body. Pulling from the rear of the tick carries a risk of leaving the head in situ, increasing the possibility of infection. If a rash develops around the site of the bite, consult a doctor. Long trousers and a good repellent reduce the chances of picking up ticks.

There are few other biting creatures; mosquitoes are easily kept at bay with insect repellent. Snakes are common in mountain areas of Slovenia, particularly the adder, but there are no deadly ones and they pose little threat to walkers, as they usually seek cover the moment they sense danger.

LANGUAGE

Slovene (or Slovenian) is spoken throughout the country; it is a Slavic language related to Croatian, Polish and Russian. An introduction to the pronunciation and translation of common words used on Slovenian maps and signs and a glossary of useful Slovene words and phrases are given in Appendix B.

The Slovenes are the first to admit that their language is complex and difficult to learn, but they are always pleased when a visitor makes an attempt! However, foreign language learning is considered a high priority in Slovenia and most Slovenes will speak at least one foreign language, and many speak four or five. English is the most commonly spoken foreign language, especially among the young, followed by German, Italian and Croatian.

MAPS

Recommended hiking maps are as follows:

- Kranjska Gora (Sidarta) 1:25,000 – Walks 1–12, 22, 28–29
- Triglav (Sidarta) 1:25,000 – Walks 1–8, 10–15, 19–22, 28–29, 36
- Bohinj (Sidarta) 1:25,000 – Walks 13–22, 30, 35–36
- Bovec-Trenta (Sidarta) 1:25,000 – Walks 7, 10–11, 19–20, 23–31, 38
- Krnsko pogorje (Planinske zveze Slovenije) 1:25,000 – Walks 30, 37–38, 40

These maps are available online (www.sidarta.si) and locally at tourist information offices, bookshops and Triglav National Park information centres. In the UK, also check out the map suppliers Stanfords and The Map Shop.

Walks 32, 33, 34 (Bled area) and Walk 39 (Stol) are not on a large-scale map. These can be found on the Julijske Alpe 1:50,000 map (Planinske zveze Slovenije) – this map covers the entire area of the Julian Alps of Slovenia but the scale is perhaps a bit big for walking.

A useful tool to use in addition to maps is the maPZS app (https://mapzs.pzs.si), which shows all of the mountain trails in Slovenia managed by Alpine Clubs and the Alpine Association of Slovenia. The app provides detailed trail information, including updates on the status of trails, reporting any closures or damage. The version released in October 2020 is still undergoing testing (Beta) but is already very popular and used by hikers.

Waymarking and navigation

Generally, routes in the Julian Alps are very well marked and signposted. Signs often give times to the next destination. The usual waymark is the Knafelc blaze – a red circle with a white dot painted on trees, rocks, buildings and so on, and there are occasional red direction arrows.

Lower-level routes can be marked with different signs and numbers that correlate with routes on the local sheet map. These local routes don't necessarily follow exactly the same paths as the routes in this book, and our routes may overlap several local routes with different numbers.

Much of Slovenia is covered with forests that contain a plethora of

Part of the walk to Vogel, dotted with flowers (Walk 16)

In Slovenia, the common waymark consists of a red circle with a white dot. Known as the Knafelc blaze (Knafelčeva markacija), it was created by Alojz Knafelc (1859–1937), who, in 1922, based on numerous experiments and suggestions, established a uniform sign for marking mountain paths. Over the decades, the Knafelc blaze has become a symbol of Slovenian mountaineering, and in 2016 it became a protected trademark. It has been calculated that there are around 50,000 Knafelc blazes in Slovenia. Legend has it that its creator was inspired by the markings on the wings of the Apollo butterfly (*Parnassius apollo*), a mountain moth that prefers meadows, flower-filled valleys and rocky slopes.

tracks and paths. One of the charms of many of the valley paths and tracks in this country is that they are as likely to be used by locals on their way to the shops as by a fully togged-up hillwalker! However, this can mean, especially on forest or lower valley walks, that there are numerous potentially misleading paths.

When in doubt about the way forward, consult the route description and the route map and compare this to the sheet map. Significant landmarks along the route that appear on the accompanying map are shown in bold in the text to help with navigation.

EQUIPMENT

Weather conditions in the mountains are notoriously changeable, and while you may spend your entire holiday in T-shirts and shorts, it's important to carry appropriate equipment and clothing in case its required. Good footwear and waterproof clothing are essential and, even in summer, a windproof jacket is a mandatory item on high-altitude hikes.

In addition to general hiking equipment, in your rucksack you should also have the following: a hat, suncream and lip salve, sunglasses, first aid kit, rain cover, tick repellent, light gloves, cap, power adapter/converter plug, cell phone for GPX, phone charger, passport, sleeping bag liner (if staying in a hut), enough water and food for the day, torch and batteries, whistle, map, compass, camera, binoculars, trekking poles, spare clothes and rubbish bags.

A helmet is strongly recommended for high-level routes, and if you are planning to do any routes with via ferrata, you will need to bring self-belaying equipment and stout gloves. An ice axe and crampons can be useful on high-level routes in the early part of the walking season. Mountain equipment can be hired locally from some sports shops and outdoor agencies by prior arrangement (but check with the tourist information offices first).

Junction on the path up the Vogel (Walk 16)

This equipment list is by no means comprehensive and is offered as a guide only; obviously, you will need to be selective depending on weather conditions and route choice.

USING THIS GUIDE

The aim of the guide is to appeal not only to experienced hill walkers but also to more casual walkers who wish to explore some of Slovenia's fine pathways. Each section contains routes for walkers of all abilities – from easy short orientation walks and visits to viewpoints, waterfalls and alpine villages through to full mountain days. Also included are longer routes with more difficult peaks that demand all the skills of a mountaineer; some of these may require two days to complete.

Arrangement of routes

Kranjska Gora, Bohinj and Bovec are the main bases for the high mountain routes, while Bled and Kobarid are situated in the foothills of the main range and, therefore, have somewhat easier routes.

Within each section, easier walks can be used as an orientation of the area before tackling harder and lengthier routes.

Walks follow a circular route wherever possible, to heighten the interest and to cover more of the area, but in some cases, for example, Walk 39 (Stol), the only practical return is by the way you came. For some of the longer routes, an overnight stay in one of the mountain huts is recommended.

Walk information

Each section of the guide begins with a short introduction to the area, giving details of its location, access, the range of tourist facilities available and a brief summary of the routes.

Each route begins with an information box showing the start and finish points, distance, grade and approximate ascent; a short introduction provides the highlights and 'feel' of the route.

Some walks follow an easy path with little height gain, while others require alpine experience, a good level of fitness and a head for heights.

Distances are given in kilometres – if the route is out-and-back, the distance includes both directions. Distance is less useful for higher routes; on steep or difficult ground it could take many hours to cover a few kilometres. When planning your walk, consider the distances in conjunction with the time given in the box.

The time given for each walk is a guide only and takes no account of rest stops or taking photographs and so on. Usually, the timings coincide with those suggested by signposts.

Each walk has been given a grade of 1 to 4 to indicate its length and difficulty. Of course, this is subjective and is intended as a guide only – it does not correspond directly with international grading systems. Some walks are easier or more difficult than others, even within the same grade; any particular difficulties are mentioned in the individual walks.

The start point is also the finish point, unless stated otherwise. Where the start point is not situated at the main base of the section, details on how to access the route are given in the information box. If the route involves an overnight stop, accommodation information is provided.

Route grading

- **Grade 1**: an easy walk, without much height gain, usually of short duration (not more than 3–4hr). These routes are ideal as an introduction to the area around each base.
- **Grade 2**: a longer route over rougher ground, with some height gain. There are no scrambling sections, but some parts of the path may be steep and/or rocky.
- **Grade 3**: a full mountain day with significant height gain, rough ground and possibly a short section or two of easy scrambling.
- **Grade 4**: a serious, high route, long and strenuous, often exposed and usually with sections of fixed protection, such as steel pegs and cables. Self-belaying equipment and a helmet are strongly recommended. A high level of fitness and competence in general mountaineering skills are required.

GPX TRACKS

GPX tracks for the routes in this guidebook are available to download free at: www.cicerone.co.uk/1215/gpx.

Although a GPS device is a great navigational aid, you should always carry a map and compass and know how to use them. Although every effort has been made to ensure the accuracy of the GPX files, neither the publisher nor the author accepts any liability for their accuracy.

SECTION 1
KRANJSKA GORA

The impressive lower falls of Martuljek (Walk 3) (photo: Roy Clark)

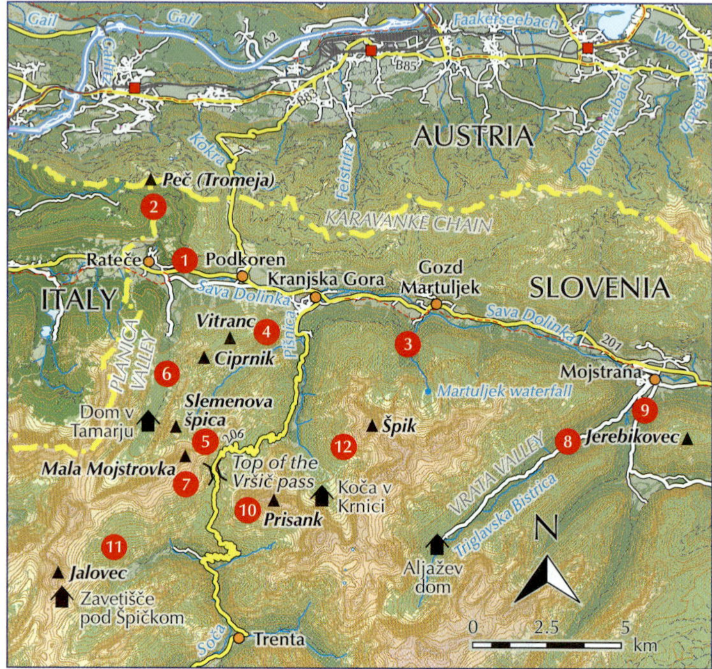

The resort village of Kranjska Gora (806m) lies near the head of the Zgornjesavska dolina, the Upper Sava valley, and is an excellent centre for walking and mountaineering. It is only a few kilometres from both the Italian and Austrian borders, in the far north-west corner of Slovenia. Surrounded by the northern mountains of the Julian Alps and the Karavanke range, the village has a wonderful setting and it has managed to retain its attractiveness in spite of well-developed tourist infrastructure. Kranjska Gora is one of the best known of Slovenia's mountain resorts, particularly in relation to skiing, which is plentiful in a good year.

Visitors can explore the local area by a series of numbered and waymarked walks, several of which feature in the 12 routes described in this section. The proximity of the Vršič pass (1611m) means that several mountain routes can be shortened by taking a bus or car to the top of the pass, making the most of the height gain. A number of mountain huts offering accommodation are within comfortable walking distance of Kranjska Gora.

Access to the resort is by the main road running from Jesenice, Route 201, which continues into Italy, or from Austria via the Karavanke tunnel, south of Klagenfurt, which joins this road. Alternatively, the Korensko sedlo (Wurzenpass, 1077m) is a steep road pass over the Karavanke range from Villach. Slovenia's highest road pass, the Vršič, links Kranjska Gora with Bovec and, ultimately, Nova Gorica to the south, and boasts 50 impressive hairpin bends built by Russian prisoners of war during World War 1. In summer there are several buses a day over the Vršič pass to Bovec, but the pass is usually closed in winter. Improvement works are planned along the Vršič pass road. They are expected to be completed by 2026 and will include a new transit arrangement for vehicles (www.kranjska-gora.si). Kranjska Gora doesn't have a train station (the railway closed in 1966 and is now a cycle track), but hourly buses link the resort to the international railway station at Jesenice. Additional bus services and free shuttles are provided in the summer, making the walks even more accessible. Timetables can be found on the local tourist office website www.kranjska-gora.si. A local taxi service can also provide transport to the start of some of the walks if required.

The whole range of tourist accommodation can be found in Kranjska Gora and its immediate surroundings, including several large hotels and a number of smaller hotels and *penzions* (guest houses). Private rooms are

The top of the Vršič pass and the imposing Prisank beyond (Walk 10)

plentiful both within Kranjska Gora and nearby villages, and hostel-style accommodation is also available. The Upper Sava valley has three campsites: an eco-camp in the woods just opposite Kranjska Gora and two in the neighbouring villages of Gozd Martuljek and Dovje-Mojstrana. Kranjska Gora and the surrounding villages have plenty of places to eat, from a quick pizza to a traditional Slovenian meal.

The village is centred on the church and has a full range of tourist services, including a health centre and pharmacy. The tourist information centre is in the large Vitranc Sports Hall.

Kranjska Gora is busy in high season, but a quieter village atmosphere can be found in Mojstrana, 13km down the valley. Situated on the bus route between Kranjska Gora and Jesenice, Mojstrana has a range of accommodation, along with a supermarket, post office and ATM. It is the base for Walks 8 and 9 and is home to the Slovenian Alpine Museum.

THE ROUTES

Twelve routes are described in this section – all within easy reach of Kranjska Gora.

- Walks 1, 3, 6 and 8 are delightful walks in the Upper Sava valley, with an abundance of flower meadows, old villages and views of the surrounding mountains.
- Walks 2, 4, 5 and 9 take in the lower peaks in the area – excellent for orientation and views.
- Walks 7, 10, 11 and 12 are high mountain routes to some of the most well-known summits of the Julian Alps.

MAPS

The 1:25,000 Kranjska Gora map, which also shows the numbered walks referred to above, and Triglav 1:25,000 cover this area.

Mount Jalovec in the early morning light (Walk 11)

WALK 1

Zelenci

Start/finish	Church in Kranjska Gora (806m)
Time	3hr 45min
Distance	14.5km
Total ascent/descent	260m
Grade	1
Maps	1:25,000 Kranjska Gora, 1:25,000 Triglav
Refreshments	Plenty of bars and restaurants along the way

This easy walk visits the main sites of interest between Kranjska Gora and the village of Rateče, in particular the wonderful emerald-green pools of Zelenci, with its mountain reflections and cathedral-like peaceful atmosphere. This is a place not to be missed during your visit to Kranjska Gora; if you don't have time to do the walk, drive or take a taxi to the car park on the road between Podkoren and Rateče and stroll the 250m to see the pools.

But a far nicer way to visit is to follow the marked paths and trails described here, which pass through beautiful flower meadows as well as the unspoilt historic villages of Podkoren and Rateče, with stunning mountain vistas all around.

From the church in Kranjska Gora, walk east through the pedestrian area to another square, with the Hotel Kotnik on the right. Turn left (north) here, following a sign for Podkoren (local) routes 3 and 4, and walk on past the culture centre Dvorana Vitranc. Reach a T-junction and turn right then immediately left past the entrance of the Penzion Lipa at the bus stop.

Take the narrow walkway between the restaurant and houses for a short distance to come out opposite the excellent cake shop, Slaščičarna Kala. Turn right and take a track across the fields for about 200m. Cross the main road that bypasses Kranjska Gora and then cross the **Sava river**. Take the track directly opposite, past some hayracks, signed (local) routes 4 and 10. A sign advertising the Natura Eco campsite points the same way (**10min**).

Continue into woods with a field to the right, skirting the crags of the little hill Peči. A narrow path, (local) route 10, heads up left here, but carry on along the broad track, past the **campsite** and a row of horse stables. Arrive at a large hayfield

ITALY
SLOVENIA
AUSTRIA
N
0
1
km
Korensko sedlo (Wurzenpass) road
201
Rateče
painted beehives
202
Zelenci pools
Podkoren
plaque
Zelenci nature reserve
former Rateče-Planica railway station
cycle track
Sava Dolinka
Peči
201
Kranjska Gora
Pišnica
SF
ski slopes
PLANICA VALLEY
Planica ski jumps
Hotel Dom Planica
Planica Nordic Centre
206
Vitranc
1637m
Ciprnik
1747m

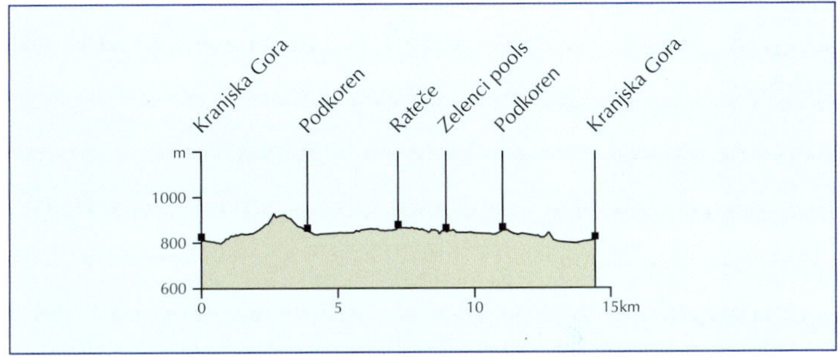

where the track forks to the right, but continue straight on, following a sign for Podkoren, to cross the meadow on a grassy track. At the very far end the track passes through a line of trees and continues into another much smaller meadow with a tiny wooden chalet about 50m to the right.

For a more **direct route to Podkoren** from here, take the main track going straight on, soon passing houses to reach the Korensko sedlo road on the edge of Podkoren. From there, do not cross the road but turn left and walk down the track parallel to the road for 100m, then turn right, through an underpass, and follow the road into the village.

A signpost for (local) route 4 directs you to the right on a narrow tree-lined path; leave the broad track and walk up here, past the chalet, for about 150m, and then turn left onto a broad track once more. After 500m carefully cross the **Korensko sedlo** (Wurzenpass) road at a hairpin bend and begin to walk down what was once the old road into **Podkoren** (**1hr**). The steep ski slopes opposite, on Vitranc, host World Cup slalom competitions each year in February.

The village of **Podkoren** dates back to medieval times, and its wealth was built around trade, which flourished because of the proximity of the pass into Austria. Heavy horses could be hired here to haul laden goods carts over the pass. New buildings have sprung up, but among them you can still recognise the old wooden houses and barns. At Podkoren 63, a house on the right as you walk down the road, a plaque commemorates Sir Humphry Davy, the English inventor of the miner's safety lamp, who lived here.

Carry on to a small square with an ancient linden tree, and the Hotel Vitranc if you are ready for some refreshment. Cross the square and walk down the narrow lane straight ahead, which continues on the other side of the main road to reach the young Sava river at a small bridge. Continue straight on for 100m to reach the **cycle track**, which was originally the railway line (closed in 1966).

Turn right (signs for Rateče and Tamar) and continue along the cycle track for about 2km, ignoring two paths to Zelenci on the right. Further on, a wonderful view of the Planica valley opens out on the left. Finally, reach houses which are the remnants of the **Rateče-Planica railway station** and turn right at a junction, signed to Rateče. At first, the people of Rateče were not in favour of the construction of the railway, so the station was built far away from the village. In about 300m meet the main road again. Cross over, enter the village and soon reach a T-junction (**2hr**). It is well worth a detour to the left to explore the pretty village of Rateče with its two churches and attractive square; there are several restaurants in the village as well.

Follow the road to the right signed Kranjska Gora and walk down this lane, past attractive houses. By the last house on the left there is an example of **painted beehives**, with information boards about this Slovene tradition. The painting of beehives began in the middle of the 18th century. Beekeepers placed coloured wooden panels on the front of the hives to distinguish theirs from others. Continue along the old road, with good views up the Planica valley, and join the main road once more. Turn left and walk about 250m along the road before crossing it to the Zelenci car park, where there is also a snack bar. The **pools** are signed along an easy track through beautiful woodland.

After visiting the pools, return along the path towards the car park, but take the first left. Cross a small wooden footbridge and after 100m reach a fork – take

Village of Podkoren (photo: Roy Clark)

THE ZELENCI POOLS

The pools are generally regarded as the source of the Sava, Slovenia's longest river, which crosses the country into Croatia, eventually flowing into the Danube at Belgrade. The true source is at Nadiža, a waterfall near Dom v Tamarju (Walk 6), whose waters disappear underground almost immediately to emerge again at the Zelenci pools. The springs can be seen at the bottom of the pools, stirring up the silt like miniature volcanoes. The temperature of the water is 5–6°C all year round; the water never freezes no matter how cold the air temperature.

The position of the pools is spectacular, against the backdrop of the mountains of Ponca and Jalovec. In spite of the proximity of the road, the area has a wonderful sense of peace and calm, and it is a place to linger a while to watch the wildlife. The whole area around Zelenci is a nature reserve.

the left path signed Kranjska Gora, crossing another bridge and continuing on a good path through the woods of the nature reserve to eventually rejoin the cycle track. Turn left and walk for 1km or so to reach the little bridge over the Sava by the turn-off to Podkoren (**3hr**).

The cycle track continues back to Kranjska Gora from here; to walk it would take 30min. However, it is more interesting to return to the square in Podkoren by turning left, crossing the main road and retracing your steps up the lane. This time turn right in the square and then, as the road bends round to the right, continue straight ahead. Go through an underpass under the Korensko sedlo road to a track on the other side. Turn right and continue down the track, parallel to the main road, then turn left as the track joins a minor road by two houses.

After 200m or so take the left fork, past some more houses, and cross a stream on a little wooden bridge. The track becomes unmade and crosses some meadows. Where the track turns right, continue straight ahead on a grassy path and at the edge of the trees turn right, following a sign for Kranjska Gora, and follow the line of a stream for about 100m before turning left and crossing it on a plank bridge. The path bears slightly right and crosses a small meadow. After 100m re-enter the wood and bear left uphill, following a sign for Kranjska Gora (local) route 3, ignoring a track to the right which leads past a house.

Continue through the wood for 150m to a signpost, turn right and continue to a T-junction where you turn right again. The path descends a little, curving round to the left, then crosses a stream and enters a meadow. Cross the meadow and join a track running parallel to the main road for a few hundred metres before reaching the hayracks where you crossed the road earlier. Retrace your steps from there into **Kranjska Gora**.

Ponca reflected in the Zelenci pools – lower-level walks can be spectacular in winter

Haflinger ponies near the summit of Tromeja, with Dobratsch in the background (photo: Roy Clark)

WALK 2

Peč (Tromeja)

Start/finish	Bus stop in Rateče (865m)
Time	3hr 30min
Distance	8.7km
Total ascent/descent	660m
Grade	2
Maps	1:25,000 Kranjska Gora, 1:25,000 Triglav
Refreshments	None on the route; restaurants in Rateče
Access	Rateče can be reached by an hourly bus from Kranjska Gora; alternatively, walk along the cycle track (about 1hr 15min)
Note	This walk could be combined with the Zelenci walk (Walk 1) for a longer day out

This summit is marked as 'Peč' on the map, but it is known locally, and indicated on all the signposts, as Tromeja (literally 'three border point'). It is not in the Julian Alps, being the first peak of the 120km-long Karavanke chain marking the border between Slovenia and Austria, but it is included in this book for three good reasons. Firstly, it is a fine walk; secondly, it offers terrific views of both the northern Julian Alps and the mountains of southern Austria; and, thirdly, it is just about as symbolic a peak as any mountain can be. On its summit meet not only the borders of Slovenia, Italy and Austria but also the three great linguistic traditions and cultures of Europe – the Germanic, Romance and Slavic. It was here that representatives of the three governments of Italy, Austria and Slovenia met to welcome Slovenia into the EU in 2004.

From the bus stop in Rateče, turn left and walk along the main road through the village, past a small store and a church. Continue on to the attractive square and then turn right, seeing ahead of you a building with a sign on it indicating, Tromeja 2hr. Walk up this lane and cross a little river before arriving at a track heading off right between two houses, signed Tromeja. Walk between farm outbuildings to a fork where you take the right-hand path, again signed Tromeja. Continue through woodland and pasture for about 10min to emerge on a forest road opposite a field (**25min**).

Seltschach
Kokra
AUSTRIA
Monte Comizza
1302m
Peč (Tromeja)
1508m
1423m
Dreiländereck-Hütte
KARAVANKE MOUNTAIN CHAIN
Petelinjek
1552m
Rio Chiusa
Monte Coppa
1496m
Cima Cavallar
1352m
ITALY
SLOVENIA
Trebiža
Rateče
SF
202
Zelenci pools
Zelenci nature reserve
cycle track
N
0
1
km
PLANICA VALLEY
Rio Vaisonz
Rio Apnen

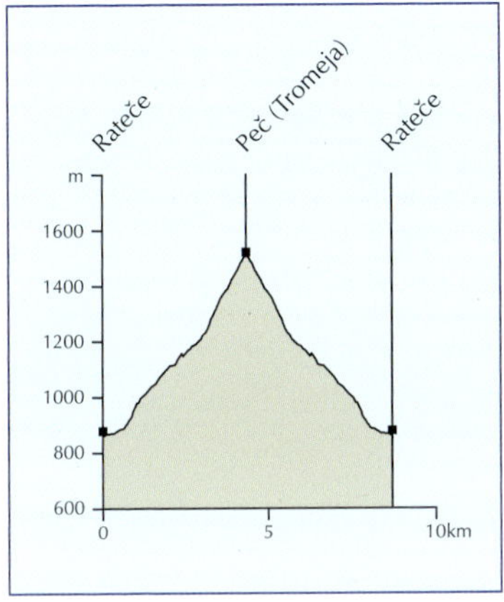

Turn right and follow the forest road gently uphill. Ignore several side tracks; the correct way is well signed or waymarked. After about 2km there is a sign for Rateče to the right. The route continues up the forest road and soon reaches a sharp right-hand bend (**1hr 10min**). A sign directs you onto a path climbing into the forest – this is the *krajša pot* (short route). It is also possible to continue up the road on the *daljša pot* (long route); this way is less steep but also less interesting.

The final section is quite steep, zigzagging up through the forest, following the line of a swathe of open land about 30m across which marks the border between Slovenia and Italy. The path weaves in and out of the forest, so at each alternate hairpin you see more and more of the stupendous view of the Julian Alps opening out behind you.

The short route that climbs into the forest is steeper but more interesting

Emerge onto the summit of **Peč** (1508m, **2hr**) to find that the forest which covers the Slovenian side has given way to a small ski resort on the Austrian side.

Peč is the westernmost peak of the 120km-long Karavanke mountain chain, and there is a good view along the ridge. The view into Austria is extensive. Directly opposite is Dobratsch (2166m) with its large aerial, while the Wörthersee lake near Klagenfurt is visible in the distance about 30km away, along with other hills and mountains near and far. There is a marked difference between the comparatively rounded hills of this part of Austria and the steep limestone peaks of the Julian Alps.

The return route takes the same path back to **Rateče**.

MONUMENT TO PEACE

Built in 1994, a monument stands just below the summit of Peč on the Slovenian side, with text in Italian, Slovene and German. It says:

TROMEJA
The Mountain of Peace by Šri Činmoj
Mountains are a symbol of peace, tranquillity and inner depth. Mankind needs all these virtues on its way to growing worldwide harmony.
'FINDING ONE'S INNER PEACE IS MAN'S GREATEST NEED.'
May this monument to understanding and friendship among nations be erected at this important meeting point of three great language groups and cultures.
Tromeja has become a link in the chain of several hundred different monuments dedicated to peace. There are buildings, mountains, bridges, cities, parks and natural phenomena which should encourage harmonious coexistence of people and nations, improve harmony and help to overcome both inner and outer borders.
PEACE DOES NOT ONLY MEAN NO WAR. PEACE MEANS THE RULE OF HARMONY, LOVE, SATISFACTION AND UNITY.
(translated by Rosvita Veselič)

WALK 3

Slap Martuljek (Martuljek waterfall)

Start/finish	Bus stop in Gozd Martuljek (750m)
Time	3hr 15min
Distance	7.6km
Total ascent/descent	500m
Grade	2
Maps	1:25,000 Kranjska Gora, 1:25,000 Triglav
Refreshments	Brunarica pri Ingotu farm at Jasenje
Access	Hourly buses run from Kranjska Gora to Gozd Martuljek. Or walk along the cycle track from Kranjska Gora for about 3km to reach the meadow with the pylon by a sidetrack to the right
Warning	It's advisable to bring a helmet as the gorge is prone to rockfall. In 2023 the section from the lower to the upper falls was closed due to trees felled during a storm. It's hoped that the trail will reopen (see https://mapzs.pzs.si for trail status updates)

This walk passes through natural forest to reach two waterfalls beneath the massive rock walls of the Martuljek peaks. The lower fall (*spodnji slap*) is at the head of a gorge, where it cascades 29m from the cliff and can be observed from a well-maintained path and viewpoint. The higher fall (*zgornji slap*) drops a total of 130m in three stages. The last part of the route to its foot involves a steep, protected scramble. Be sure to make the short detour to Jasenje, a stunningly beautiful *planina* (alp) surrounded by forest, with views up to the sheer rock spires of the mountains, where Brunarica pri Ingotu offers delicious home-made food and drinks.

From the bus stop 'Zgornje Rute' in Gozd Martuljek, walk back towards Kranjska Gora (for about 50m) and take a track on the left, signed 1., 2. Slap. Leave the houses behind and walk across open meadows for about 300m before walking under the cycle track under an old stone bridge. Skirt the edge of another pasture, where the view is unfortunately marred by a big pylon, to reach the forest by a **charcoal-burning site** used for demonstrations, with information boards and a picnic area (**15min**). Charcoal burning was a critical industry in the past when iron was first produced from the iron ore found in the Karavanke hills.

Just after the charcoal-burners' area, the tracks divide at a sign – the right-hand track is the descent route, while the left-hand track leads in 5min to a bridge at the lower end of the gorge, where there is a man-made waterfall built to control the flow.

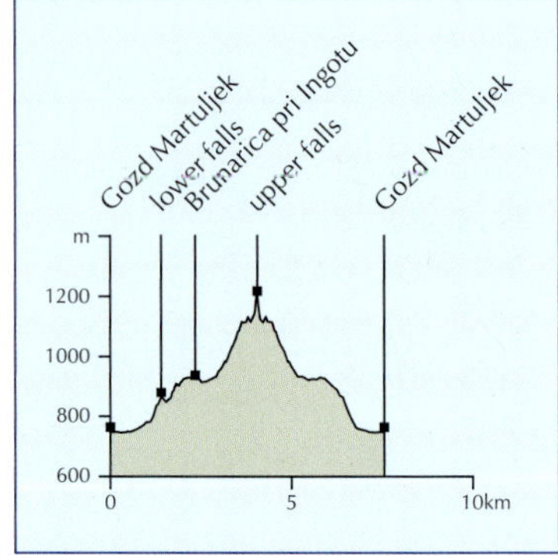

The path continues on the left-hand side of the **gorge**, with the impressively steep walls closing in on either side. After about 200m, the route crosses one or two simple wooden foot-bridges over the now narrow river. This is followed by a steep ascent up wooden steps to cross another bridge above the river, and the path continues up to a good viewpoint for the **lower falls** (850m, **35min**) from another wooden bridge.

Carry on along the waymarked path quite steeply for about 15min to the top of the gorge and reach a T-junction with the broad gravel track. Turn left along it, signed Brunarica pri Ingotu 15min. After 100m ignore a path on the right, signed Pod Špik 1hr, and continue on the main track, signed 2. Slap. In another 5min, cross a stream bed and just beyond ignore a path to the right, signed 2. Slap and continue on towards Brunarica pri Ingotu. In another 20m cross a wooden bridge and walk up to reach the planina (930m, **1hr 5min**).

From the hut, follow the grassy track straight ahead on the right-hand side of the planina, and at the end of the field keep right and take a broad track. In 20m reach an amazing tree – Mama Lipa (lime) and her seven daughters. Another 100m brings you to a **wooden chapel** and a memorial listing those who have lost their lives in these mountains. Now walk down into the stream bed, crossing it on a small wooden plank, and continue through the wood for about 50m then turn left to join the waymarked path to the second waterfall passed just before the bridge.

Soon afterwards the path bears right, away from the river, and begins to ascend, with a small stream to the left. In another 5min the path turns left and crosses the stream then continues to climb steadily through the woods.

After a further 10min, the path begins to rise more steeply, ascending a small rocky bluff, and then continues climbing through the woods for another 10min to reach a path junction by a bench. Ignore the path heading right to Za Ak (which leads to a bivouac hut) and continue bearing left, following a Slap 2 sign, along

the now narrow path, traversing the steep, wooded hillside, with the sound of the river down below. After 300m the path descends quite steeply, with the aid of a cable handrail, to reach the fast-flowing water. Cross the small footbridge and

Brunarica pri Ingotu at Jasenje provides home-produced food and drink (photo: Roy Clark)

ascend carefully over steep, eroded ground to a good viewpoint for the impressive **upper falls** (1150m, **2hr**). The protected ascent to the foot of the main cascade climbs a steep cleft to the left of the falls for about 25m – it's an awkward scramble and you may find it even more difficult coming down! The best time to visit the waterfalls is in the late spring, when they are at their most abundant due to the melting snow.

Return by the same route, and when you reach the river-crossing to the chapel, continue on down the waymarked path if you don't wish to revisit the hut. Retrace your steps down to the junction where you joined the gravel track and continue straight on, steeply down, for about 15min. The track levels out at the charcoal-burning area, close to the starting point of the walk.

WALK 4

Vitranc and Ciprnik

Start/finish	Church in Kranjska Gora (806m)
Time	6hr 30min
Distance	15.7km
Total ascent/descent	1005m
Grade	2/3
Maps	1:25,000 Kranjska Gora, 1:25,000 Triglav
Refreshments	Restaurants and cafés near Lake Jasna, Mojčin dom na Vitrancu, Hotel Dom Planica
Warning	The path is steep in places and can be dangerous and slippery in snow

This beautiful walk takes in an excellent viewpoint and is a good route for orienting yourself within the area. Be sure to make the short detour to beautiful Lake Jasna (meaning 'clear'), which lives up to its name with the mountain backdrop reflected in its clear waters.

It is also possible to shorten the route by using the chairlifts to Vitranc from Kranjska Gora but check in advance at the tourist information office that they are open. The main walk along the ridge from the top of the second chairlift to the viewpoint at Ciprnik (1747m) takes about 50min one way; to follow the descent from Ciprnik to Kranjska Gora described here, allow 2hr 30min–3hr.

From the church in Kranjska Gora, follow the sign to Jasna, (local) route 21, and walk down the narrow street to reach the **Pišnica river** at a wooden bridge. Turn right after the bridge and continue along this path, keeping the river on your right for about 20min, until you reach the Vršič pass road at a sluice gate complex. Cross the road and turn left at a small dam to reach **Lake Jasna** in 100m, where a statue of Zlatorog, the golden-horned ibex, stands on the shore (**25min**).

Retrace your steps to the small dam and take the path signed Vitranc–Mojčin dom and Ciprnik. The route follows the riverbank for a short distance then reaches a concrete embankment which leads into the woods. Here the path begins to climb, following waymarks. Continue up the marked path, ignoring side paths, for about 5min to reach a fork where you turn left, following a sign to Vitranc, (local) route 20. The path now begins to zigzag steeply uphill then turns right,

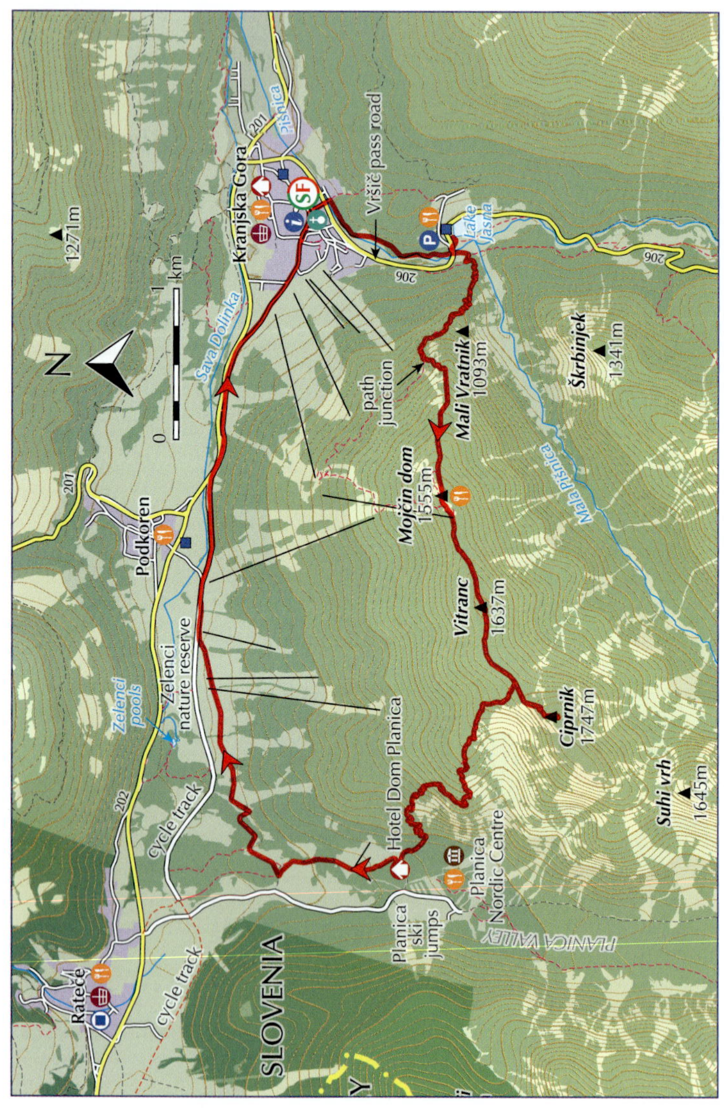
N
0
1
km
1271m
Kranjska Gora
SF
201
Pišnica
Vršič pass road
Lake Jasna
206
Sava Dolinka
path junction
Mali Vratnik
1093m
Škrbinjek
1341m
Mojčin dom
1555m
Mala Pišnica
201
Podkoren
Vitranc
1637m
Ciprnik
1747m
Zelenci nature reserve
Zelenci pools
Hotel Dom Planica
Suhi vrh
1645m
202
cycle track
Planica Nordic Centre
Planica ski jumps
PLANICA VALLEY
Rateče
cycle track
SLOVENIA

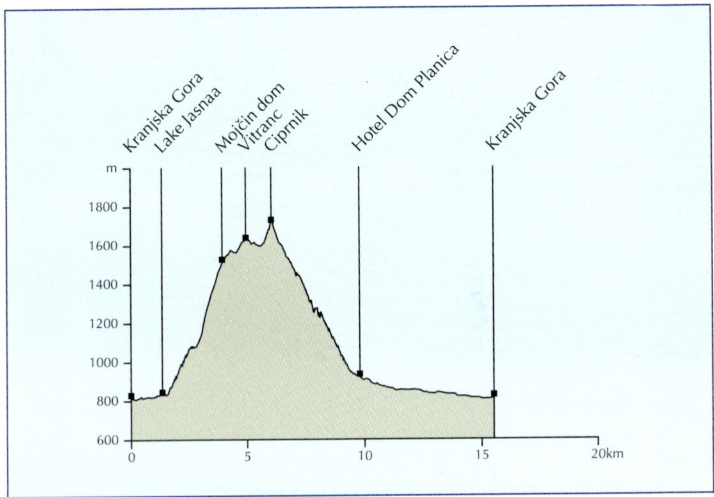

crossing the slopes of Vratnik (the eastern ridge of Vitranc), with fine views down to Kranjska Gora. Continue uphill in hairpins until you reach a **junction** (about **1hr 30min** from Kranjska Gora) where you turn left, following the path signed Vitranc and Ciprnik, (local) route 20a (the right-hand route offers an alternative ascent to Vitranc across the Kranjska Gora ski slopes).

Carry on along the path quite steeply to join the crest of the ridge. Further on, the path continues on or slightly by the ridge until it emerges onto a large forest road. Walk up the road for 50m then take a path on the left, signed Mojčin dom and Vitranc, to reach in 10min the tiny **Mojčin dom** (1555m, **2hr 30min**). Continue left for a short distance to reach the top of the chairlift and take the path behind signed Ciprnik. The new chairlift follows the route of the former one-seater chairlift Vitranc II, which was one of the oldest in the world.

The summit of **Vitranc** (1637m) passes unremarked among the undulations of the ridge. The last steep section to Ciprnik seems almost out of character with the level, shady forest path; the route suddenly emerges from the forest onto more-open land with rocky steps and dwarf pine. A little viewpoint on a shelf of the path, not far below the summit, looks directly down on the emerald pools of Zelenci, and in another 20m the waters of Lake Jasna come into view below to the left. Continue up the last short, rocky section to reach the summit of **Ciprnik** (1747m, **3hr 25min**).

The statue of Zlatorog, the golden-horned ibex, on the shore of Lake Jasna

The **view** from the summit is spectacular. In the Planica valley far below, you can see the ski jumps and the Tamar dom. Jalovec, looking like a magnificent single crystal, bars the head of the valley, with Ponca to its right; the ridge joining them forms the border with Italy. East of Jalovec are Velika and Mala Mojstrovka. Razor and Stenar form the foreground of Triglav, which appears somewhat subdued by the nearer peaks. Down below is Kranjska Gora and the whole sweep of the Zgornjesavska dolina. To the north are the Karavanke and the lower hills of eastern Austria beyond.

To continue the walk, reverse the route from the summit for about 10–15min until you see a path dropping down to the left with a sign to Planica painted on a tree. The path descends, at times steeply, through the wood, following the edge of crags falling to the Planica valley. There are good views through the trees of amazingly complex limestone rock scenery, with Ponca behind and the sentinel of Jalovec standing guard. After about 15min the path veers away from the edge back into the woods, where it continues to descend, following waymarks.

At around 1350m, just above the height of the topmost ski jump, the path traverses the hillside for about 5min (walking here is less enjoyable as the path is occasionally covered in fallen trees) before beginning to zigzag down on the far side of another, smaller, side valley full of strange rock scenery, with clefts, gullies and needles. A short detour from the path brings you to a viewpoint looking directly across to the ski jumps. During ski jumping events, this is where TV broadcasters place one of their cameras to film the jumps and the crowd from above.

The path comes out behind the **Hotel Dom Planica** (934m, **4hr 50min**). A short detour following the track east from the Hotel Dom Planica takes you to the ski jumps. From here follow Walk 6 (Tamar and Planica) back to **Kranjska Gora**.

WALK 5

Slemenova špica

Start/finish	Top of the Vršič pass (1611m)
Alternative finish	Church in Kranjska Gora (806m)
Time	2hr 30min (with extension 5hr 15min)
Distance	4.9km (with extension to Kranjska Gora 15.9km)
Total ascent	410m (with extension 410m)
Total descent	410m (with extension 1200m)
Grade	2 (with extension 3)
Maps	1:25,000 Kranjska Gora, 1:25,000 Triglav
Refreshments	On the extension route to Kranjska Gora: Dom v Tamarju and Hotel Dom Planica
Access	Regular buses run from Kranjska Gora and Bovec to the top of the Vršič pass in the summer season. See www.kranjska-gora.si for times or check at the bus stop. There are car parks at the top of the pass, but they fill up quickly in high season. A new transit arrangement for vehicles is expected to be in place in 2026
Warning	It's advisable to bring a helmet due to the risk of rockfall near Tamar waterfalls on the extension route to Kranjska Gora

Without doubt this is one of the most beautiful walks in this book. The height gain from the top of the Vršič pass is relatively modest, but it is still enough to give you a feeling of being in the high mountains. The route is delightful in every way, with a new vista around each corner and a lovely sense of seclusion as you turn away from the bustle of the day trippers in the Vršič area. The path crosses high alpine meadows among white limestone rock before rising to the summit of Slemenova špica (1911m).

Just below the summit, a high pasture offers stunning views of Jalovec reflected in three or four tiny pools. It is a lovely place to sit for a while and soak up the sun and the scenery. However, if you go at a weekend or at peak holiday time you may find that most of Slovenia is there with you!

The walk can be extended by returning to Kranjska Gora via Tamar and the Planica valley. This option over the Slatnica saddle takes about 4hr and offers unsurpassed alpine scenery below the north walls of Mojstrovka and Travnik.

Rateče
202
201
Zelenci pools
Podkoren
cycle track
cycle track
Zelenci nature reserve
Sava Dolinka
SLOVENIA
ITALY
Planica ski jumps
Hotel Dom Planica
Mojčin dom 1555m
Kucerji 1619m
Planica Nordic Centre
Vitranc 1637m
PLANICA VALLEY
Ciprnik 1747m
MALA PIŠNICA VALLEY
Mala Pišnica
Škrbinjek 1341m
Suhi vrh 1645m
Ponza Grande - Visoka Ponca 2274m
N
Mavr 1272
Kumlehova Glava 1785m
Vavovje 1810m
Grlo 1516m
0 1 km
Izvir Nadiže 1232m
Slemenova špica 1911m
Dom v Tamarju 1108m
Slatnica saddle 1815m
Prednje Robičje 1941m
206
Vratica saddle 1799m
TAMAR VALLEY
waterfall
Mala Mojstrovka 2333m
Erjavčeva koča 1525m
Prednja Glava 1684m
gully
Velika Mojstrovka 2366m
Vršič 1737m
SF
Tamar waterfalls
Top of Vršič pass 1611m
P
Poštarski dom na Vršiču 1688m
Tičarjev dom na Vršiču 1620m
Travnik 2378m
Mali Prisank 2223m
to Bovec
206
Prisank 2547m

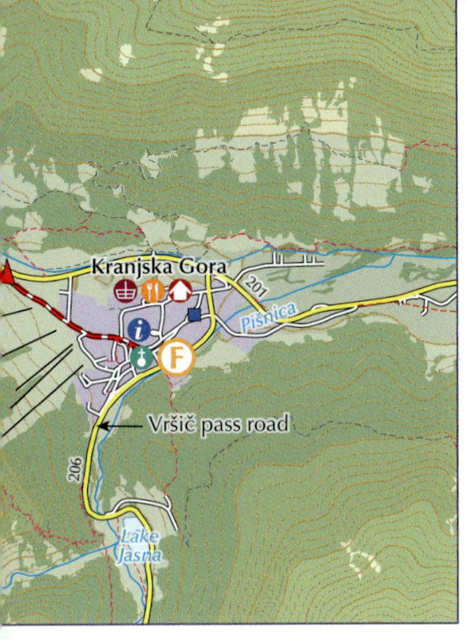

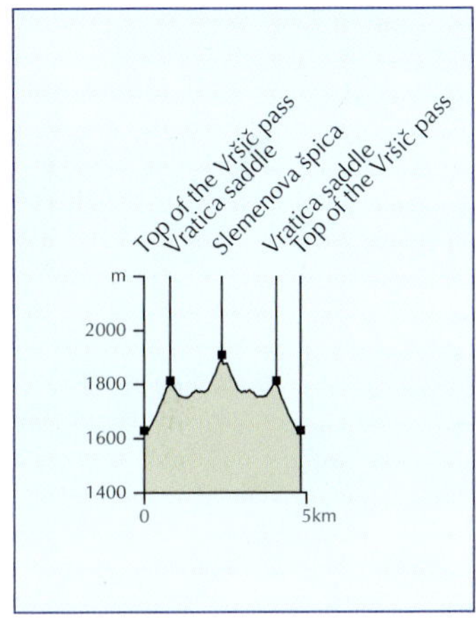

At the top of the Vršič pass, look for a metal sign on the right indicating Sleme 1hr 30min, with an arrow to the right and a waymark on a rock. The route soon enters dwarf pine, climbing steadily up to the right. Cross several quite steep scree gullies on the stable path to reach **Vratica saddle** (1799m, **30min**). Here the path divides: left leads to the Hanzova pot, a difficult protected route on the north face of Mala Mojstrovka, and right leads to Slemenova špica. It is worth lingering in this very attractive spot for a few moments, with its dwarf pine and larch trees beneath the crags of Mojstrovka.

Take the Slemenova špica path, which descends slightly at first and then bears left to reach a pleasant balcony section after 10min, with wonderful views to the Mala Pišnica valley, Ciprnik, the Karavanke and the mountains of Austria beyond. After about 500m, the path crosses the top of a large scree gully which falls steeply down to the right. The summit of Slemenova špica is now visible ahead. Just before you start to climb again, a path heads down to Tamar on the right, signed Grlo (this is another possible route for extending the walk and returning to Kranjska Gora, but the path is more difficult and less well maintained compared with the option via the Slatnica saddle).

Continue straight ahead on the waymarked path, which becomes rockier and begins to ascend. At a junction, bear right and climb steeply for a short distance to reach the open pasture with its tiny pools, about 10min below the summit (here a sign painted on a rock points left to Vršič – this is the route for extending the walk via the Slatnica saddle).

View of the northern slope of Mala Mojstrovka along the route

The beauty of the surrounding mountain scenery makes this a lovely place to relax for a while, and while it can often be busy, there are views enough for everyone. Continue easily to the summit of **Slemenova špica** (1911m, **1hr 30min**), where the slopes fall away on all sides to give views of Tamar, almost vertically below, and the mountains of the north-west Julian Alps.

The walk back to the Vršič pass takes about 1hr.

Extension via the Slatnica saddle

Retrace your steps down to the open pasture with its tiny pools and the sign for Vršič. Take this path and continue for 5min to reach the **Slatnica saddle** (1815m). Follow a sign for Tamar, 1hr 30min from the saddle, and begin to descend the other side, with excellent views of the north wall of the ridge extending from Mala Mojstrovka and Travnik all the way to Jalovec. The path descends pleasant grassy slopes through small open glades and stands of old larch. After 15–20min arrive at a group of boulders. A scramble up the largest provides access to an impressive picnic stop below the north face of Travnik, with the crystal-shaped rock spire of Jalovec forming a beautiful backdrop.

The path passes the boulders to the right and continues down, the beautiful flowers combining with the mountains in a backdrop of classic alpine scenery. Pass a waymark on a rock and cross a scree-filled watercourse, shortly followed by a second one. Another 10min of descent through woods brings you to the top of the steep ravine of the Tamarski slapovi (**Tamar waterfalls**), known locally as Črna voda (black water).

Descend steeply into this ravine, skirting the foot of the cliffs, with a view of the waterfall in the corner. Despite the low altitude, snow often lies in this gully until late in the summer. The path turns right and continues straight down, keeping to the right-hand side of the gully; the loose rock requires care, and this part, mainly in spring time, is exposed to rockfall. Towards the bottom, the path bears to the left and another waterfall comes into view on the right (this is a popular ice-climbing area in winter). Continue following waymarks across stony ground until you join a more obvious broad path heading towards **Dom v Tamarju** (1108m, **3hr 10min**). Follow Walk 6 (Tamar and Planica) to return to **Kranjska Gora**.

Descending from the Vratica saddle in the direction of Slemenova špica

WALK 6

Tamar and Planica

Start/finish	Church in Kranjska Gora (806m)
Time	5–6hr
Distance	21km
Total ascent/descent	370m
Grade	1
Maps	1:25,000 Kranjska Gora, 1:25,000 Triglav
Refreshments	Hotel Dom Planica; café in the central building of the Planica Nordic Centre; Dom v Tamarju

This pleasant walk takes you along easy tracks, through beautiful alpine scenery of mountains and flower meadows, to Planica, where one of the biggest natural ski jumps in the world rises high above the valley floor. The route continues through mixed forest to Dom v Tamarju (1108m), a picturesque mountain hut with a superb view of Jalovec, and then visits Izvir Nadiže (1232m), the source of the short Nadiža river, which soon disappears underground to resurface at Zelenci (Walk 1).

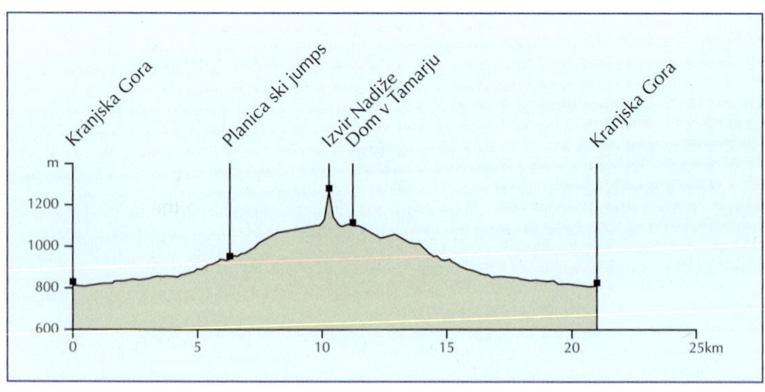

Walk west from the church, past the shops, towards the ski lifts. Where the main road bends sharply right, continue straight ahead, past the chairlifts and parking

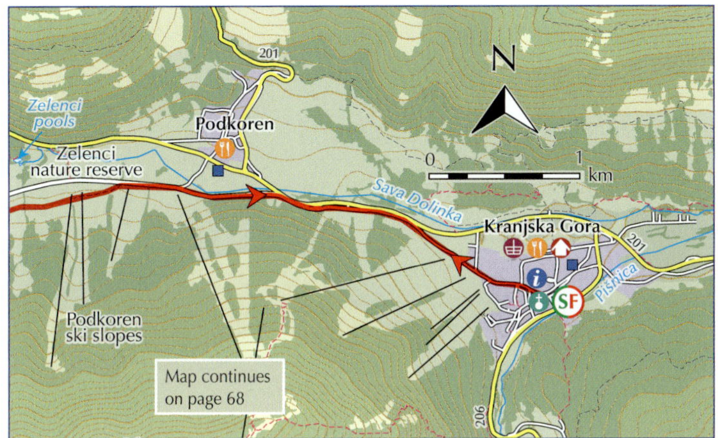

places. The road soon narrows to become a **cycle track** (once the railway) and cars are permitted access only (**15min**). After about 2km, pass a house that was once the railway station at Podkoren, continue for about 100m to a yellow signpost and then take a rough track bearing left, gradually rising away from the cycle track (**45min**).

At a fork, bear left, signed Tamar, and continue across the **Podkoren ski slopes** masquerading as flower meadows in the summer. Where the track turns left and follows the chairlift up the slope, continue straight ahead on a slightly rougher track across the fields, with Visoka Ponca (2274m) dominating the view ahead.

As the track begins to approach the forest, it passes through a second belt of trees and bushes and meets a track curving up and down. Cross this track and continue straight ahead on a narrow path, passing a waymark on a tree. A dry riverbed comes into view on the right. Continue past a small wooden building and begin to ascend slightly, heading into the forest. Emerge from the trees and turn right down a grassy slope. After a short distance arrive at the riverbank and turn right, ignoring a marker for (local) route 9 that points left (**1hr 10min**).

The path now crosses the river and bears left again into woods. Continue for 5min to reach an open pasture with some wooden buildings and here turn left on the grassy track, which brings you across the field to a forest road that re-enters the wood. Walk through a gate and shortly afterwards reach a junction where you turn left, following a sign for Tamar and Planica.

Continue south, cross over the river again and walk through woods to reach an open meadow with a ski lift. At the **Hotel Dom Planica** (934m), bear right past the

buildings and reach a road where you turn right and soon reach a T-junction opposite the winter sports complex at Planica, with its massive ski jumps (**1hr 40min**).

The **Planica ski jumps** are a national icon in Slovenia; the Ski Flying World Cup, held here, is a four-day festival that draws enormous crowds. Planica saw the first 100m jump in 1936, and in 1994 it recorded the first skier to pass 200m; records continue to be broken here. The area continues to be developed with more facilities for winter sports. The Planica Museum, located in the central building of the complex, provides an insight into the heritage of Slovenian Nordic skiing.

Turn left up the road, past the ski jumps, to reach the end of the vehicular valley road just before a wide, dry torrent bed. Two forest trails can be seen on the other side of the watercourse; both of these go through the forest to reach Tamar. Take the right-hand trail. The left-hand track is used as the service road to the hut.

As you approach the attractive **Dom v Tamarju** (1108m, **2hr 45min**), with a small chapel just in front of it, you can see Izvir Nadiže (the true source of the river Sava) up to the right and the mighty crystal-like profile of Jalovec at the head of the valley. A track crosses the *planina* (alp) to the foot of Izvir Nadiže, where a path leads up steeply to the source with the help of a steel handrail. It is well worth the 30min detour from the hut to see the crystal-clear waters gushing wildly from the dark rock.

Return to **Kranjska Gora** down the service road for the hut (not open to private vehicles).

The source of the Nadiža river

The upper part of the Planica valley extends into the Tamar, one of the most beautiful ends of the valley in the Slovenian Alps

WALK 7

Mala Mojstrovka

Start/finish	Top of the Vršič pass (1611m)
Time	3hr 30min
Distance	4.1km
Total ascent/descent	700m
Grade	3
Maps	1:25,000 Kranjska Gora, 1:25,000 Triglav, 1:25,000 Bovec-Trenta
Refreshments	Tičarjev dom na Vršiču (at the top of the Vršič pass)
Access	Regular buses run from Kranjska Gora and Bovec to the top of the Vršič pass in the summer season. See www.kranjska-gora.si for times or check at the bus stop. There are car parks at the top of the pass, but they fill up quickly in high season. A new transit arrangement for vehicles is expected to be in place in 2026
Warning	It's advisable to bring a helmet as the section in the gully near the Vratca saddle is exposed to falling rocks

Mala Mojstrovka (2333m) is a wonderful introduction to the high mountains in the Kranjska Gora area. The bulk of the height gain to the top of the Vršič pass can be achieved by bus or car, so this is an ideal mountain walk for the beginning of a holiday, allowing both body and head to acclimatise to the area. The views are quite extensive and provide a measure of the complexity of the Julian Alps range and an opportunity for orientation. There is a striking contrast between the lush valley and the bare rock, which at first glance looks as though there's nothing living on it – yet during the summer, a surprising number of flowers flourish.

The route starts from the top of the Vršič pass, at the kiosk on the right-hand side as you approach from Kranjska Gora. Bear right behind the kiosk to a red sign: Mala Mojstrovka to the right and Jalovec to the left. Follow the path to the right as it meanders enjoyably up through dwarf pine, quickly gaining height and turning left after about 10min. Continue over the dwarf pine roots entangled in the path before crossing loose rock and scree and arriving at the bottom of a wide **gully** (**30min**).

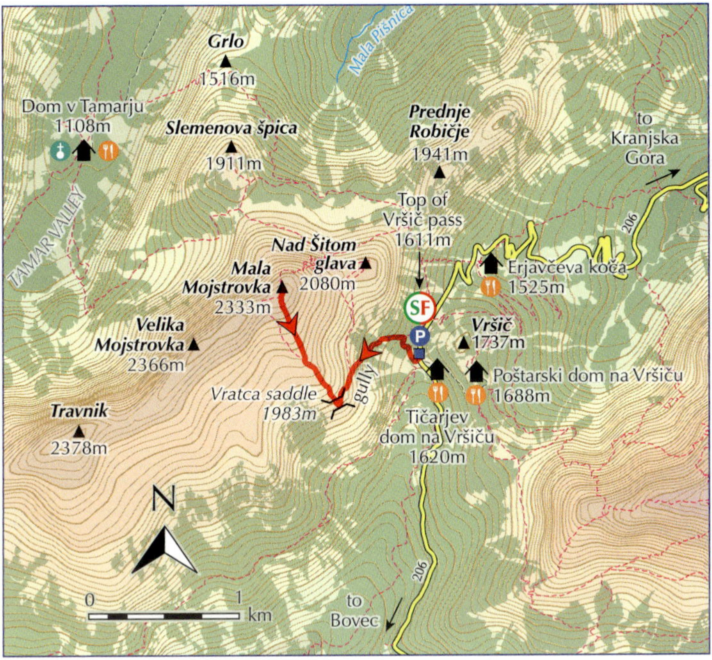

Climb steeply over the loose ground before reaching the final section, which can be somewhat slippery due to erosion; a cable and a few steel pegs provide some protection. From the small grassy saddle of **Vratca** (1983m, **50min**) at the top of the gully, there are good views of the Vršič pass and the mountains stretching into the distance both north and south.

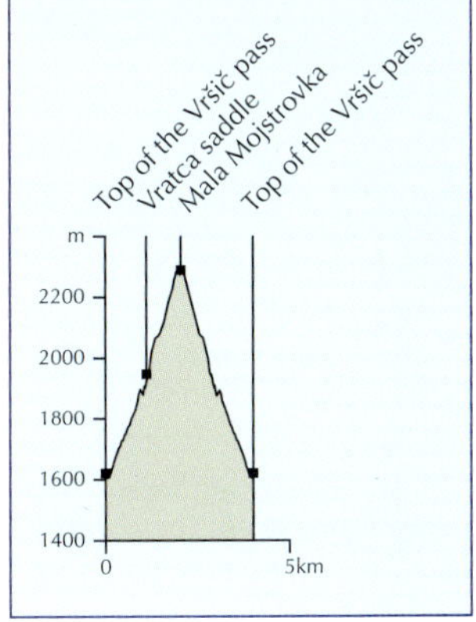

The path turns right at the top of the gully and follows waymarks over some steepish rocky steps intermingled with easier-angled sections to regain the edge – more an escarpment than a ridge – at a little group of cairns (**1hr 15min**). From here

View from the grassy Vratca saddle

a track bears left but keep to the right and ascend quite close to the escarpment edge, as countless boots have caused many deviations from the left-hand route.

The summit is now about 45min away, over broken and slabby, although not very steep, ground. On this section there are no waymarks, but the ascent on the panoramic ridge is easier than the left track, which climbs up the scree. Continue up past the group of large boulders that lie just below the summit of **Mala Mojstrovka** (2333m, **2hr**) on the right, with the craggier top of Velika Mojstrovka to the left.

From the top, **extensive views** stretch in all directions, showing the great expanse and complexity of the Julian Alps massif, as well as the nearby mountains of Austria and Italy. To the west is Velika Mojstrovka, with Mangart beyond, and then Ponca, with the peaks of North-East Italy behind. To the north are Peč and the Karavanke ridge, with the view extending into Austria. To the north-east the view is straight down the Mala Pišnica valley to Jezero Jasna, marking the edge of Kranjska Gora. On the opposite side of the Vršič pass are Prisank, Špik and Škrlatica. To the south lies the Trenta valley and the huge pyramid of Bavški Grintavec. Only Jalovec is missing to the west, hidden behind the bulk of Velika Mojstrovka.

To descend, retrace the route.

An extension to Velika Mojstrovka (2366m) looks enticing – but its ascent is not recommended. There are no waymarks on the route, and small changes over past years, caused by minor rock slides and freeze-thaw action, have made the route more difficult.

WALK 8

Vrata valley

Start/finish	Supermarket in Mojstrana (661m), 13km east of Kranjska Gora
Time	5hr 45min
Distance	19.9km
Total ascent/descent	370m
Grade	2
Maps	1:25,000 Kranjska Gora, 1:25,000 Triglav
Refreshments	Koča pri Peričniku and Aljažev dom
Access	Buses run hourly from Kranjska Gora to the Mojstrana-Dovje bus stop on the main road to Jesenice (10min walk to the starting point). During the summer season, shuttle buses run from Kranjska Gora to the village of Mojstrana and from Mojstrana to Aljažev dom. See www.kranjska-gora.si for times or check at the bus stop

The route up to the Aljažev dom is a delightful walk up the Vrata valley, gateway to the northern Julian Alps, with something of interest around every corner. Don't be tempted to simply walk up the road, which is relatively dull apart from the Peričnik waterfall; the Triglavska Bistrica Trail was developed in 2006 to take advantage of local tracks and is well supplied with information boards explaining the fascinating geology and wildlife of the area.

If you have time, make sure you visit the Slovenian Alpine Museum in Mojstrana, which covers the history of mountaineering in the Slovenian Alps.

Walk along the road, passing a car park and a Triglav National Park (TNP) sign, to reach a couple of houses at **Pri Rosu** and, just beyond them, a small weir with sluices (**30min**). To the right is an information board about the TNP and the Triglavska Bistrica Trail (TBT), with parking for a few cars. Cross the river Bistrica on a footbridge and turn right along the riverbank on a narrow path signed Peričnik, which enters woods. The path becomes narrower as it traverses a steep section a few metres above the river, but soon after this it joins a broader track by a bridge, and you continue straight ahead.

Soon pass the first information boards and continue up the track, through attractive forest carpeted with pink cyclamen and full of birdsong. After about 20min, reach signs directing you right across a footbridge to Slap Peričnik (Peričnik waterfall). On the other side of the river, rejoin the valley road, turning left, and walk up here for 5min to reach **Koča pri Peričniku** (750m, **1hr 15min**) and a car park at the base of the waterfall.

Although you can see the **waterfall** from the road, it's well worth the detour to have a proper look. The upper fall is 16m high and the lower one drops 52m, and you can actually walk behind the lower one. In winter it forms a vast curtain of icicles across the cliff.

After the waterfall, walk along the road for about 25min then leave the tarmac to take a track on the left, following the sign for the TBT. In about 5min take the right-hand fork, with an information board about the galleries (shallow caves in

Slap Peričnik (photo: Roy Clark)

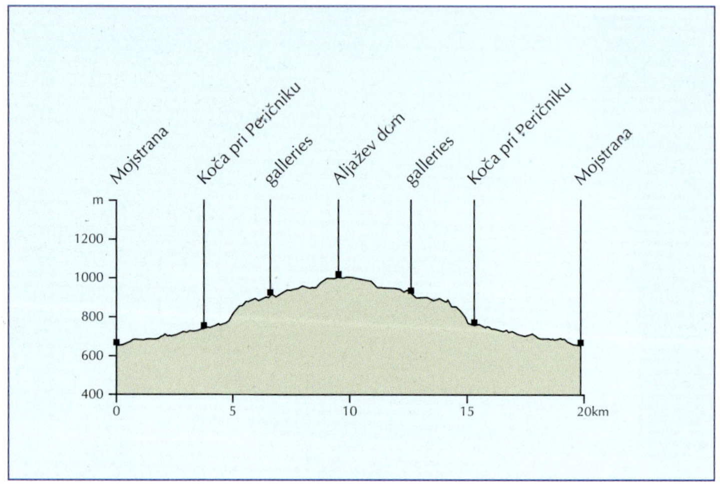

the cliffs), now high above the river (**1hr 45min**). The way leads you beneath the **galleries**, with the cliffs above the path sometimes dripping with water. The forest relents a little here so you can see not only the hillside of Mlinarica opposite but also, slightly ahead, the big pyramid of Cmir with its steep rock walls. Up to the left there's a small 'window' in the ridge of Rjavina.

After the galleries, continue walking along a pleasant broad forest path, passing the **Poldov rovt** *planina* (alp), and in just over 5min rejoin the road and turn left (**2hr 20min**). At a bend in the road, the summit of Triglav comes into view. After about 5min you are directed off the road again to the left. The river is now greatly reduced in size, and you ford it on stepping stones. If you want to avoid fording the river twice on stones, you can continue on the tarmac road, which the route joins later anyway.

On the true right bank, follow a track through the trees and in about 150m come to a disused wooden footbridge that once crossed the river. Ford the river again and turn left on a pretty woodland path signed Aljažev dom. Shortly afterwards, rejoin the road at **Turkov rovt**, with one or two buildings, and turn left. Walk along the road for 10min to reach the big TNP car park. It's a 10min walk from here to **Aljažev dom** (1015m, **3hr**).

Retrace your outward route to the start or, if the service is operating, take the seasonal shuttle bus back to **Mojstrana**.

SLOVENIAN ALPINE MUSEUM

If you haven't visited the Slovenian Alpine Museum yet, don't miss it! Opened in 2010, the museum is a unique mountain and mountaineering centre in Slovenia. In 11 thematic sections, you pass through the milestones in the history of Slovenian mountaineering, alpinism and mountain rescue, learning about the motives that have always drawn people to the mountains and experiencing the unique attraction and magic of the mountains. Virtual experiences are also on offer, taking you around Slovenia's 30 most popular peaks, across the narrow Triglav ridge or on a ride in the cable car from the top of Slovenia's highest mountain. The museum shop offers a range of mountaineering guides and reference books, maps and literature for all generations (for more information, see www.planinskimuzej.si).

WALK 9

Jerebikovec

Start/finish	Mojstrana-Dovje bus stop (661m), on the main road to Jesenice
Time	4–5hr
Distance	9.3km
Total ascent/descent	1000m
Grade	2/3
Maps	1:25,000 Kranjska Gora
Refreshments	None on the route; restaurants in Mojstrana
Access	Buses run hourly from Kranjska Gora to Mojstrana
Note	In 2023 this path was closed due to trees felled during a storm. It is hoped that the trail will reopen (see https://mapzs.pzs.si for updates on the status of the trail)

Jerebikovec is a fine hill lying to the south of Mojstrana, about 13km east of Kranjska Gora. At 1593m it provides an outstanding view of Triglav and its surrounding summits, which sit at the head of the three beautiful valleys of Krma, Kot and Vrata. The walk climbs steeply through beautiful forest to an old *planina* (alp), which nature is starting to reclaim, before reaching the summit.

Just above the road is a monument to **Jakob Aljaž** (1845–1927), who was the priest in Dovje and a pioneer of mountaineering in Slovenia. He bought the summit of Triglav for a nominal sum to keep it in Slovene ownership and was influential in the building of many paths and huts, including the one which bears his name, Aljažev dom.

From the bus stop, head down the lane towards Mojstrana. Cross the river **Sava Dolinka** on the road bridge and continue in the same direction, through the village, to a left turn, signed Radovna and Krma. Cross the river Bistrica and follow the road round to the left, past the post office, then take a right turn signed Bled and Krma (**15min**). The minor road climbs steeply between the houses and bears right before it becomes broader. Continue up the road, and after about 500m pass

a large metal sign for Triglav National Park. Another 400m after the sign, look for a narrow path on the left and a sign indicating Jerebikovec 2hr (**35min**).

The path climbs up into the woods and after about 150m bears left. Continue climbing for 30–40min through the trees to reach the edge of a forested ridge. There is a good view here down to the village of Dovje on the other side of the valley, with the Karavanke hills behind. The path turns right and continues on through fine beech and spruce forest for a further 30–40min before arriving

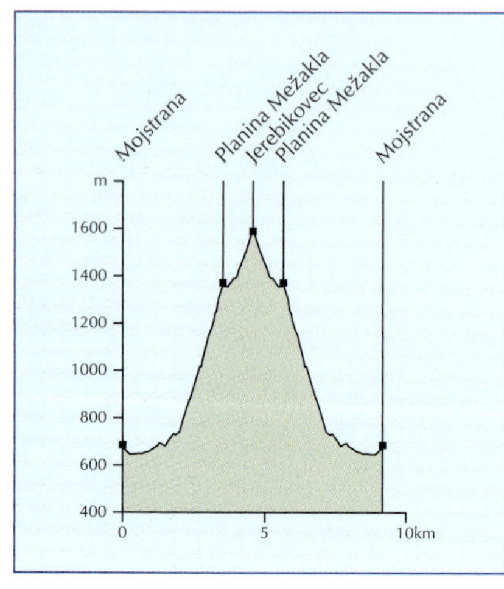

at Planina Mežakla, where there is a bench and a **partisan memorial** (**2hr**). The planina was abandoned in 1969.

The path continues beyond the planina, signed Jerebikovec. It soon joins a broader track which ascends gently for about 350m to reach a level col (1330m, **2hr 10min**). Turn left and almost immediately take a path on the right going up into the woods, again signed Jerebikovec. Climb up through the woods for about 15min onto the west ridge and continue along the forested crest, now rockier in places. The path suddenly emerges on to the summit of **Jerebikovec**, clear of trees, with its wonderful panorama (1593m, **2hr 45min**).

From the summit, the **view of Triglav** is magnificent, and Stol, the highest summit of the Karavanke, is visible to the east, although other peaks of the range are somewhat obscured by trees.

The descent to **Mojstrana** is by the same route.

Looking south up the Krma and Kot valleys to Triglav (photo: Roy Clark)

WALK 10

Prisank

Start/Finish	Top of the Vršič pass (1611m)
Time	6hr
Distance	8.3km
Total ascent/descent	950m
Grade	4
Maps	1:25,000 Kranjska Gora, 1:25,000 Triglav, 1:25,000 Bovec-Trenta
Refreshments	Tičarjev dom and Poštarski dom na Vršiču (both at the top of the Vršič pass)
Access	Regular buses run from Kranjska Gora and Bovec to the top of the Vršič pass in the summer season. See www.kranjska-gora.si for times or check at the bus stop. There are car parks at the top of the pass, but they fill up quickly in high season. A new transit arrangement for vehicles is expected to be in place in 2026
Warning	This is a true mountaineering route; via ferrata kit and helmet are strongly recommended

Prisank (2547m), also known as Prisojnik, lies to the east of the Vršič pass. It is a huge and complex mountain with many routes. Its east–west ridge dominates the skyline as seen from Kranjska Gora, its most obvious feature from here being the east 'window'. In fact, there are two windows on Prisank, and the route described here goes directly past the other, larger, western one, Prednje Prisankovo okno (meaning 'the front Prisank window'). The route is not overly difficult and all of the exposed sections are well protected. It is nevertheless a serious mountain route, so appropriate gear and experience are essential.

At the top of the Vršič pass, take the service road leading up left, past Tičarjev dom. Walk up the broad track and soon reach a bend and turn sharp left. A sign at the bend says, 'Poštarski dom 5min'. Follow the gravel road as it passes between two old military defences – a huge gun emplacement to the right and a smaller pill box to the left. As you pass them and round a corner, arrive at an information board and a terrific view of Prisank's north face (**15min**). Notice the sad 'face' in the rock of Ajdovska deklica (the pagan girl), a natural rock sculpture on the crags straight ahead.

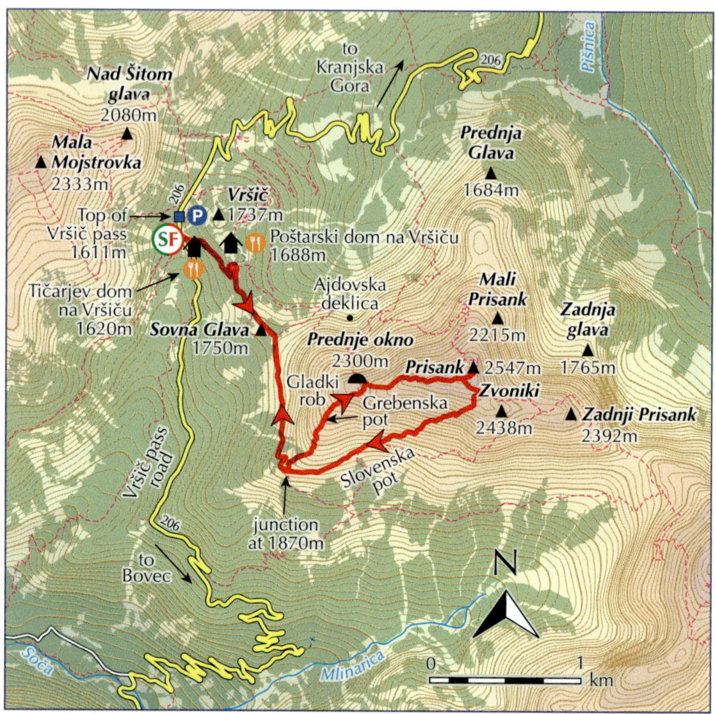

The gravel road continues a short distance to the dom, but leave it here to the right on a narrow path signed to Prisojnik (the other name for the mountain) and Razor. Another path, also on the right, signed Prisojnik via Skozi Okno 3hr 30min, descends into the larch trees, but this leads to a difficult, protected route up the north face. Carry on through dwarf pine and then over short grass as you pass close to the little top of **Sovna Glava** (1750m) and descend to arrive at a group of boulders at a level saddle (**30min**).

The waymarked path begins to ascend diagonally across fairly extensive screes before reaching the lower rocks of the south-east ridge. Continue, between dwarf pine again, a short distance to a junction at **1870m** (**1hr**). Turn left, signed Prisojnik (Grebenska pot) 2hr, and begin ascending the **Gladki rob** (meaning 'smooth edge'). The path climbs very steeply at first, and after about 20min the

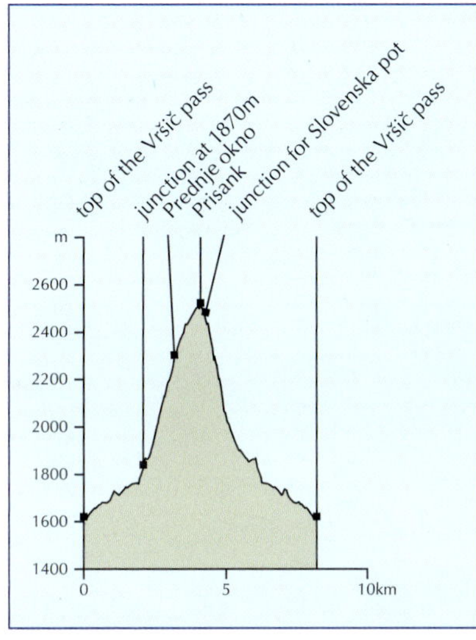

dwarf pine thins then ceases abruptly, and you continue on the stony waymarked path. There are excellent views to the left of the crags that form the huge western spur. Mangart, Jalovec and Mala and Velika Mojstrovka are on display, while through the gap in the Vršič pass you can see into Austria.

The path keeps quite close to the left-hand side of the grassy edge, climbing steadily before bearing diagonally right as it approaches the crags. Abruptly, you reach the lip of **Prednje okno** (2300m, **2hr 15min**). It is absolutely vast – a cathedral-sized gaping cavern, with the wind sometimes rushing up through it.

The route now leads up rocks on the right-hand side. After about 50m of easy scrambling on good rock, reach the first protected section: a steel cable heading up towards the ridge proper. Continue to follow the cables onto the ridge. It is quite steep and somewhat exposed in places but well equipped.

Follow the waymarks along the ridge, which gives thrilling views of Vršič lying almost vertically below. Some easy scrambling over rock steps helps keep the mind and body focused, but steel cables and pegs secure any difficulties.

The route continues, becoming easier as you gain height, and bears more to the right-hand side as you approach the summit section. Continue diagonally up to the left on good rock, and just beyond some steel cables descend a few metres to the top of another cable that heads down (this will be the descent route: Slovenska pot). Signs are painted on the rock – straight up for Prisojnik, and down for Vršič, Okno 2, Mlinarica and Slovenska. Continue straight up on fairly steep slabby rock to reach the summit of **Prisank** (2547m, **3hr 30min**). There is a wonderful panorama, not just of the Julian Alps but also of the Hohe Tauern region of Austria and even the Dolomites in Italy on a good day.

Descend to the painted signs and steel cables and head straight down from here, very steeply, following the Vršič and Slovenska waymarks. Continue down over slabby rock and stones for 10min or so to reach a junction where you turn right, following a sign on a rock for Vršič (**3hr 50min**). Descend more steeply and

Hikers on the summit of Prisank

then traverse a broad ledge that leads right, across the gully. Continue over loose, stony ground, then make a short descent of a rocky nose before suddenly turning right and dropping down through a notch into another smaller gully.

The route continues, bearing right down a series of gullies with some short sections of steep scrambling, but with all the difficulties well secured. The path keeps to the left-hand side of the final gully and exits onto a rocky, grassy spur. Down below you can see the path that traverses the flank of the hill which will take you back to Vršič. Continue down over grass and stones before traversing right, across the lower part of the gully, where the ground becomes easier and finally reaches the level path, where you turn right and soon reach the junction of the ascent path at the foot of **Gladki rob** (**5hr**).

Continue straight ahead, retracing your outward steps to the starting point.

WALK 11

Jalovec

Start/finish	Top of the Vršič pass (1611m)
Time	2 days (12–13hr)
Distance	17.6km
Total ascent/descent	1585m
Grade	4
Maps	1:25,000 Kranjska Gora, 1:25,000 Triglav, 1:25,000 Bovec-Trenta
Accommodation	Zavetišče pod Špičkom
Access	Regular buses run from Kranjska Gora and Bovec to the top of the Vršič pass in the summer season; see www.kranjska-gora.si for times or check at the bus stop. There are car parks at the top of the pass, but they fill up quickly in high season. A new transit arrangement for vehicles is expected to be in place in 2026
Warning	This is a true mountaineering route; a helmet, self-belaying equipment and possibly an ice axe are all strongly advised

Jalovec (2645m) is arguably the most beautiful peak in Slovenia, poised like a giant crystal guarding the head of the Planica valley. It dominates the skyline from the south too, rising proudly above the Trenta and Koritnica valleys. On the Trenta side of the Vršič pass stands the statue of the pioneering climber Julius Kugy, his face turned eternally towards his favourite mountain. Jalovec holds a special place in the hearts of Slovene mountaineers, not least because of its difficulty, which is significant from all directions; it is without doubt one of the more serious routes described in this book.

This route comprises a half-day's walk up to Zavetišče pod Špičkom (2064m), followed by the ascent of Jalovec (2645m) and the return on Day 2.

DAY 1

Top of the Vršič pass to Zavetišče pod Špičkom

Start	Top of the Vršič pass (1611m)
Finish	Zavetišče pod Špičkom (2064m)
Distance	6.8km
Ascent	700m
Descent	255m
Time	4hr

Of all the routes leading to Jalovec, the one from the Vršič Pass is perhaps the most popular among hikers, as it saves some altitude. The first part of the walk to Zavetišče pod Špičkom winds gently through the forests beneath the Mojstrovka peaks, with magnificent views opening up between the trees. Once out of the forest, the route begins to climb rather steeply and completely exposed to the sun, but with increasingly scenic views. Even if you do not intend to climb Jalovec, this route as far as the hut makes for an enjoyable day's walk from the top of the Vršič pass.

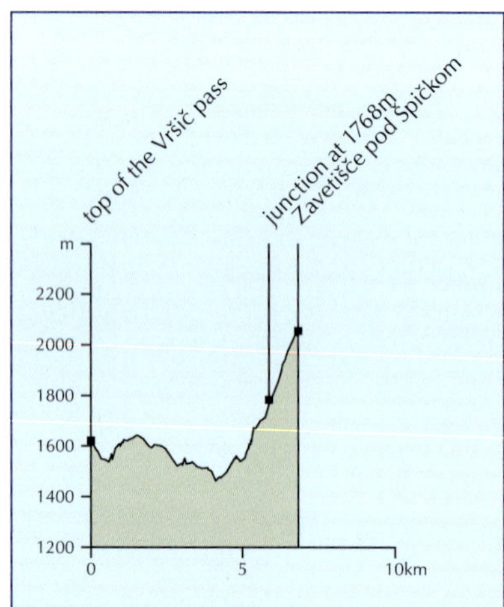

The route starts from the top of the Vršič pass, at the kiosk on the right-hand side as you approach from Kranjska Gora. Bear right behind the kiosk to a red sign: Zavetišče pod Špičkom 4hr and Jalovec 5hr to the left and Mala Mojstrovka 2hr to the right. The route to Jalovec via Zavetišče pod Špičkom is part of the Slovenian Mountain Trail (SMT) and is well waymarked and signed throughout.

Almost immediately pass a sign on a rock for Jalovec and Špiček and then descend over scree and dwarf pine to reach trees and a steep rock face. The path soon begins to climb, gently at first, then steeply, protected by two sections of steel cables – not difficult (**15min**).

After this, the path enters the forest and flattens out, winding along the slopes of Mojstrovka.

The walk is pleasant, shaded by trees and with many flowers on both sides of the path and even a few varieties of mushrooms. To the left, through the trees and the occasional open area, there are magnificent views of some of the highest peaks in the Julian Alps. First Prisank, Razor, Kanjavec and Veliko Špičje, then as you continue, Triglav comes into view. Apart from a few short climbs, the route is mostly downhill, now above the Zadnja Trenta valley. Finally, the view opens up to Jalovec and the jagged peak of Špiček, below which the hut is located (**1hr 45min**). If you look closely, you can see the hut from here.

After about 2hr from the start of the walk, reach a junction where you turn right, following signs for Mali kot and Zavetišče pod Špičkom. Ascend gently through the forest, pass a sign for Špička painted on a rock and after a few minutes

The last section of the path to Zavetišče pod Špičkom

follow another sign on a tree for Špiček, Mali kot and Jalovec. After 100m or so the path divides: right leads to Jalovec via the col of Jalovška škrbina and left leads to Zavetišče pod Špičkom and Trenta. Take the left and soon meet a path that descends left, signed Trenta. Ignore this and continue straight ahead, following waymarks (**2hr 20min**).

Shortly afterwards, the path begins to climb more steeply, gradually emerging from the forest. Continue across steep scree below crags then through thickets of dwarf pine to reach a junction at **1768m**, where a path is signed left again to Trenta. Continue straight on, following a sign for Zavetišče pod Špičkom 1hr, and within a few paces you will see **Špiček** with its hut below, looking not too far away (**3hr**).

The stony path now climbs through rocky karst scenery. After about 40min a path is signed right to Jalovec, but you continue up for another 20min to reach the overnight stop at **Zavetišče pod Špičkom** (2064m, **4hr**).

> The small **hut** is one of the most scenic in the Julian Alps, with views stretching towards the Zgornja Trenta valley, surrounded by Prisojnik, Razor, Planja and Pihavec, with Triglav visible behind the latter. Just behind the hut, Mali Ozebnik and Vrh Zelenic rise to the west and Veliki Ozebnik to the north, blocking the view of Jalovec. Be sure to rise early in the morning, as the sunrise from here is spectacular!

DAY 2

Zavetišče pod Špičkom to the top of the Vršič pass

Start	Zavetišče pod Špičkom (2064m)
Finish	Top of the Vršič pass (1611m)
Distance	10.8km
Ascent	885m
Descent	1330m
Time	8–9hr

From Zavetišče pod Špičkom, the route soon becomes serious as it climbs up the steep crags of Veliki Ozebnik. Although the first part of the ascent is well protected on the steep, rocky sections, later on, the route is poorly protected on loose rock and is exposed to falling rocks (wear a helmet!). The last section on the exposed ridge requires a strong head for heights.

The return to the Vršič Pass is long, so an early start is advised.

From the hut, descend for a few minutes along the path you came from then take the waymarked path that bears to the left towards the crags of **Veliki Ozebnik**. Shortly after, notice on some boulders the interesting inscriptions (verses) praising the mountains and Jalovec: on one of them is written, 'The beauty of the mountains; this is Slovenia. Jalovec, the king of the mountains!' Jalovec is so iconic that its triangular shape is featured in the symbol of the Alpine Association of Slovenia.

Continue over scree and rubble which bring you to the foot of steeper crags (**15min**). Start climbing and soon meet the first steel cables and pegs. This first section of the climb takes place in steep and rocky terrain, and some sections are quite exposed but well protected. After about 20min, the path turns left and climbs through a notch for a few metres before turning right again, secured by steel cables. From here on, the path becomes less protected, and crossing the steep slope below Veliki Ozebnik requires great care due to the loose rock.

Continue climbing for another 30min and you will finally see the summit of Jalovec, which is still quite far away. Shortly afterwards, the path crosses a short exposed gully secured by steel cables and then leads onto grassy terrain. The route now descends a little to reach the mountain plain of Jezerce at the head of the **Loški žleb gully** (**1hr 30min**). An ice axe might well be required here, as the snow lies late at the head of the gully.

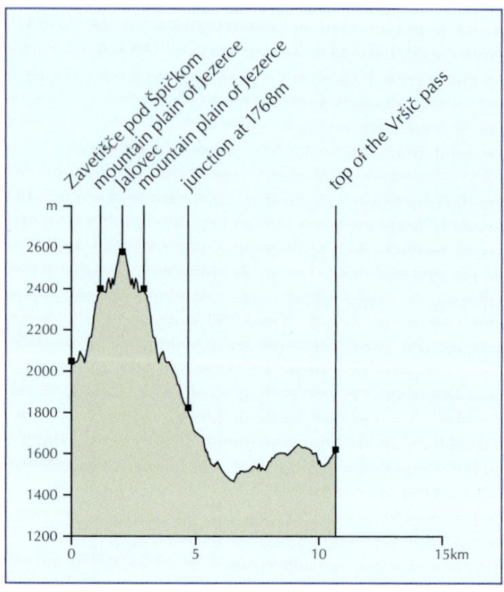

Pass a path heading right to Jalovška škrbina and reach the foot of the lower rocks of the summit section of Jalovec. Continue over rocky ledges with abundant flowers among the rocks and, although there are no real difficulties, follow the waymarks carefully as it is easy to end up on very tricky ground if you lose your concentration. Follow a shallow gully with rock steps to reach the crest of the south ridge, with spectacular views of the Koritnica valley and Mangart.

Continue along the exposed ridge for about 10min, keeping to the right (east) side when not on the crest, to reach a notch. Pass through to the left side of the ridge to meet a junction; a sign, Tamar 5hr, indicates a path (marked *zelo*

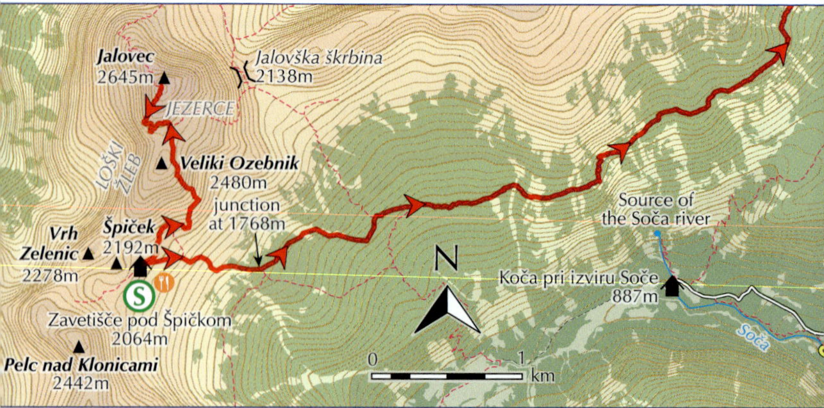

Summit of Jalovec

zahtevna pot, meaning 'very difficult route') heading down to the left. Another 5min or so brings you to the summit of **Jalovec** (2645m), marked by a metal crown symbolising its status (**2hr 30min**).

Take your time to admire the superb view of the Julian Alps of Slovenia, as well as the Italian and Austrian hills to the north and west, before returning to the Zavetišče pod Špičkom hut and the Vršič pass by the same route.

WALK 12

Špik

Start/finish	Church in Kranjska Gora (806m)
Time	10–11hr
Distance	19.1km
Total ascent/descent	1615m
Grade	4
Maps	1:25,000 Kranjska Gora, 1:25,000 Triglav
Refreshments	Koča v Krnici
Parking	There is a small parking area at the bridge, which reduces the total walking time by about 1hr 30min
Warning	On this route, a helmet is recommended. Make sure you take plenty of water, as this is a long walk across arid mountainside

The shapely pyramid of Špik (2473m) can clearly be seen towards the right of the great cirque of mountains viewed from Gozd Martuljek. There are no walkers' routes on the northern side but the western approach is not so precipitous, and this fine route can be completed in a day from Kranjska Gora. The route gives a close-up view of the dizzying cliffs and ridges of this northern spur of the Julian Alps, and although it is steep and has some short sections with cables and steel pegs, it is not overly difficult and self-belaying techniques are not required.

It is a long and tiring route, but it is possible to stay overnight in Koča v Krnici (1hr 40min from Kranjska Gora) and continue early in the morning from there.

From Kranjska Gora, follow Walk 4 to **Lake Jasna** (**25min**). Just before the lake, cut across the car park to a walking track that goes past the lake on the right. Follow this until it rejoins the road, then continue on the road to the bridge across the **Pišnica river**. Don't cross it, but take the broad track to the left, heading south alongside the river and signed Krnica and Vršič (**40min**). After about 25min from the bridge, pass a large rock with Špik painted on it to the left of the track and a sign indicating, Pot na Špik via Skozi Kačji graben 4hr; this marks the descent route. About 10min later, reach two metal gateposts (with no gate) just before a wide, dry watercourse. Cross over and walk along the broad trail (**1hr 15min**).

201
Sava Dolinka
Kranjska Gora
Pišnica
201
Gozd
Martuljek
N
0
1
km
206
Lake
Jasna
Mala Pišnica
Črni vrh
1481m
Škrbinjek
1341m
Kurji vrh
1762m
Vršič pass road
Rigljica
2040m
Rušica
Vrh nad Rudo
2108m
Mavrinc
1272m
206
Špik
2473m
Na pečeh
2039m
Mihov dom
na Vršiču
1085m
Kačji
graben
Lipnica
2417m
Pišnica
Velika
Ponca
2602m
memorial
shrine
V Klinu
TARMANOVA
ŽLEFA
Gamsova špica
1931m
Prednja
Glava
1684m
GRUNTOVNICA
Škrlatica
2740m
Mali
Prisank
2215m
Koča v Krnici
1113m
Mizica
1711m
Spodnja
Dolkova špica
2541m
Zadnja glava
1765m

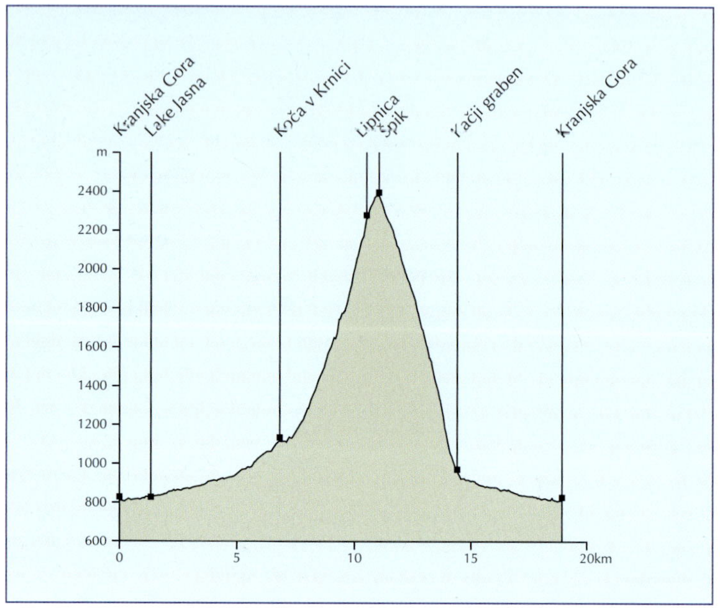

Within another 150m come to a junction close to a **memorial shrine** and join a track that links with the one coming down from hairpin bend 3 on the Vršič road. The track bears left towards the dry river courses, which just here are at right angles to each other. Cross the first tributary watercourse and walk a few metres up the right-hand side (looking ahead) of the other, main, one. Almost immediately there are waymarks for a narrow path turning right into the forest, and a little further on, waymarks indicate the continuation of the forest road. Either of these will bring you to **Koča v Krnici** (1113m) in 20–25min (**1hr 40min**).

At the hut, the path is signed Špik 4hr. It is well waymarked and signed throughout. The route initially heads off to the north-east, entering the wood and descending a little to cross a dry riverbed. It then begins a gentle ascent through the woods before crossing another watercourse. The well-trodden path then ascends through dwarf pine on the right-hand edge of the **Gruntovnica valley**. Looking up the valley, you can see the sheer rock faces of Škrlatica and its satellite tops.

About 20min from the hut, the path bears right to cross a dry riverbed. Continue ascending on the right of the watercourse, following the waymarks on the rough scree- and boulder-covered path. As the watercourse steepens and starts to narrow, waymarks lead you across to the left-hand side, which you follow for a further 150m before finally exiting on the left.

The path now climbs up and bears sharply left, past a boulder waymarked Špik, and begins a long rising traverse under the crags of **Gamsova špica**, over scree and boulders (**3hr**). After the traverse, back in dwarf pine and larch, ascend a steep trough, initially staying on the right-hand side. Before reaching its head, traverse left and continue zigzagging up quite steeply to exit on the left into the upper part of the wider Tarmanova žlefa valley.

The dwarf pine has thinned out and you are now on grass and rock, with the little craggy top of Gamsova špica close by on the right. Continue to a small col with an amazing view into a steep chasm on its south side (**4hr 30min**). Turn left and continue to another small col, where the route bears left once more. The path steepens and becomes rockier and soon reaches the 20m or so of cables on Lipnica; the initial 5m are steeper than anything that follows. The angle eases again over the remaining rocks and the path broadens, decorated with bright blue gentians, to climb easily to the summit of **Lipnica** (2417m). Špik stands close by to the north, looking like the spear that gives it its name. There are spectacular views to the right, with the rock faces of the Škrlatica group dropping into the depths.

Continue the short distance down to the rocky saddle between Lipnica and Špik, without much height loss. The route keeps to the left-hand side, below the

Koča v Krnici

rocky crest; there are some steel cables and pegs on the traverse but it is not too difficult or exposed. Start to ascend again and pass a waymark for Črna voda pointing down – this is the descent route. Continue to the top of **Špik** (2473m) via fairly steep rocks, taking care not to dislodge the loose stones (**6hr 15min**).

The **summit** is surprisingly roomy but drops off dramatically to the north, with excellent views east to the Gozd Martuljek cirque. A little to the south is Škrlatica, then Razor and Prisank. In the Sava valley you can see Podkoren and Gozd Martuljek, although Kranjska Gora is hidden behind the ridges of Špik's north-west spur.

Retrace your steps to the sign for Črna voda. The first 100m or so of descent from here is awkward because the ground is steep and the scree makes it unstable. As you reach the more forgiving scree, the path begins to bear right, traversing to avoid some crags. After passing the crags, it turns left and continues down. Pass some house-sized boulders and, at the end of this long descending traverse, reach the start of the treeline (**7hr 30min**).

Continue descending pleasantly but quite steeply into woods. There are a few short sections with cables and pegs over small rocky steps and bluffs. The descent is long and consistently steep, but eventually you hear the rushing of the river Pišnica in the bottom of the valley.

Finally, the angle eases and there is a dry, rocky watercourse on your right – **Kačji graben**. Shortly afterwards, cross the watercourse and carry on; ahead and to the left on the other side of the river you can see the pleasant green *planina* (alp) of V Klinu with its wooden buildings. Continue over stony ground with dwarf pine before entering the final section of woodland to reach the forest road (**10hr**). Turn right, back towards the bridge over the Pišnica, and retrace your steps to **Kranjska Gora**.

SECTION 2
BOHINJ

Aljaž's tower on the summit of Triglav (Walk 21)

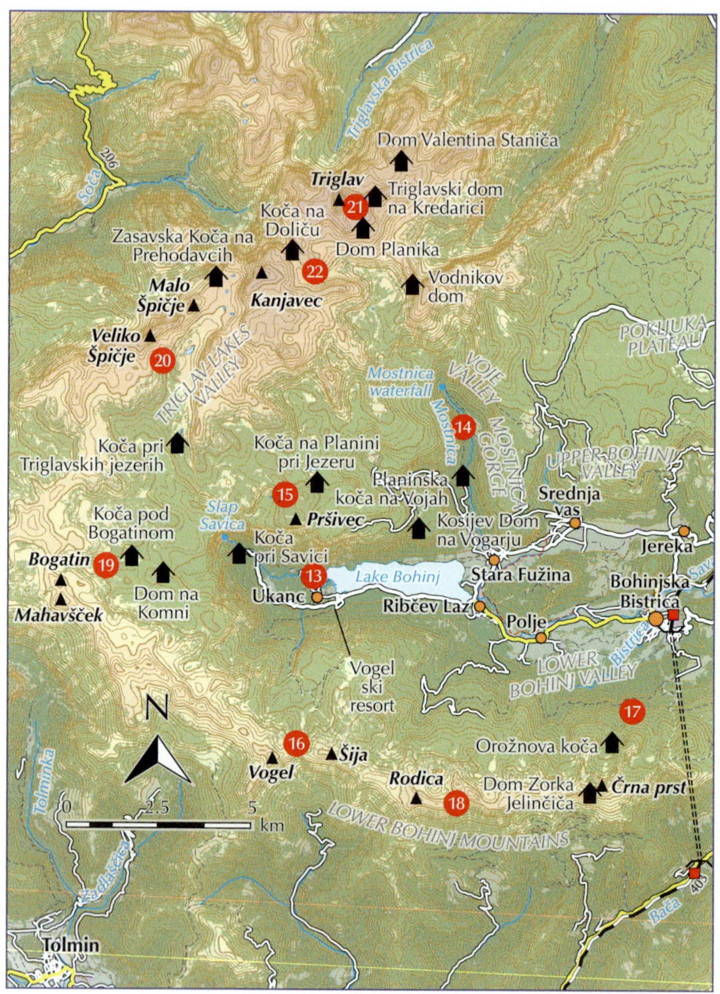

Bohinj (525m) is the largest of Slovenia's permanent lakes. The glacial lake in its long valley, surrounded by high mountains, is one of the great sights of Slovenia in its own right, but the valley is also an excellent base for mountaineering in the Julian Alps. The axis of the lake is east–west – to the south lies the ridge of the Lower Bohinj mountains with their wonderful natural flower gardens, while to the north the high mountains begin in cliffs and plateaus that rise up almost from the lakeshore. The village of Ribčev Laz at the eastern end of the lake, with its beautiful stone bridge and church, is the classic viewpoint, and here too is a well-known statue celebrating the four men who first climbed Triglav.

There is no large centre for tourism here (and no town called Bohinj). Instead, a number of villages, particularly Bohinjska Bistrica, Ribčev Laz and Stara Fužina, supply visitors with all their needs: hotels, apartments, hostels, campsites, shops and tourist information. A number of tourist farmhouses also offer accommodation. However, don't expect large hotels and apartment blocks – Lake Bohinj sits firmly inside Triglav National Park, and so development is limited. In fact, a good deal of the area's charm originates in its undeveloped feel, and the villages have retained their alpine way of life. Here the old houses and barns of the villages nestle together as if to ready themselves for the harshness of the alpine winter, and the new buildings, thankfully, maintain a similar style.

Plentiful iron ore in the area ensured Bohinj's prosperity from early times until competition closed the last of the smelters in the late 19th century. Fortunately, the opening of a railway link in 1906, which connected Bohinj with the coast, brought new opportunities for tourism and trade. For centuries, the area has also been important for alpine dairy farming and cheese-making.

Access to Bohinj is mainly via a good road from Bled; it takes about 25min. Regular buses run throughout the year from Ukanc to Ribčev Laz and Bohinjska Bistrica, and the area is well served by direct buses to Bled and Ljubljana. Especially in the summer months, a car is not really necessary here; to encourage green mobility, additional public transport lines and free shuttle buses to the main starting points of the trails are generally available from June to September (for more information, visit www.bohinj.si). Arriving in Bohinj by train from Nova Gorica and the Soča valley is a wonderful experience. The Bohinj railway line, which connects Nova Gorica to Jesenice via Bohinjska Bistrica, is one of the most picturesque and historically rich in Slovenia. Several daily car trains also run on this line from Most na Soči to Bohinjska Bistrica: this service saves a lot of time for those travelling by car between Bohinj and the Soča valley.

The Triglav National Park Information Centre, with its permanent exhibition 'The Lake', is located in the village of Stara Fužina, a 15min walk from the lake. The centre has a leisure room, with a view of Lake Bohinj, and a shop selling local products.

Lake Bohinj from Ribčev Laz (Walk 13)

THE ROUTES

Bohinj is an excellent base for all kinds of outdoor activities. The 10 walks described in this section include both easy routes that provide a flavour of the valley, its villages, viewpoints and waterfalls (Walks 13 and 14) and harder and longer ones that include the mountains of the Lower Bohinj range on the south side (Walks 16, 17 and 18) and several peaks in the Julian Alps, including Triglav (Walks 15 and 19–22). The ski resort of Vogel (1535m) is situated at the far end of the lake to the south, and its skiers' cable car can be used in the summer to gain height for some of the walks or simply to marvel at the unsurpassed view of Triglav and its mighty neighbours. There are also almost unlimited possibilities for hut-to-hut routes in the Bohinj area.

MAPS

All the routes in this section are covered by 1:25,000 Bohinj, and all except Walks 16–18 are on 1:25,000 Triglav.

WALK 13

Tour of Lake Bohinj

Start/finish	Bridge at Ribčev Laz (532m)
Time	3hr 45min (with extension 5hr 45min)
Distance	11.6km (with extension to Savica waterfall 19.2km)
Total ascent/descent	205m (with extension 530m)
Grade	1 (with extension 1/2)
Maps	1:25,000 Bohinj, 1:25,000 Triglav
Refreshments	On the extension route to Savica waterfall: Koča pri Savici and Planinski dom Savica (both open only during the tourist season)
Access	Regular buses run from Bohinjska Bistrica via the Upper and Lower Bohinj valleys to Ribčev Laz, and shuttle buses are usually added to regular services in high season. See www.bohinj.si for times or check at the bus stop. If you arrive by car, there are several car parks in Ribčev Laz (parking fee)

Bohinj is one of the classic beauty spots of Slovenia, and this tour around the lake gives ample opportunity to absorb its delights. The lakeshore can get busy in high season, so this route mostly follows quiet paths through the forest, which, particularly on the south side, leave the day trippers behind so that you can appreciate the wonderful natural scenery in peace.

There is an option to extend the walk to Slap Savica (Savica waterfall), one of the main attractions of the Bohinj area and arguably the best-known waterfall in Slovenia. The water slides 38m down an angled gully and then falls free for a further 51m. The extension starts in Ukanc and follows the main signposted route to the fall; an entrance fee is charged for the final section and viewpoint. The route returns through meadows and forests to Ukanc from where you can continue the tour of the lake.

Walk away from the bridge on the road heading west towards Ukanc and follow the lakeshore, past the car parks, to the **statue of Zlatorog**.

Zlatorog is the golden-horned animal god of Slovenian legend whose realm was among the peaks of Mount Triglav. Whether it was a chamois or an ibex

Grıva 1758m
Vrtec 1811m
PLANINA VIŠEVNIK 1625m
Vodični vrh 1621m
Stador 1688m
Rigelj 1768m
Kamen 1028m
N
Črno jezero 1319m
Pršivec 1761m
Kosijev Dom na Vogarju 1054m
KOMARČA
Studor 1002m
0
1
km
MOSTNICA GORGE
Slap Savica
Koča pri Savici (653m)
pay kiosk
Govic
Stara Fužina
Triglav National Park Information Centre
beach
Na Jami
gravel walkway
Lake Bohinj
beach
beach
gravel walkway
Savica
Ukanška glava 574m
Planina Blato
Camp Bohinj
Ukanc
statue of Zlatorog
Vogel cable-car station
hunting trail
Ribčev Laz
Veliki Grad 684m
hunting trail
to Bohinjska Bistrica
209
Sava Bohinjka
Konjski Vrh 1739m

depends on which statue you see and which story you read. Here the statue is a chamois – at Lake Jasna in Kranjska Gora, it's an ibex!

About 100m further on, there is a small mooring on the right and a crag on the left hung with the fixed ropes of a sport-climbing venue. A **gravel walkway** by the road starts on the left and just by it there is a sign to Ukanc (local route 2) along the gravel walkway, or Ukanc – *lovska pot* (**hunting trail**) on a small path climbing a little into the woods above the road (**5min**).

The way described here continues along the small path, which is far more pleasant and peaceful. In 2023, the hunting trail was seriously damaged by falling trees during a storm but is now clear and passable again.

As you climb away from the lake, the noise of a busy summer gradually recedes until the only sounds are those of the forest. About 15min from the lake, cross a little wooden bridge over a pretty stream bubbling among mossy boulders and, shortly after this, pass a tiny spring on the left which tumbles over a miniature cliff. The path then continues its traverse, crossing many stream beds, usually dry, on wooden bridges. Ignore logging tracks to the right and left; the path is obvious throughout its 3.5km length and indicated by yellow target waymarks.

After about 1hr reach a viewpoint with a bench. Thanks to the presence of some electricity cables, the trees give way to a beautiful view. Take a moment to admire the first good view since entering the forest; you can see the lake and the cliffs of Komarča (Walk 20) at the head of the valley. About 10min further on, the path begins to descend gently. Cross a deep, dry riverbed filled with large boulders carried down by the torrent during floods, and about 5min later a yellow sign across the path directs you right and down to the **cable-car station** (**1hr 40 min**).

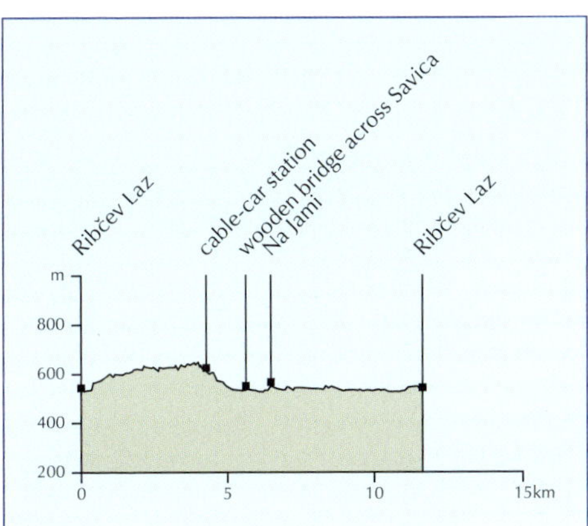

Turn right and walk down the tarmac road at the end of the car park to a crossroads and carry straight on along the road, for about 100m, to the entrance of Camp Bohinj. Follow the road and as you pass the end of the campsite grounds, turn right on a track. After a short distance come to an open meadow and cross it on a path. Continue on this path to reach the riverbank and the **wooden bridge** across the Savica (**2hr**).

Cross the bridge and turn right on a track about 30m further on, signed Ribčev Laz and Lake (note a sign pointing left to Savica – the extension to the waterfall starts here). Follow the track through trees and then pass an open area with some cottages on the left to reach a junction. Turn left here, signed Lake, and after 30m go through a gap in a fence and continue to the lakeshore. Re-enter the trees and turn to the east, following the obvious path (**2hr 10min**). Directly opposite is a good view of the span of the Vogel cable car.

Cross a couple of scree slopes, close above the deep water of the lake, and continue below massive prows of rock. About 500m from the western end of the lake come to a fork and branch left, away from the water's edge. The route now crosses a small peninsula of land called **Na Jami**.

At times of high water, a torrential waterfall bursts forth from **Govic cave**, 130m above in the cliffs, bringing with it rocks and boulders which have built the land out into the lake.

Cross the (normally) dry watercourse and continue past a couple of buildings in a field on the left. At the end of the field, rejoin the shore by a small beach and notice an interesting shrine on the left made of a dead tree trunk still in situ.

Continue pleasantly through the forest and pass a series of concrete water tanks at a disused fish farm (**2hr 45min**). Shortly after, the path opens out into a broad track, which you follow past a number of small beaches. Pass through another short section of woodland and continue past fields, with views of the village of Stara Fužina and the steep slopes of Studor and Rudnica, their profiles making a textbook U-shaped valley. Looking back along the length of the lake, you can see the Lower Bohinj mountains to the left, Dom na Komni on the skyline straight ahead and Pršivec to the right. About 50min from the disused fish farm, cross a car park to a tarmac road, which you follow for 300m through trees before branching right across a small open area to the bridge at **Ribčev Laz**.

Extension to Slap Savica

This extension route is a pleasant circular walk in itself, taking about 2hr from the village of Ukanc, which is well served by buses. At the junction after crossing the wooden bridge across the Savica, turn left, following a sign for Slap Savica. Carry straight on past pretty chalets and flower meadows, with views of Vogel up to the left. Where the tarmac lane makes a sharp curve down to the left, continue straight ahead on the gravel path, signed Slap Savica. Almost immediately, cross a small stone bridge and continue along the gently ascending path.

The well-made gravel path continues, ascending gently past regular waymarks. After 300m notice a water trough with a picnic table and benches on the right. As you head on through the attractive forest, occasional glimpses of the steep rock walls of Komarča can be seen through the trees, and the rush of the fast-flowing river on your left becomes louder. Ignore any paths on the left of the track and arrive at a trail leading up the forested slopes on the right – this is the path to Komarča (**45min** from the wooden bridge). Continue for another 100m and cross the river on a scenic wooden bridge. Just beyond the bridge, to the left, is **Koča pri Savici** (653m), but turn right and walk through the car park, past a restaurant and the small souvenir shop opposite. Follow the signs past the restaurant and in another 250m reach the pay kiosk, cross the bridge and continue ascending a well-made path with steps to eventually arrive at the main viewpoint for **Slap Savica** (836m, **1hr 10min** from the wooden bridge).

Slap Savica is the source of the Savica river, which flows into Lake Bohinj. The outflow at the eastern end is the Sava Bohinjka, which joins the Sava Dolinka (whose source is at Zelenci, near Kranjska Gora – Walk 1) just beyond Bled. Together they form Slovenia's longest river, the Sava, which eventually empties into the Danube at Belgrade. Slovenia's greatest poet, France Prešeren, contributed greatly to the recognition of this waterfall with his poem *The Baptism at the Savica.*

The church of St John the Baptist and the old bridge at Ribčev Laz

At weekends in high season the road down from Savica can be very busy, so it is better to return to Ukanc by your outward route. To return, walk past the bridge and Koča pri Savici and follow the road gently downhill, with some good views of the river through the trees. After about 15min, cross a pretty, mossy stream on a bridge and almost immediately afterwards turn left on a gravel road, passing a small building. After a further 100m the track reaches **Planina Blato** – walk between the buildings of the farm into open meadows. Go straight across the meadow to reach the end of the field at the edge of the wood and carry on, going slightly uphill into the forest, passing waymarks.

The track, sometimes a little overgrown in parts, soon descends into a dip that can be very boggy early in the season. If it is too wet, make your way about 20m to the left to reach drier ground and a narrow path that avoids the worst of the marshy area. In a few metres join the main path again at a fork. Take the right-hand, waymarked, path and make another short ascent, followed by a descent to cross a dry riverbed. A little further on, reach an open pasture with a couple of buildings on the left. Keep going in the same direction, passing more houses in the pretty little hamlet of **Ukanc**, to arrive at a junction. Turn left and continue for 100m to reach the **wooden bridge** across the Savica.

Savica waterfall

WALK 14

Korita Mostnice

Start/finish	Supermarket in Stara Fužina (551m)
Time	3hr 30min
Distance	11.3km
Total ascent/descent	305m
Grade	2
Maps	1:25,000 Bohinj, 1:25,000 Triglav
Refreshments	Planinska koča na Vojah and restaurant Okrepčevalnica Slap
Access	Regular buses run from Bohinjska Bistrica via the Upper and Lower Bohinj valleys to Stara Fužina, and shuttle buses are usually added to regular services in high season. See www.bohinj.si for times or check at the bus stop. If you arrive by car, go left at the crossroads, where the road turns right over the bridge in Stara Fužina, and drive up the hill for about 700m to a car park (parking fee). Take the trail signed for Korita Mostnice and Dolina Voje and walk along the level path for 250m to reach Hudičev most

This lovely walk follows the river Mostnica to the head of the Voje valley. The first section runs alongside the deep gorge, which has been formed by the river (there is an entry charge). The route then goes on to visit the waterfall at the end of the valley before circling back through the open *planina* (alp) with its wooden buildings and flower meadows. The route is beautiful throughout, varying between woods and open land, and is full of interest, with wonderful views of the surrounding peaks.

From the supermarket in Stara Fužina, walk north and go straight ahead at the crossroads, following a sign to Korita Mostnice and Dolina Voje, with the river on your right and passing pretty houses on both sides. After crossing the river, turn left at a T-junction and walk up the lane. Soon after the large Rabič apartment building on your left, go through an iron gate, where the track is joined by another from the right, and continue round to the left across a small open pasture to reach **Hudičev most** (the Devil's bridge, **15min**). The Mostnica gorge is much deeper than expected as you look down from the bridge!

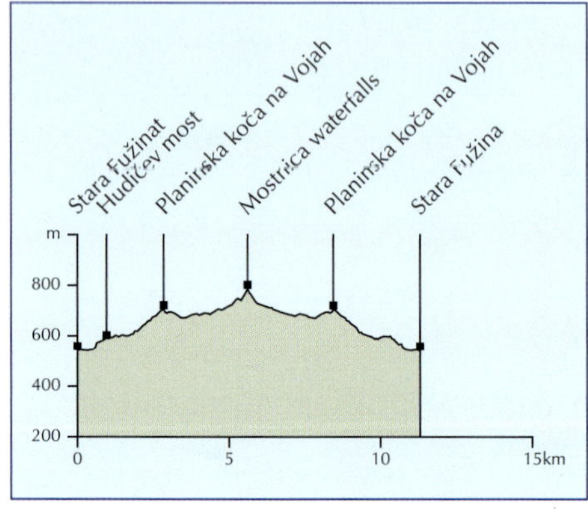

From Hudičev most, walk up the track on the west bank of the Mostnica river for a short distance to a big orientation sign describing the gorge and take the path straight on, descending slightly into the woods, with the gorge falling away to your right. Walk through pleasant forest to the **pay kiosk** and turn right to cross a bridge, with more views down into the deep gorge. Further along from this bridge, the gorge becomes much shallower and the path runs to the right of the extremely pretty river.

The phrase '**crystal clear**' is somewhat overused to describe rivers but this one genuinely merits it – it sparkles like diamonds and in places is so clear that you have to look twice to see if there is any water there at all. At times it reflects startlingly green where the bottom is sandy, while elsewhere there are potholes, small rapids and little waterfalls. At a sign that says, 'Slonček' (Elephant Rock), pointing towards the river, there is an enchanting deep green pool with a natural little rock arch.

The path continues through beech woods, bending slightly away from the river, and the gorge gradually deepens again. Reach a viewpoint of a section of the gorge where the rocks are almost overhanging – the top ones are barely a metre apart. Further on, a stone bridge takes you back onto the west side, again with good views into the depths, where you take the right-hand path climbing steeply away from the river into the forest, signed Dolina Voje. Follow the waymarks, with the noise of the river on your right.

About 15min from the bridge, the path joins a tarmac road coming up from Stara Fužina. Turn right and about 200m further on reach **Planinska koča na Vojah** (690m, **50min**), where you can enjoy refreshments while gazing at the view out into the open valley, with the shapely peak of Draški vrh in the background. Next to the hut there is a bus stop: during the summer months, shuttle buses run from Stara Fužina to the hut and back.

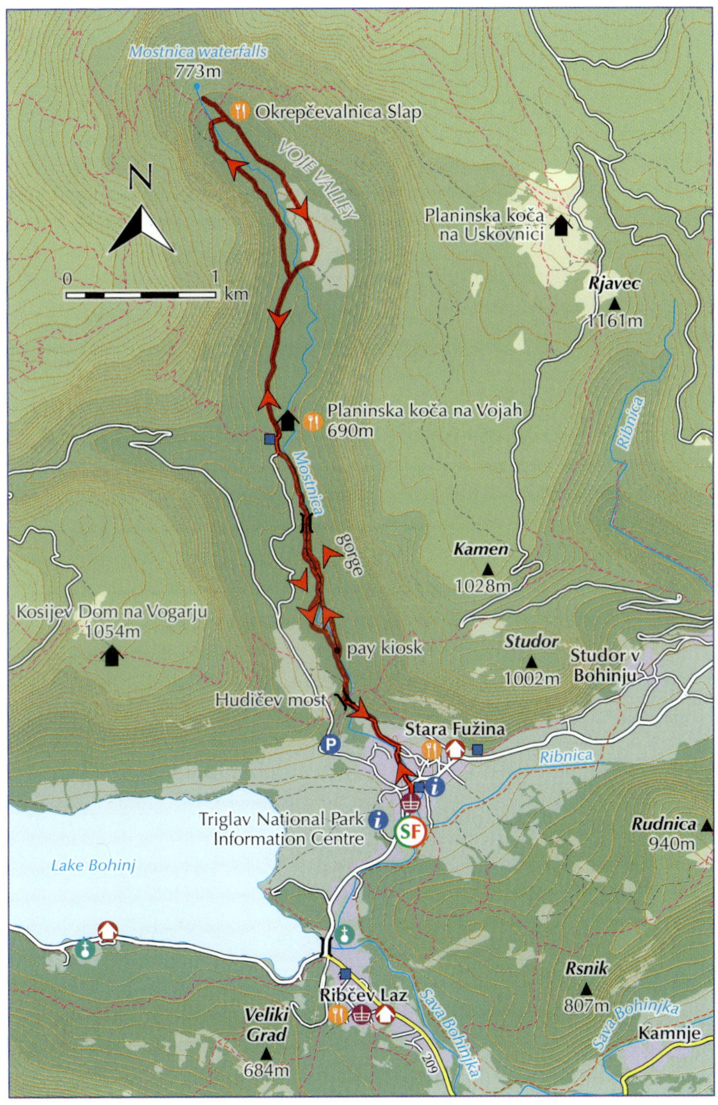
Mostnica waterfalls
773m
Okrepčevalnica Slap
VOJE VALLEY
N
0
1
km
Planinska koča
na Uskovnici
Rjavec
1161m
Planinska koča na Vojah
690m
Mostnica
Ribnica
gorge
Kamen
1028m
Kosijev Dom na Vogarju
1054m
pay kiosk
Studor
1002m
Studor v
Bohinju
Hudičev most
Stara Fužina
Ribnica
Triglav National Park
Information Centre
SF
Rudnica
940m
Lake Bohinj
Rsnik
807m
Ribčev Laz
Veliki
Grad
684m
Sava Bohinjka
Kamnje
209

After the hut the road becomes unmade and you continue north along it. Carry on along the main track to a building where the track forks; the right-hand trail is signed to Slap Mostnice (*krožna*, meaning circular) and Planinska koča na Uskovnici, while the left is signed to Vodnikov dom na Velem polju and Triglav.

Take the left fork, which keeps to the left-hand side of the valley and emerges near the valley head in an open area. A little further on come to a sign 'Slap Mostnice', indicating a path heading right. Take this path and soon reach a bridge; cross it and continue straight ahead for 100m to come out opposite the restaurant Okrepčevalnica Slap, where you can get refreshments. Turn left onto a broad path and walk for about 5min to the viewpoint for Mostniški slapovi (**Mostnica waterfalls**, 773m, **1hr 40min**). The falls are in two tiers, dropping into deep green pools deeply shaded by the trees.

Return down the path and continue straight on, past Okrepčevalnica Slap, through the delightful open planina of **Voje**. At the end of the planina the road enters the forest once more and soon crosses the river to return to the building where the track forks on the outward route. Continue the way you came to return to Planinska koča na Vojah and carry on down to the stone bridge (**2hr 45min**). To return to Hudičev most, don't cross the bridge but instead continue straight on, following signs for Stara Fužina. The path now runs on the other side of the gorge, giving you more views down into the river. Continue on this path to reach the pay kiosk and then return to **Stara Fužina**.

Elephant Rock

WALK 15

Pršivec

Start/finish	Supermarket in Stara Fužina (551m)
Time	7–8hr
Distance	18.1km
Total ascent/descent	1350m
Grade	3
Maps	1:25,000 Bohinj, 1:25,000 Triglav
Refreshments	Kosijev Dom na Vogarju, Bregarjevo zavetišče na Planini Viševnik and Koča na Planini pri Jezeru
Access	Regular buses run from Bohinjska Bistrica via the Upper and Lower Bohinj valleys to Stara Fužina, and shuttle buses are usually added to regular services in high season. See www.bohinj.si for times or check at the bus stop. If you arrive by car, there are several car parks in Stara Fužina (parking fee)

If you like walking through forests, then this mountain is for you. Almost the entire trail is through the trees, the mixed woodland of the lower slopes gradually giving way to pine, spruce, larch and finally dwarf pine. It is even better in the autumn as the larch trees begin to shed their needles in a golden rain shower against the impossibly blue skies and the beeches burn red and orange in the valley. The views from the summit are even more rewarding for the lack of them on the way up – when you finally emerge from the trees, the panorama is startling in its extent.

It is perfectly feasible to climb Pršivec and return the same way, but it is worth making the circular route described here. Although the return trail is slightly longer, the charms of Planina Viševnik, with its shepherds' huts tucked beneath the cliffs, and Planina pri Jezeru, with its beautiful lake, will more than repay the extra effort.

From the supermarket in Stara Fužina, walk north and go straight ahead at the crossroads, following a sign to Korita Mostnice and Dolina Voje, with the river on your right and passing pretty houses on both sides. After crossing the river, turn left at a T-junction and walk up the lane. Soon after the large Rabič apartment building on your left, go through an iron gate, where the track is joined by another

Mizčna glava 1622m
Planina Blato 1147m
Planinska koča na Vojah 690m
Voje Valley
Rjavec 1149m
Planina pri Jezeru
Griva 1758m
Planina Viševnik
Vrtec 1811m
Bregarjevo zavetišče 1625m
Koča na Planini pri Jezeru 1453m
Vodični vrh 1621m
Rigelj 1768m
Pršivski kras
Majska jama
Pršivec 1761m
Komarča
Planina Zgornji Vogar
Planina Spodnji Vogar
Kosijev Dom na Vogarju 1054m
Mostnica Gorge
Mostnica
Kamen 1028m
pay kiosk
Studor 1002m
Hudičev most
Stara Fužina
Ribnica
N
0 1 km
Lake Bohinj
Triglav National Park Information Centre
Savica
Ukanška glava 574m
Ukanc
Vogel cable-car station
Sava Bohinjka
to Bohinjska Bistrica
Ribčev Laz
Rsnik 807m

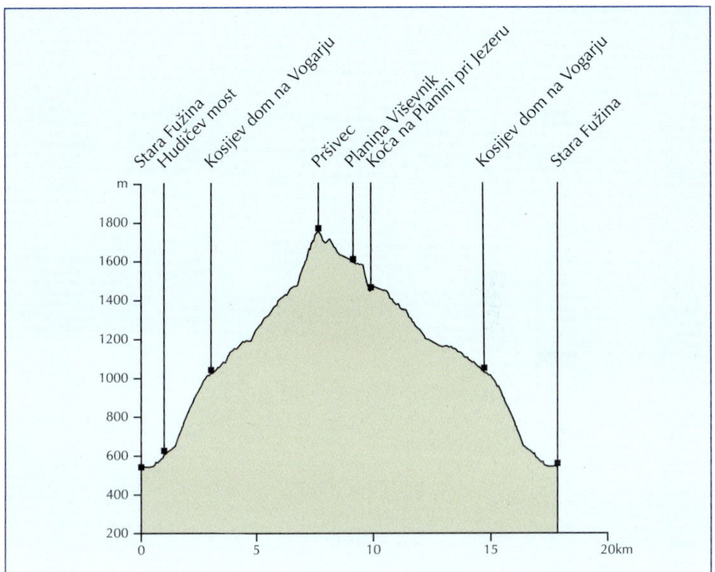

from the right, and continue round to the left across a small open pasture to reach **Hudičev most** (the Devil's bridge, **15min**).

Cross the bridge, take the track on the west side of the river and walk uphill, following signs for Vogar and Korita Mostnice. At an information board about the Voje valley, do not take the track that leads down right to Korita Mostnice, but keep walking up the road, signed for Vogar on a rock. Keep on the track as it gently climbs to meet a minor tarmac road. Turn right and walk up the road for about 30m to the waymarked track that continues on the left-hand side (**30min**). Follow a sign for Kosijev dom 1hr and Pršivec 3hr 30min.

Walk up between wire fences on an open grassy pasture and then climb up through the woods; it's steep but the height gain is a pleasure because of the well-laid stones of the old mule track that still survive in many places. Eventually, as the gradient eases, a path leads left, signed *Spomenik* (memorial), which leads to a launch site for paragliders. It is worth the 30m detour to get an excellent view of the lake.

Return to the main path and continue up it, passing a small pasture with two beautiful old buildings. The broad track continues past a water trough and between more attractive buildings at the lower end of Planina Vogar, all of them roofed with the traditional wood shingles of the area. Soon arrive at **Kosijev Dom**

The old mule track to Kosijev Dom na Vogarju

na Vogarju (1054m, **1hr 30min**). The walk to the dom is a pleasant walk in itself, taking about 2hr 30min for the round trip from Stara Fužina.

Continue up and past the hut and then level out near more buildings to reach a signed junction. The broad track bends sharply to the right here but leave it to the left on a path, signed Pršivec 2hr 30min. The path is narrow and almost immediately leads into the forest, heading uphill. It continues to rise gently and very enjoyably through primarily beech forest, becoming almost level. After about 20min arrive at a fork in the track and, ignoring a path that leads steeply up to the right, continue straight ahead to arrive at a small open marshy glade filled with butterburs with their broad, rhubarb-like leaves (**2hr**). A small stream flows into this flat glade from the right, forming this little marshy habitat.

The track crosses the glade and on the other side begins to climb steeply again. Follow the waymarks, ignoring any tracks off to the right or left. The path levels and bears sharply left while another broader muddy track swings up to the right into the wood. Stay left on the waymarked path as it skirts a hollow about 50m wide, the delightful woodland route providing enjoyable walking.

The forest gradually begins to change, with increasing stands of conifers. In about 10min turn left onto a broader track with a sign for Pršivec. Continue for 25min, following the waymarked track which has been broadened for logging activity, again ignoring any tracks off to the right or left. As you reach a large open area with many felled trees, the path steepens (**3hr 10min**); take care to follow the waymarks showing the direct route, as various shortcuts can be misleading.

After about 10min reach a junction where an overgrown path heads off right to Planina Viševnik but continue straight ahead, following a sign on a rock for Pršivec. Just 25m beyond the junction, the path crosses the top of a steep gully bounded on its left by a huge prow of rock, offering precipitous views down to Ukanc. Beyond this, there are some short sections of easy scrambling with no real difficulties; nevertheless, there is a feeling of exposure and care should be taken if the rock is wet.

The view really opens out now, and the path continues over easier ground, still covered with lush plant growth and small trees whose twisted roots and branches encroach on the path. After a further 10min ascent, the narrow path passes a small rise or subsidiary top and continues between rocks and small larch trees for another 5min before arriving at the open summit of **Pršivec** (1761m, **4hr**).

The top of **Pršivec** is marked by a stone cairn and a metal box containing the summit book and stamp. The fabulous 360-degree panorama is all the more appreciated due to the restricted outlook on the way up. To the west is Bogatin and the Komna plateau, and to the north is Triglav. Continuing clockwise, the Karavanke ridge stretches away into the distance towards the Kamnik-Savinja Alps, while to the south lie Vogel and the Lower Bohinj mountains.

The route leaves the summit to the north, following a narrow path and sign on a rock for Viševnik, and drops down through dwarf pine. The waymarked path descends over typical limestone rock steps with many small crevices, and care should be taken if it is wet, as it is easy to twist an ankle on this terrain. About 10min after you leave the summit, pass the entrance to **Majska jama**, one of the deepest caves in the area, which has been explored to a depth of over 592m. Special equipment is needed for the exploration of the cave. About 100m further on, the path rises briefly before dropping down through the interesting limestone landscape (marked as Pršivski kras on the map). In spite of the rocky ground, the trees still manage to flourish, with a great variety of plants nestled in the rocky niches.

Around 20min brings you to **Planina Viševnik** (1625m, **4hr 30min**) – an extremely scenic little *planina* (alp) nestling under the cliffs of Griva, with wooden huts topped with shingled roofs, one of which offers refreshments in summer. Follow the sign to Planina pri Jezeru and within another 100m arrive at a fork. Both paths are waymarked and signed Planina pri Jezeru – take the path to the right, signed 20min. Continue on into the wood, the path soon dropping steeply over rocks and gnarled tree roots to skirt beneath a large crag, and reach **Planina**

pri Jezeru (1453m) with its charming lake, herders' huts and big mountain hut (**4hr 50min**).

Take the broad track that leads away from the mountain hut, signed Planina Vogar 1hr 30min, which enters the wood after 100m. In another 150m reach a junction where a narrow path heads right, signed Planina Vogar 1hr 45min, and the main track goes straight on for Stara Fužina and Planina Vogar 1hr 30min. You can take either path, but the way described here continues straight on along the broad stony track. In another 5min go through a gate and continue down, passing log benches where a path heads steeply down to the left.

About 30min after leaving the dom, reach a junction at a sharp left-hand bend in the track, where a path is signed to the right, Planina Vogar 1hr. Take this, descending into the wood, and in about 15min leave the track for a narrow path that bears right, following a waymark on a tree (**5hr 35min**). The path runs quite level as it passes through beautiful mature beech woods and, in another 20min, emerges onto a tarmac road. From here Planina Vogar is signed 20min and Stara Fužina 1hr 20min, so continue along the road and soon pass a small planina with two pretty cottages. About 200m after this arrive at a junction, leave the forest road and continue straight ahead on a broad gravel track signed Koča na Vogarju 10min.

Pass more attractive cottages as you enter the upper end of **Planina Vogar** and arrive back at the junction 5min from the Vogar dom, where the path to Pršivec leads off into the forest to the right. Continue along the broad track the short distance to the Vogar dom (**6hr 20min**), and from here reverse the ascent route back to the start.

Planina pri Jezeru

WALK 16

Vogel

Start/finish	Top station of the Vogel cable car (1540m)
Time	4–5hr
Distance	10.4km
Total ascent/descent	720m
Grade	3
Maps	1:25,000 Bohinj
Refreshments	Bars and restaurants near the top cable-car station
Access	The bottom cable-car station is near Ukanc, at the western end of Lake Bohinj, and is signed from the road. Regular buses run from Bohinjska Bistrica via Ribčev Laz to Ukanc, and shuttle buses are usually added to regular services in high season (the bus station is located 50m from the cable-car station, next to Camp Bohinj). See www.bohinj.si for the times or check at the bus stop. If you arrive by car, there is a car park next to the cable-car station

The ascent of Vogel (1922m) is made easy by using the ski resort cable car, which also runs in the summer (see www.vogel.si for opening times). Most people who arrive at the top cable-car station only look north at the admittedly magnificent view of Triglav and the Julian Alps, as the view south to Vogel is made unpleasant by the ravages of the ski lifts and the runs that are so popular in winter. However, the mountain massif of Vogel is complex, and there are places to be found with views and alpine meadows that are as beautiful as anywhere in the Julian Alps.

This tour descends slightly from the cable-car station before climbing to the summit of Vogel via a stunningly beautiful, secluded valley. The return is by a high-level balcony path that avoids the ski slopes until the very last section, making an excellent short mountain day. It's not worth trying to tackle the walk up from the valley floor – the ski slope is miserably steep to ascend in places.

From the top cable-car station, walk past the former Ski Hotel and continue on the broad ski service road and past a restaurant/pizzeria, following signs for Vogel

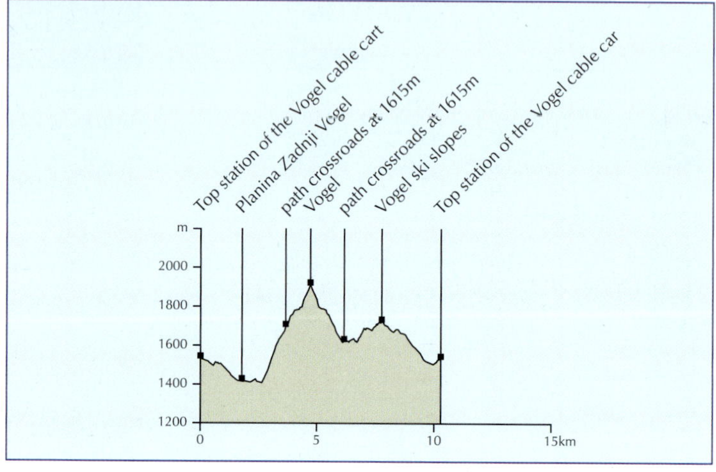

and Planina Zadnji Vogel. About 350m from the cable car, turn right at a junction, signed Komna and Ukanc. Soon afterwards pass a right-hand junction, which is the way down to the valley, after which the track, signed Planina Zadnji Vogel, bears slightly right and down. Do not take this track but instead head uphill for a short distance on a track bearing left, which brings you to a sign for Planina Zadnji Vogel indicating a narrow path entering the forest to the right (**15min**).

This pretty path lined with flowers and old trees provides a pleasant 10min alternative to the service road. All too soon it begins to descend a little and you can see the service road below, which you eventually rejoin, continuing in the same direction. Another 10min on the road brings you to **Planina Zadnji Vogel** (1413m, **35min**). Leave the forest road, which heads down to the right, and cross the open area past the *sirarna* (cheese-making building), continuing straight ahead on the now grassy track.

> **Bohinj cheese** is famous in Slovenia – cheese-making began again at this *planina* (alp) in 2009 after a decline following World War 2. Cheese and other dairy products are made and sold in the summer season.

Shortly afterwards come to a prominent rock, signed to the left, Vogel 2hr. Head left on the narrow path, through dwarf pine, alpine flowers, larch and spruce trees. After a few hundred metres enter a small, open valley with steep rocky sides covered with trees, while flowers of all hues carpet its floor in what

can only be described as an alpine garden. Walk due south across the valley and ascend the rocky path at its head. Half an hour's delightful walk brings you almost to the top of the valley and another prominent boulder, signed Vogel to the left, which you follow in more or less the same direction. Pause a moment to look back at the excellent view of Triglav, which looks vastly bigger than its neighbouring peaks. The lower peak of Pršivec (Walk 15) is straight ahead on the other side of the Bohinj valley.

A further 10min climbing brings you to a **path crossroads** (1615m, **1hr 30min**). To the left is the return route to the cable car, while to the right the path winds all the way to Komna. Continue straight ahead to Vogel as the path traverses the left-hand side of a rocky scoop. On the skyline is a dramatic notch on the craggy ridge, and further to the right along the ridge is the summit pyramid of Vogel. After 10min you will reach the ridge at a col with the first view of the Primorska (south) side, which is much steeper and craggier.

The path turns right and continues on the northern side, below the ridge. The ridge path, signed '1', is part of the Slovenian Mountain Trail (SMT). Looking back now, you can see along the ridge of the Lower Bohinj mountains. The path continues, keeping well below the crest to the right-hand side and, in about 10min, brings you to a second col, with the bulk of the summit of Vogel right in front (**1hr 50min**). Make a short scramble up the lower rocks of the ridge; it is not difficult but it is a little exposed and protected by a steel cable. The path then traverses screes, again on the northern side, before turning left at a junction to reach the western ridge which it follows to the summit of **Vogel** (1922m, **2hr 30min**).

The **view** from the summit is spectacular: to the south-east a stratified ridge links Vogel to nearby Žabiški Kuk (1844m). The hills of the Lower Bohinj mountains continue towards Bogatin (Walk 19), while Triglav and his companions dominate the view to the north. To the east stretches the enticing ridge that leads all the way to Črna prst (Walks 17 and 18).

Retrace your steps to the **path crossroads** at 1615m (**3hr 15min**) and turn right onto the return route to the cable car signed Orlova Glava and Rjava skala (Ski Hotel). As an alternative return route, take high-level route 1, which follows the ridge east to Šija, where you turn left to descend the ski slopes. The path traverses the hillside through dwarf pine and alpine flowers, with excellent views to the north and west. A short uphill section takes you to the crest of a ridge (of the subsidiary summit of Skakavec) covered with a thicket of dwarf pine, which edges the last side valley before the main ski area. To avoid the descent and ascent of an ugly ski slope, turn right, following waymarks where the path divides, and traverse round the head of the rocky valley (**3hr 35min**). A side path from the head of the valley makes a short diversion to the summit of Šija (15–20min to the top).

Part of the route winds through an enchanting small open valley

Continue round and pass under the ski lift and shortly afterwards see a sign on a rock signed Ski Hotel (**4hr**). Continue on the path, which winds down through limestone rock formations and dwarf pines. Meet the ski lift again, and then, unfortunately, the ski slopes can no longer be avoided. Ascend slightly, passing underneath the ski lift, and make your way down, following the pistes. You can see the former Ski Hotel below, along with wonderful views of Triglav, one reason the slopes are so popular in winter. It is about 20min from here back to the **top cable-car station**.

WALK 17

Črna prst

Start/finish	Main crossroads in Bohinjska Bistrica (512m)
Time	6hr
Distance	14.8km
Total ascent/descent	1375m
Grade	3
Maps	1:25,000 Bohinj
Refreshments	Orožnova koča and Dom Zorka Jelinčiča na Črni prsti
Access	Regular buses run from Bohinj Lake to Bohinjska Bistrica, and shuttle buses are usually added to regular services in high season. Check the times in the tourist information office (www.bohinj.si) or at the bus stop. If you arrive by car, there are several car parks in Bohinjska Bistrica

The real beauty and attraction of this mountain lie in the fact that its flanks and summit are home to a diverse collection of flowers, which start at around 1400m and continue all the way to the top at 1844m. The route passes through them as if through a perfectly planted border carefully tended by expert gardeners. Here, though, the only gardeners are natural selection and the climate, combined with unusual soil conditions – Črna prst means 'black earth'. There are wonderful views, too: north towards Triglav and the white limestone Julian Alps, and south across Primorska, with its softer, steep-sided, tree-covered hills.

From the main crossroads in Bohinjska Bistrica, looking south towards the Lower Bohinj mountains, turn left and walk along the road, round a right-hand bend, to the house at 10 Jelovška cesta. Turn right and take the rough track on the right, signed Ravne, up past some gardens and across a field to reach a **military cemetery**.

The **military cemetery** has 285 marked graves of soldiers of different nationalities. Between 1915 and 1917, Bohinj was an important military base behind Austro-Hungarian lines in the high mountains of the Krn front, and there were two military hospitals in Bohinjska Bistrica. Patients were transported to hospital by rail, and the dead were buried here in late 1917.

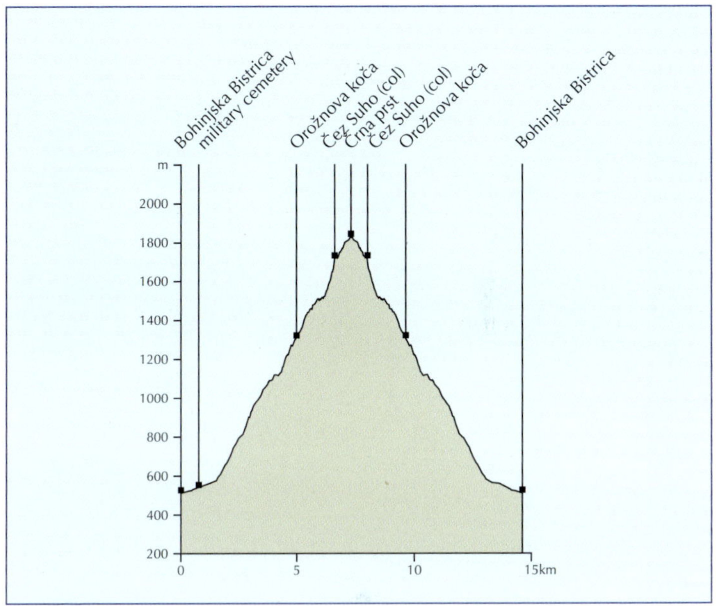

Continue across more fields, following a grassy track which brings you to an open pasture with farm buildings. Pass them and reach a forest road where you see a sign for Črna prst pointing up the hill, heading south. Walk quite steeply up the rutted and usually muddy track for 15min then as the route levels out in a tiny field, continue in the same direction on a narrow path. Another 15min climb brings you to a wide track where you turn left. This quickly turns into a path across a small pasture and comes out on another wide track. Turn left again and, after a few paces, reach the forest road (**1hr**).

Turn right this time, ignoring signs to the left for Črna prst and Orožnova koča, and after about 150m pass a sign on a rock, 'Črna prst 2hr 30'. Just after this, turn left onto an obvious path heading left up into the woods. After about 5min the route makes a slight detour as it crosses a scree-filled gully – in 2014 the original line of the path was covered in fallen trees, the result of a major ice storm. Within 40m join the original path again and climb steadily on this pleasant trail, trending diagonally right across the forested hillside.

After about 30min the path looks as if it carries on traversing, but a sign on a tree for Črna prst and Orožnova koča directs you up quite steeply to the left.

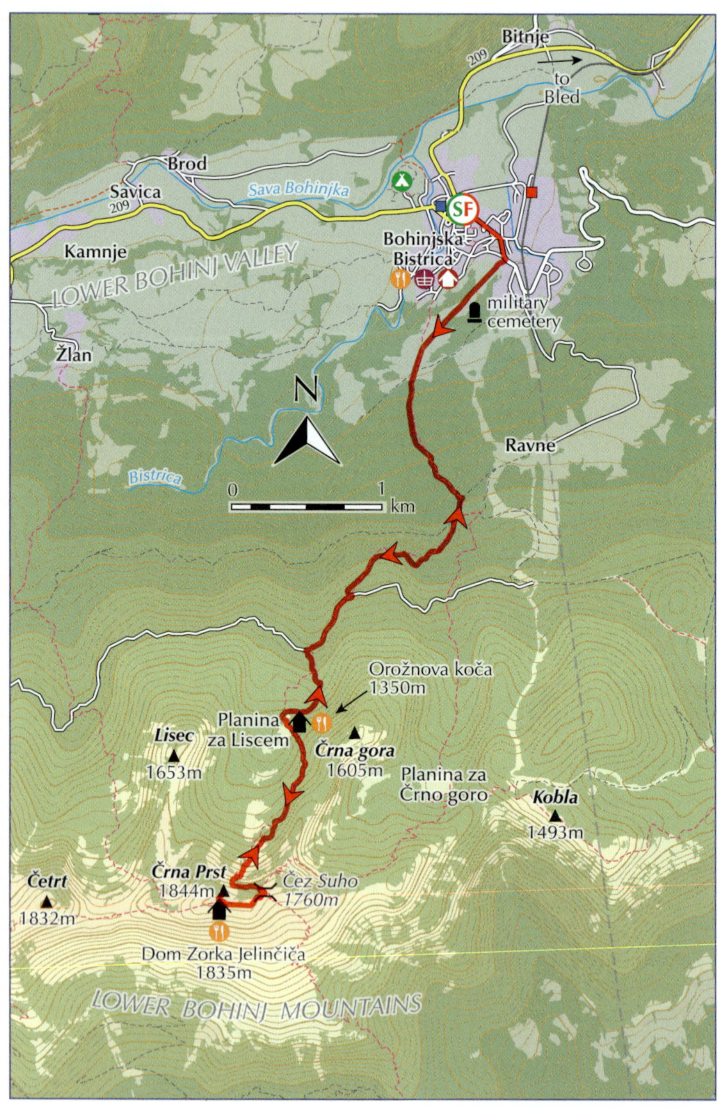
Bitnje
209
to
Bled
Brod
Savica
209
Sava Bohinjka
Kamnje
Bohinjska
Bistrica
SF
LOWER BOHINJ VALLEY
military
cemetery
Žlan
N
Ravne
Bistrica
0
1
km
Oražnova koča
1350m
Planina
za Liscem
Lisec
1653m
Črna gora
1605m
Planina za
Črno goro
Kobla
1493m
Četrt
1832m
Črna Prst
1844m
Čez Suho
1760m
Dom Zorka Jelinčiča
1835m
LOWER BOHINJ MOUNTAINS

About 5min more brings you to the upper forest road, where Črna prst is signed to the right. Within 100m you will see Lisec (1653m) straight ahead, looking like a forested cone from here, and as you round the next corner, Črna prst looms into view to the left of it.

Continue on the forest road for about 5min to a tree with a waymark, signed Črna prst and Orožnova koča to the left but also Črna prst and Orožnova koča along the forest road to the right. The route described here goes left up into the forest, directly south towards Črna prst. After 15–20min of steady climbing, come to a more level section through mixed woodland with thick undergrowth and, in another 5min, reach some small crags where there is an extraordinary pair of trees, a conifer and a beech growing tightly together on top of a rock. The path continues, still climbing but more easily now, past the crags to some final zigzags up to the *planina* (alp).

Just before the trees part to reveal the planina, a path goes right, down towards Bohinjska Bistrica and Polje. On the return, this could provide an alternative descent route to the valley. Just up ahead you can see **Orožnova koča** (1350m, **2hr 30min**), rebuilt in 2004. The original hut was the very first owned and used by the Slovene Alpine Club, built in 1894 and destroyed in 1944. In front of the hut is the basin of Planina za Liscem, with a tiny pool in the bottom, Lisec on the right (not quite as cone-shaped now) and Črna prst up ahead.

Follow waymarks left into the wood and pass a Triglav National Park sign and information boards about the special plants of the area. The track quickly gains height and then begins to level out a little as it traverses the rocky side of the high planina, and you walk through a mass of different perennials and small shrubs, mostly above knee height. It pays to linger along this beautiful balcony path through the flowers, with extensive views north towards Triglav.

You are now at the bottom of the summit slopes – the 'gardens' continue up quite steeply to the base of the crags. As the height increases the species gradually change, but there is always the same incredible range of colours. The path continues pleasantly up, and just below the summit crags it traverses to the left beneath them.

Looking down, you have quite a **view** of the planina with the hut, Bohinjska Bistrica on the floor of the valley and behind that the Pokljuka plateau. Planina Zajamniki with its row of herders' cottages can be seen in the distance straight ahead, while behind is the dark forested ridge of Debela peč and the peaks of the Julian Alps, with Triglav very much in charge. Over to the right is the inevitable line of the Karavanke, always on the edge of the view, and then the Kamniško-Savinjske Alpe. Babji zob, the craggy top above Bled, marks the gorge of the Sava Bohinjka where it divides the plateaus of Pokljuka and Jelovica.

Oroznova koča

The path begins to traverse away from the summit cliffs, heading left along a rocky ramp which soon enters a small thicket of low trees and plants. Keep traversing left and then come out into the open again where a path signed to Planina za Črno goro continues straight ahead. Turn right here and ascend the final few metres to the small col of **Čez Suho** (1760m). Now you can see the summit not far away, with Dom Zorka Jelinčiča beneath it on the south side. Turn right along the ridge; the last 10–15min is a pleasant stroll along the south side, with excellent views to Primorska down an amazing, uniformly steep grassy slope, still covered with lush vegetation. The hut supply cableway, coming up from the little village of Stržišče, can be seen. Behind the dom, scramble a metres up easy rocks to the top of **Črna prst** (1844m, **3hr 30min**) for a truly panoramic view.

To descend, retrace your steps of the ascent.

WALK 18

Spodnje Bohinjske Gore (Lower Bohinj mountains)

Start	Top station of the Orlove glave chairlift (1670m), Vogel ski resort
Finish	Polje (523m), on the road between Bohinjska Bistrica and Ribčev Laz
Alternative Finish	Bohinjska Bistrica (512m)
Time	9hr
Distance	17.3km (alternative 18km)
Total ascent	595m (alternative 625m)
Total descent	1740m (alternative 1755m)
Grade	3
Maps	1:25,000 Bohinj
Refreshments	Dom Zorka Jelinčiča and, on the alternative descent, Orožnova koča
Access	Take the cable car near Ukanc at the western end of Lake Bohinj to the top station and continue on the Orlove glave chairlift, which runs directly from the top station. For access to the bottom cable-car station, see Walk 16. To return to the starting point it is necessary to take a bus (several buses a day go from Bohinjska Bistrica via Polje to Ukanc – check the times on www.bohinj.si) or a taxi. If you are a group with two cars, you can leave one at the end before you start
Warning	Check the weather forecast before you go, as the ridge is no place to be in a thunderstorm

This excellent high-level ridge walk marks the southern edge of the main Julian Alps. It runs from Vogel to Črna prst, never quite reaching 2000m but never falling below 1700m. The walk makes use of the Vogel cable car and chairlift to gain height and then follows the Lower Bohinj mountain ridge from Šija to Črna prst. Apart from the excellent views to the north and south, a major attraction of these mountains is the wonderful variety and abundance of flowers, which catch the eye on every side. Just beyond Rodica, a narrow section on the ridge can feel quite airy due to the very steep grassy slopes, particularly on the south side, but apart from this there are no major difficulties.

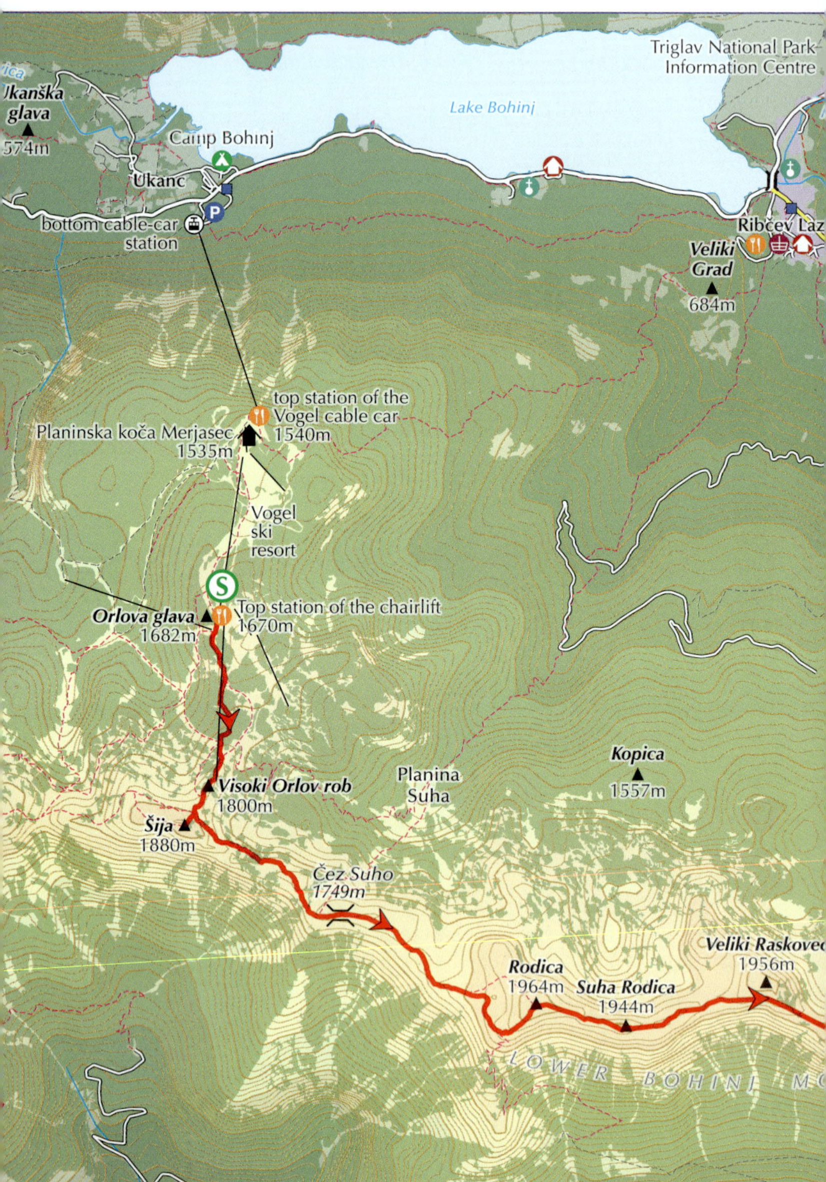
Triglav National Park Information Centre
Lake Bohinj
Ukanška glava
574m
Camp Bohinj
Ukanc
bottom cable-car station
Ribčev Laz
Veliki Grad
684m
top station of the Vogel cable car 1540m
Planinska koča Merjasec 1535m
Vogel ski resort
Orlova glava 1682m
Top station of the chairlift 1670m
Visoki Orlov rob 1800m
Šija 1880m
Planina Suha
Kopica 1557m
Čez Suho 1749m
Rodica 1964m
Suha Rodica 1944m
Veliki Raskovec 1956m
LOWER BOHINJ MO

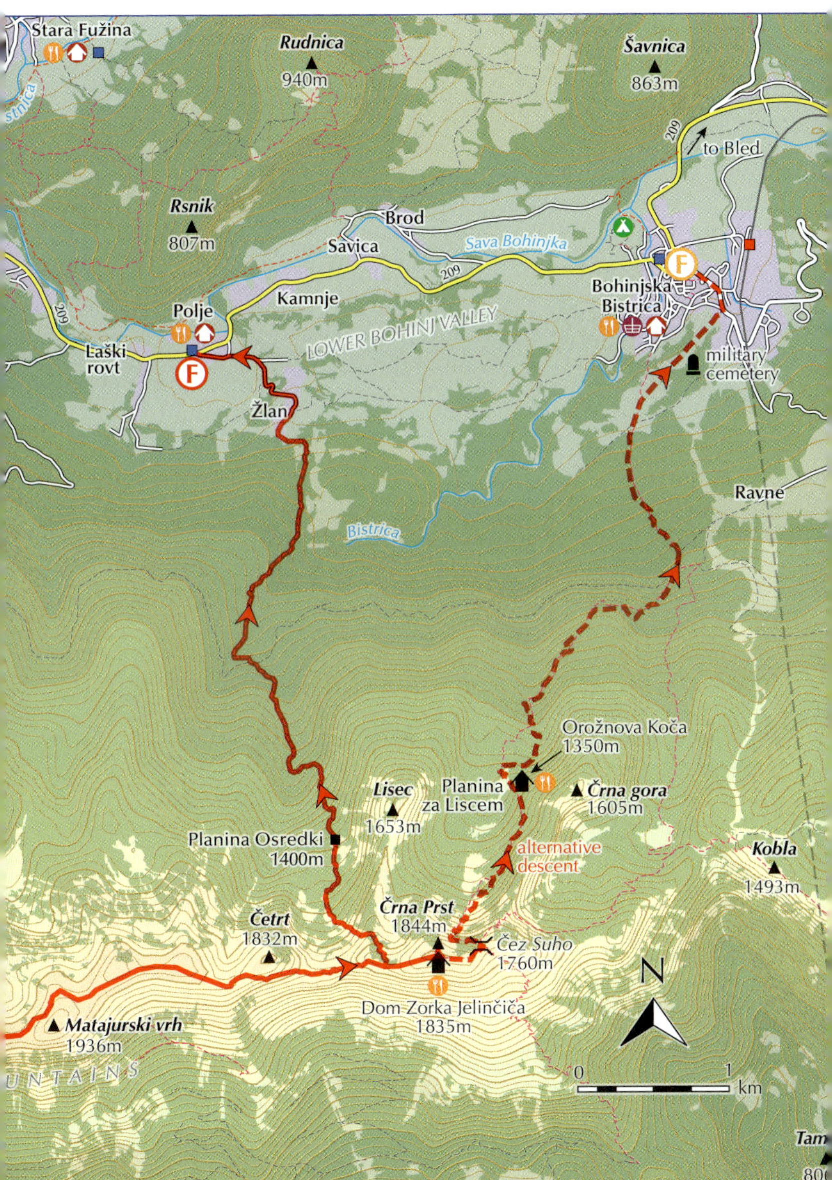

Stara Fužina
Rudnica
940m
Šavnica
863m
to Bled
209
Rsnik
807m
Brod
Savica
Sava Bohinjka
Bohinjska
Bistrica
Kamnje
Polje
LOWER BOHINJ VALLEY
Laški
rovt
Žlan
military
cemetery
Ravne
Bistrica
Orožnova Koča
1350m
Planina
za Liscem
Lisec
1653m
Črna gora
1605m
Planina Osredki
1400m
alternative
descent
Kobla
1493m
Črna Prst
1844m
Četrt
1832m
Čez Suho
1760m
N
Dom Zorka Jelinčiča
1835m
Matajurski vrh
1936m
UNTAINS
0
1
km
Kal

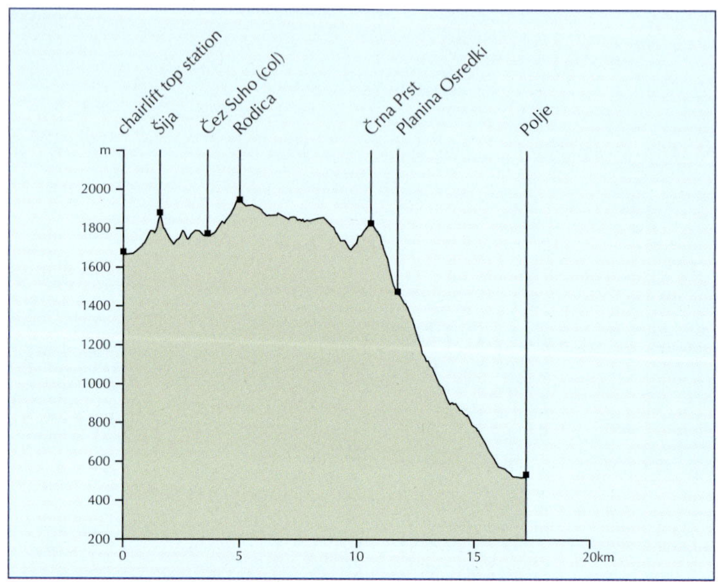

From the top of the chairlift, walk up the path through dwarf pine to reach a junction, where paths go left and right – turn right for Šija.

Follow the stony track, between the piste fences and over the little top of Orlova glava, to eventually reach the top of the second chairlift at **Visoki Orlov rob** (1800m, **30min**). The path continues just to the right of the little cabin here, at first descending slightly and then beginning the ascent of **Šija** (1880m). Reach a junction with SMT Route 1 signed left to Rodica, but for now go straight on and continue climbing steadily. Reach the grassy summit (**1hr**), with good views to the south and along the ridge east to Rodica and west towards Vogel.

Return to the junction with the SMT and turn right for Rodica. The path traverses the hillside, descending gently for 10min, and then climbs over a few rocky steps and dwarf pine roots to reach the broad grassy ridge. The path continues along the gently rising ridge, which is covered with flowers, including edelweiss.

Another 10min brings you to the top of Zad. Suha at 1796m. From here the rocky path drops down between dwarf pine to reach the grassy col of **Čez Suho** (1749m, **2hr 10min**). Just beyond the col there is a cairn at a T-junction, where you keep straight on. A possible escape route here turns left to descend to Planina Suha, where a waymarked path continues down to Ribčev Laz at the eastern end of Lake Bohinj.

The path continues easily along the broad grassy ridge, eventually dropping a little to wind between two karst sinkholes, and from here another 20min of ascent brings you to the summit of **Rodica** (1964m, **3hr**).

From the summit the ridge ahead narrows, but a good path continues along the crest, with steep slopes on either side. After about 100m the path drops down a little to the right-hand (southern) side and continues just below the rocky crest. Further on, the path takes to the left-hand (northern) side to pass below the craggy top of **Suha Rodica** (1944m, **3hr 30min**), and continues more easily now as the ridge begins to broaden out again.

Begin to ascend once more and cross back to the south side of the ridge to traverse below the summit of **Veliki Raskovec** (1956m). From here you can see Črna prst with its hut in the distance. Continue, rejoining the crest for a short while, before dropping back to the north side, just below the crest. The path traverses well below the summit of the next peak, **Matajurski vrh** (1936m, **4hr 15min**), with the large stony corrie of Matajurc on your left. Pass another big sinkhole to the left and join the grassy crest again, carpeted with flowers.

The next section is one of the most pleasant parts of the walk, as the route wanders along easily to the right of the level ridge, with an airy feeling of space above the steep grassy slopes falling uniformly down to the forest in the valley. The path follows either the crest or the right-hand side of the ridge and passes below the summit of **Četrt** (1832m). The village of Stržišče can be seen below in the valley to your right. As you approach the unique plant habitat of Črna prst, the flowers become larger and more colourful and varied.

The chairlift 'Orlove glave'

A brief scramble up some rocky steps brings you to a short section with a steel cable handrail and a painted sign on a rock, Koča Črna prst 20min. Continue steeply up, with more cable handrail on the eroded path but no real difficulties, to reach the crest of the ridge, noticing a path going down on the north side signed Polje, Žlan and Planina Osredki, which you will take on your

Beginning the descent from the ridge (photo: Roy Clark)

return. To reach **Črna Prst** (1844m) and **Dom Zorka Jelinčiča**, just below the summit, continue ascending east along the ridge for another 15min (**6hr**).

Return to the path for Polje mentioned above. Begin the descent from the ridge through dwarf pine and shrubs and within 10min reach a grassy notch at the foot of the satellite ridge that leads to Lisec. Pass through the notch, following a sign on a rock for Planina Osredki, and descend the stony path, still surrounded by the tall, lush plants. You may see and hear marmots in the boulder- and scree-filled corrie to your left.

About 20min from the notch, the path passes through a level open area of grass. Pass a small cattle watering hole as the narrow path enters thickets and shrubs and then descends again. The two attractive wooden buildings of **Planina Osredki** (1400m, **7hr**) come into view, sitting on a grassy rise above a small pool, with the beautiful backdrop of Triglav and the Julian Alps behind.

Walk down the small *planina* (alp), where you may need to step over/under a wire cattle fence before you enter mixed forest. After 25min of steep descent from the planina, cross a forest road, following waymarks and a sign on a tree (Polje), and continue down the path. After another 15min pass a track heading right to Orožnova koča and continue straight down to reach a broad gravel road. Turn left and continue along the gravel road for about 100m, then turn right onto the path signed Polje (**8hr**).

Continue down the now broad forest track, which in 150m crosses a dry stream bed on a concrete ford as it bears right. After a further 15–20min of descent, the track ends and you continue down, bearing left, on a narrower path into the wood.

In a few more minutes reach a dry watercourse that crosses the path. Straight ahead is another stony watercourse. Follow the waymarked path on its right bank for a few metres; it soon heads further to the right into the woods before bearing left across a small clearing. Arrive at another grassy clearing with a weekend cottage and just as you are passing the cottage, notice a tree with a waymark to the left and follow a narrow path that heads down towards trees. You may need to negotiate a temporary cattle fence here but continue to follow waymarks on the narrow path that descends through the wood and bears left.

The roofs of Žlan soon come into view below and the path emerges at a gravel turning point. Within a short distance the gravel road becomes tarmac and passes between the houses and old wooden *toplars* (hayracks) of the village of **Žlan**. Continue down the road for almost 1km to reach the main road at **Polje**, just by the bus stop.

Descent to Bohinjska Bistrica

From Črna prst descend east to reach the grassy col of **Čez Suho** (1760m) then follow signs for Orožnova koča and Bohinjska Bistrica. The path leads down left then bears right as it traverses above Planina za Liscem before arriving at the **hut** (1350m, **1hr 15min** from Črna prst). From the hut, zigzag down through the woods, following waymarks and signs for Bohinjska Bistrica and Ravne (skozi Snežno konto).

The path soon forks – take the right fork and follow the path as it passes below small crags and through shrubby undergrowth before descending steadily for about 10–15min to reach a forest road. Turn right along the road and ignore a path signed Bohinjska Bistrica that almost immediately bears left; instead, follow the forest road and in 5min take the waymarked path on the left that leads steeply down through the forest for another 25min to meet a forest road again. Turn right and continue along it for about 150m before turning left and heading down a track that becomes a path as it crosses a small open meadow just below the road.

Continue down, following waymarks on a track, then turn right onto a path, signed Bohinjska Bistrica, passing a small open area then dropping down more steeply on a rutted track to come out into the open at a gravel road. Cross the road and head down a grassy track across the open pasture to reach, in 150m, a sign pointing left to Bohinjska Bistrica. Don't take this track but instead turn right on a grassy path which brings you in 5min to a **military cemetery**.

From here another 5min brings you to a road (Jelovška cesta) where you turn left to reach the main crossroads in **Bohinjska Bistrica** (**3hr** from Črna prst).

WALK 19

Bogatin and Mahavšček

Start/finish	Koča pri Savici, west of Ukanc (653m)
Time	9hr
Distance	22.7km
Total ascent/descent	1455m
Grade	3
Maps	1:25,000 Bohinj, 1:25,000 Triglav, 1:25,000 Bovec-Trenta
Refreshments	Koča pri Savici, Dom na Komni and Koča pod Bogatinom (all also offer accommodation)
Access	During the summer season, shuttle buses run to Savica waterfall and Koča pri Savici (see www.bohinj.si for times or check at the bus stop). Koča pri Savici can also be reached by a 45min walk from Ukanc (described in Walk 13), which is well connected with a regular bus service. If you arrive by car, there is a car park near Koča pri Savici (parking fee)

Bogatin (1977m) is closely linked to one of Slovenia's favourite legends, that of Zlatorog, the Goldenhorn. The treasure he guarded was supposed to lie under this mountain, and so it is close to the hearts of Slovene mountaineers. Local stories aside, this shapely mountain, combined with its close neighbour Mahavšček (2005m), introduces the walker to the area around Komna and makes a fine day out from the Bohinj valley.

Walk through the car park and past the restaurant, where a sign points towards Dom na Komni and Koča pod Bogatinom. Just before the Savica waterfall **pay kiosk**, the path branches left, again signed Dom na Komni and Koča pod Bogatinom. Walk up the good path through beech woods, quickly gaining height in sweeping hairpins. There are a couple of places where it is possible to get a good view of the lake. At the top of the hairpins the path continues, heading through the wood (**1hr 30min**).

For a while the hut cableway can be seen overhead, but it later disappears into the trees as the route to the hut meanders away from it. Look out for a glimpse of Dom na Komni through the trees, ahead and on your left. After about 2hr 30min

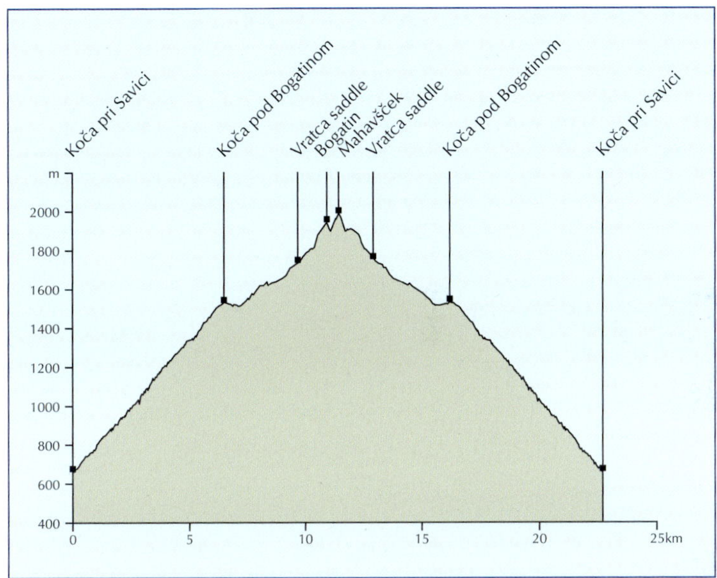

ignore a waymarked path on the right, signed Črno jezero, and continue on the main track. Shortly after, the route emerges from the trees to reach another junction signed Dom na Komni 5min and Koča pod Bogatinom 15min. Follow the sign for the hut or make the short detour left to **Dom na Komni** for refreshments.

The **view** opens out and is stunning. Although you are now above the beech and spruce, there are still plenty of dwarf pine and rowan, and the bare tops on the skyline are reminiscent of the Scottish Highlands. All the peaks above Komna can be seen across a tree-filled valley, with the summits of Mahavšček and Bogatin to the left of the Vratca saddle (Bogatinsko sedlo).

Reach **Koča pod Bogatinom** (1513m, **2hr 45min**) and after 100m, at a junction, bear left (signed Bogatin) and continue along an excellent path which was once a military road. Concrete and stone defences can be seen around the hut – which was used as a military hospital for a while during World War 1 – and below the pass. Just below the **Vratca saddle** (called also Bogatinsko sedlo, 1804m) the path divides, with a steeper path heading up to the right and traversing some rocky outcrops to reach the saddle, while the main path keeps left and makes an

Planina Viševnik
1625m
Vrtec
1811m
Rigelj
1768m
Stador
1688m
KOMARČA
Črno jezero
1319m
waterfall viewpoint
Slap Savica
836m
Koča pri Savici
653m
SF
P
pay kiosk for Savica waterfall
Savica
Blato
to Lake Bohinj and Ribčev Laz
Vrh Korit
1664m
WW1 military monument
Dom na Komni
1520m
Planina Na Kraju
Koča pod Bogatinom
1513m
Planina Govnjač
SPODNJA KOMNA
Kraj Kala
1855m
Srednji Vrh
1874m
Bogatin
1977m
Mahavšček
2005m
Vrh Škrli
1924m
Vratca saddle
1804m
Lanževica
2003m
N
0
1
km

A hiker descending from Mahavšček in the direction of Bogatin

easier zigzag; you can take either route. At the saddle (**4hr**) there is a signpost, an old military building and an old boundary marker. The border between the Kingdom of Italy and the Kingdom of Serbs, Croats and Slovenes once ran through here according to the agreement of superpowers in 1920.

From the saddle, bear left and begin to climb the ridge. Climb quite steeply but easily up the ridge, although care should be taken as the rock is loose and broken. Look back over your left shoulder for good views of Triglav. The path levels for a while before the final steep section, which is narrow for about 40m with steep drops on both sides, and while it is without real difficulty it might seem intimidating on a windy day. It is **4hr 30min** to the top of **Bogatin** (1977m) from Koča pri Savici.

From the top the **vista** is excellent – all of the northern Julian Alps can be seen, as well as a very clear view of Lake Bohinj. To the south-east the ridge continues towards Vogel and the Lower Bohinj mountains, and in the distance are the Karavanke, the Kamniške Alpe and beyond.

Mahavšček lies enticingly close to the south, and its ascent offers excellent views of the deep Tolminka valley and surrounding peaks that cannot be seen

Koča pod Bogatinom

from Bogatin. From the summit of Bogatin, the path drops down quite steeply at first, with a few rocky steps, before reaching easier, though still loose and broken, ground. This brings you to a saddle between the two peaks. Continue easily up the rocky ridge, which is not quite as steep or narrow as that of Bogatin, to reach the summit of **Mahavšček** (2005m, **5hr**).

Retrace your steps to the saddle. You can avoid ascending to the summit of Bogatin again by taking an easy path from the saddle that traverses the western side of Bogatin below the summit, leading you back to the Vratca saddle (**5hr 30min**). Reverse the ascent route to reach the valley or stay overnight at either Dom na Komni or Koča pod Bogatinom.

A circular route heading south-east down the ridge from Mahavšček and then east via Planina Govnjač to Dom na Komni looks enticing on the map but is not recommended. The route is little used and therefore quite overgrown in places, making route-finding awkward, especially in poor visibility.

WALK 20

Triglav Lakes valley and Veliko Špičje

Start/finish	Koča pri Savici, west of Ukanc (653m)
Time	2 days (12–13hr)
Distance	24.4km
Total ascent/descent	1955m
Grade	4
Maps	1:25,000 Bohinj, 1:25,000 Triglav, 1:25,000 Bovec-Trenta
Accommodation	Koča pri Triglavskih jezerih (Triglav Lakes hut)
Access	During the summer season, shuttle buses run to Koča pri Savici. See www.bohinj.si for times or check at the bus stop. Alternatively, from Ukanc follow Walk 13 as far as the turn-off for the Komarča path (just before Koča pri Savici). If you arrive by car, there is a car park near the hut (parking fee)
Warning	A helmet is recommended on this route

The Triglav Lakes valley, containing a string of seven lakes, is one of the highlights of the Julian Alps. Each lake, surrounded by steep mountains and, in the lower part of the valley, by rich mixed forest, has its own character. This route comprises a half-day's walk up to the Triglav Lakes hut (Koča pri Triglavskih jezerih, 1685m), followed by the ascent of Veliko Špičje (2398m) via its north-eastern ridge and the return on Day 2. For a more leisurely tour, you could stay a second night at Zasavska Koča na Prehodavcih (2071m).

Enjoying spectacular views from the summit of Bogatin

DAY 1

Koča pri Savici to Koča pri Triglavskih jezerih

Start	Koča pri Savici (653m)
Finish	Koča pri Triglavskih jezerih (1685m)
Distance	6.1km
Ascent	1085m
Descent	65m
Time	3hr 15min

The wall of crags rising up behind Koča pri Savici can look daunting, but a well-laid-out route makes relatively easy work of the ascent. From the top, the waymarked path leads gradually through fine woods until you reach Koča pri Triglavskih jezerih in its glorious Alpine lakeland setting. If you don't have much time to explore the Triglav Lakes valley, this route as far as the hut makes for an enjoyable day's walk from Bohinj.

From the hut, a sign directs you over the bridge to Črno jezero 1hr 40min and Koča pri Triglavskih jezerih 3hr 15min. About 100m past the bridge, reach the sign on the left for the **Komarča path** and take it, climbing steadily through beech forest. Ignore a path to the left that leads to Savica waterfall (Slap Savica), and after about 20min reach the foot of the first rocks dripping with water.

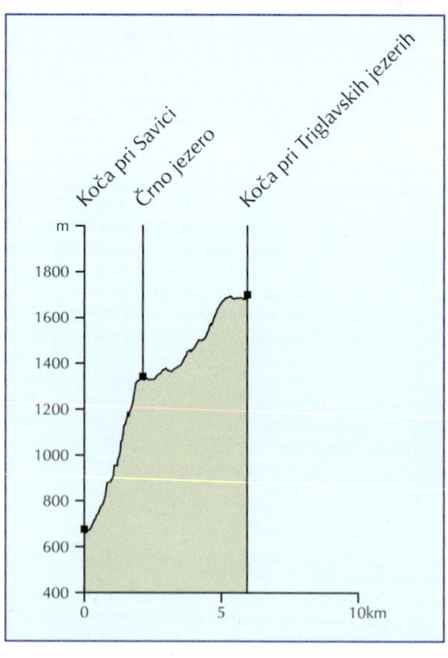

The path branches left and continues climbing steadily below crags in the trees, shortly afterwards reaching another sign for Črno jezero and Koča pri Triglavskih jezerih (**30min**). Continue up, zigzagging through

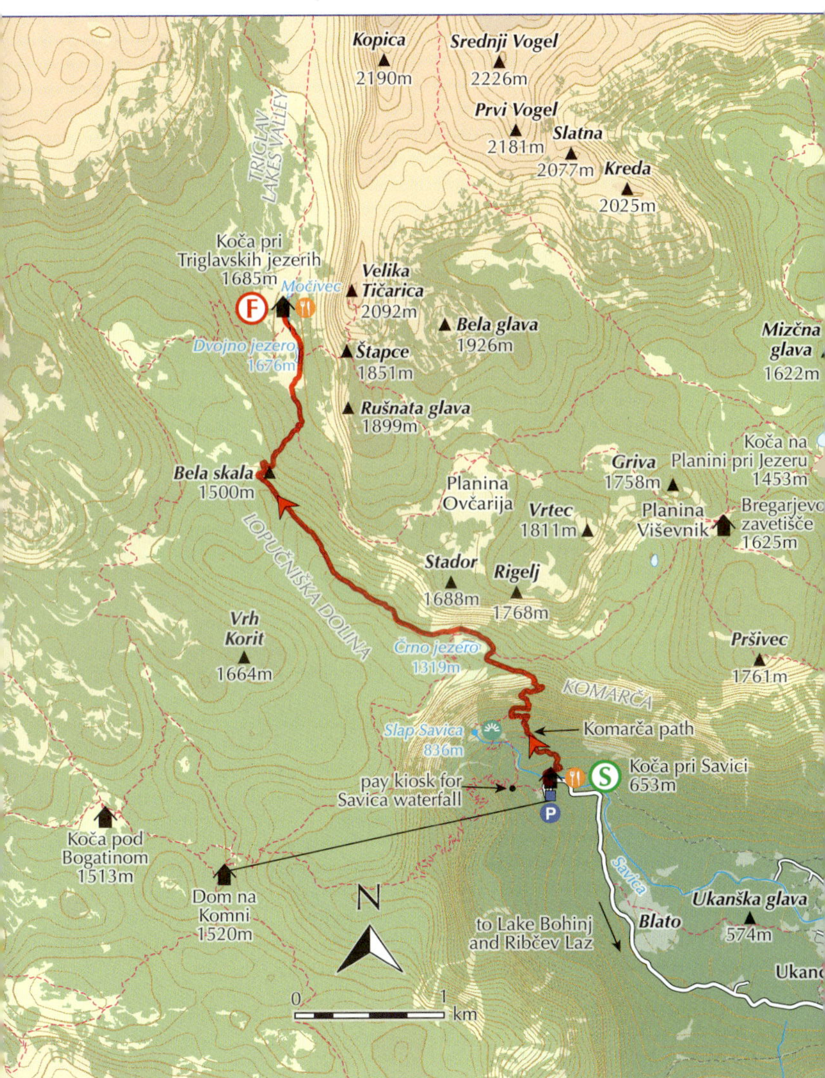
Kopica
2190m
Srednji Vogel
2226m
Prvi Vogel
2181m
Slatna
2077m
Kreda
2025m
TRIGLAV LAKES VALLEY
Koča pri Triglavskih jezerih 1685m
Močivec
Velika Tičarica
2092m
Bela glava
1926m
Mizčna glava
1622m
Dvojno jezero
1676m
Štapce
1851m
Rušnata glava
1899m
Koča na Planini pri Jezeru
1453m
Griva
1758m
Bela skala
1500m
Planina Ovčarija
Vrtec
1811m
Planina Viševnik
Bregarjevo zavetišče
1625m
LOPUČNIŠKA DOLINA
Stador
1688m
Rigelj
1768m
Vrh Korit
1664m
Črno jezero
1319m
Pršivec
1761m
KOMARČA
Komarča path
Slap Savica
836m
Koča pri Savici
653m
pay kiosk for Savica waterfall
Koča pod Bogatinom
1513m
Dom na Komni
1520m
Savica
Ukanška glava
574m
Blato
to Lake Bohinj and Ribčev Laz
0
1
km

the trees towards the crags before beginning to ascend the Komarča cliff face. The path is very well constructed, with steel cables forming a handrail in places and occasional steel pegs.

The **Komarča** (ladder) face was first explored towards the end of the 18th century, and at that time spruce trees, with their branches cut like the rungs of a ladder, were laid over the most difficult places, giving the face its name.

About three-quarters of the way up, the route meets a fast-flowing stream in a steep gully and ascends on some metal rungs for a few metres to the left of it (**1hr 15min**). There are occasional glimpses through the trees to the end of the lake and across the valley to Vogel. The path is steepest near the top, a fact that is particularly noticeable in the descent. At the top the path levels out and enters a forest of beautiful tall spruce and beech trees, reaching **Črno jezero** (the black lake, 1319m, **1hr 40min**) in less than 10min. The lake is surrounded by trees and flanked on its northern edge by the huge crags of Stador and by steep rock walls to the south.

Koča pri Triglavskih jezerih

The waymarked path branches right just before you reach the lakeshore. In another 50m reach a sign on a tree pointing to the left indicating, 'Koča pri Triglavskih jezerih 1hr30'. The path continues through the woods above the right-hand side of the lake, below the crags. Just before the end of the lake reach another junction, signed left to Dom na Komni, but the route described here keeps straight on to Triglav Lakes.

The rocky path continues through pine and shrubs along a narrow valley known as Lopučniška dolina, gradually changing to tall spruce with occasional beech. After about 1.5km the path passes underneath a wet overhanging wall and begins ascending gently along the foot of the rocks of **Bela Skala** (the white cliff). Pass a water trough that collects the refreshing water from the crags and, in another 5min or so, swing sharply right and begin to zigzag up more steeply (**2hr 40min**).

Soon the zigzags relent and the path continues climbing steadily. Reach a sign for the hut to the left at a junction. The trail becomes easy, passing through larch trees and soon reaching the pretty Dvojno jezero (twin lakes), with the hut at the far end. Continue along the right-hand side of the lake to reach **Koča pri Triglavskih jezerih** (1685m) in its dramatic setting with the towering cliffs of Tičarica on the right.

DAY 2

Koča pri Triglavskih jezerih to Koča pri Savici

Start	Koča pri Triglavskih jezerih (1685m)
Finish	Koča pri Savici (653m)
Distance	18.3km
Ascent	870m
Descent	1890m
Time	9–10hr
Refreshments	Zasavska koča na Prehodavcih

This full mountain day entails a very long descent if returning all the way to Koča pri Savici. The superb walk along the high ridge contrasts perfectly with the gentler descent past the shimmering turquoise waters of the Triglav Lakes valley.

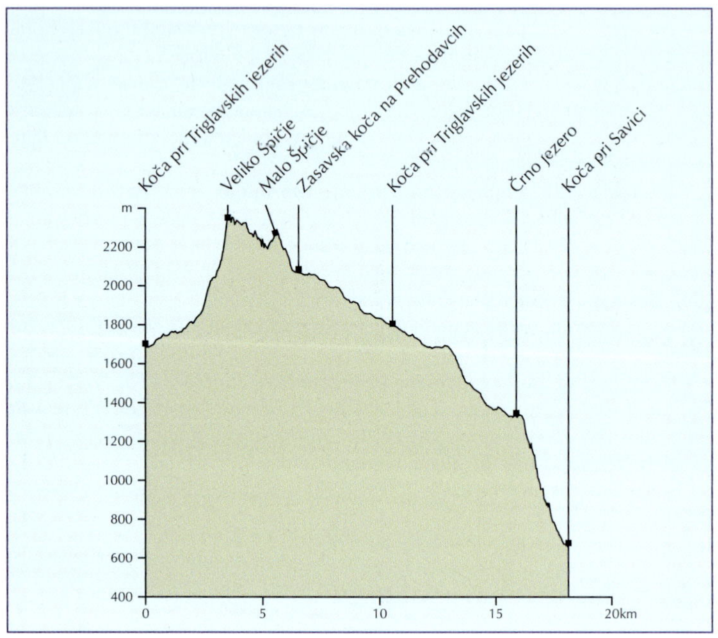

From the hut, the path leads off on the right-hand side, close to the pools of the next (man-made) lake with its small dam. The path climbs gently up between boulders and over limestone pavement slabs for about 25min to a sign for Veliko Špičje at a left-hand fork (**30min**). This path is narrower and, after about 5min, it descends a little to a karst hollow (80–100m in length) which is sometimes filled with water. Skirt the hollow by the western end and continue, following waymarks. Soon begin to ascend gently again, around karst sinkholes and through the lush vegetation and occasional larch trees. Through the trees you can see Veliko Špičje ahead. After a while the path begins to ascend more steadily to the left of outcrops of rock topped with dwarf pine. There are good views behind you of the ridge opposite and back down the valley, with the Lower Bohinj mountains on the skyline.

Pass through a shallow rocky channel, being careful to follow waymarks left, and soon afterwards begin to climb more steeply over more limestone pavement towards the rocky, grassy spur that is the ascent route. The path winds its way up this spur for the next 10–15min to reach a steel cable that protects a short but

Zasavska koča na Prehodavcih
2071m
Jezero pod Vršacem
1991m
Kanjavec
2568m
Rjavo jezero
2006m
Poprovec
2496m
Čez Hribarice
2358m
TREBIŠKI DOL
Malo Špičje
2312m
Zeleno jezero
1988m
Vrh Hribaric
2388m
Vršak
2440m
2335m
Veliko Špičje
2398m
Veliki Grad
2004m
Veliko jezero (Ledvička)
1831m
Velika Zelnarica
2310m
Zadnji Vogel
2327m
Debeli vrh
2390m
Mala Zelnarica
2320m
TRIGLAV LAKES VALLEY
Kopica
2190m
Srednji Vogel
2222m
N
Prvi Vogel
2181m
Slatna
2077m
Kreda
2025m
Žagarjeva glava
1634m
0
1
km
Močivec
Koča pri Triglavskih jezerih
1685m
S
Velika Tičarica
2092m
Bela glava
1926m
Dvojno jezero
1676m
Štapce
1851m
Mizčna glava
1622m
Rušnata glava
1899m
Koča na Planini pri Jezeru
1453m
Kraj Kala
1855m
Griva
1758m
Planina Ovčarija
LOPUČNIŠKA DOLINA
Vrtec
1811m
Planina Viševnik
1625m
Bregarjevo zavetišče
1625m
Stador
1688m
Rigelj
Vrh Korit
1664m
Pršivec
1761m
Črno jezero
1319m
KOMARČA
Slap Savica
836m
Komarča path
pay kiosk
Koča pri Savici
653m
F
P
Koča pod Bogatinom
1513m
Dom na Komni
1520m
to Lake Bohinj and Ribčev Laz
Savica

quite exposed traverse across a steep section of rock, then ascending rocky steps to reach easier ground, again on the crest of the spur. Continue on to reach the crest of the main ridge, where you turn left and follow the path for about 100m to the summit of **Veliko Špičje** (2398m, **2hr 30min**). The views from the summit are excellent; the position of Veliko Špičje between the Bohinj and Trenta peaks ensures a panorama across the whole of the Julian Alps and beyond into Austria and Italy.

Retrace your steps from the summit to the path junction and follow waymarks along the ridge towards Prehodavci. In a short distance the path drops a little to the right-hand side of the ridge, with a good view of the Triglav Lakes valley. The path momentarily joins the crest again, with a view down a vast chasm to Trenta on the other side, and then continues along the ridge, keeping mostly on the right-hand side.

Excellent views are maintained along the length of the **ridge** as the path traverses pleasantly over short grass and rocks painted with deep blue gentians, Zois' bellflower and cushions of Triglav rose. The ridge is also a regular haunt of ibex.

Make a short descent before beginning to climb again towards the peak of **Malo Špičje** (2312m, **3hr 45min**); the path bypasses the summit but you can make a 2–3min detour, signed left, to the top for a spectacular view back along the ridge and on towards the next hut.

After this the path soon begins to descend, bearing left at first before turning right again and continuing down over fissured limestone rock, avoiding steep crags barring the continuation of the ridge from Malo Špičje. Eventually, turn right at the edge of a slabby white limestone pavement for about 30m, then turn left again as you climb up onto the slabs and cross them. Reach a junction signed right for Triglavska koča 2hr (go this way if you wish to shorten the route a little, avoiding Zasavska koča na Prehodavcih) and left for Prehodavci. Turn left, and about 100m past the junction reach another one with a path heading left down to Trenta on the old military road; continue on for another 200m to reach **Zasavska koča na Prehodavcih** (2071m, **4hr 30min**).

From **Zasavska koča** you can see the highest of the seven Triglav Lakes, Jezero pod Vršacem (1991m), lying in the hollow beneath the steep cliffs of Kanjavec. It is unusual among the seven lakes in that it doesn't flow into the Triglav Lakes valley but instead towards the Soča. The six other lakes are connected underground, and their levels fluctuate widely throughout the year.

Continue descending on the waymarked path (signed Koča pri Triglavskih jezerih), with Rjavo jezero (brown lake) about 200m to the left, enveloped by the massive crags of the surrounding mountains – Kanjavec and Vršaki. The path continues descending to **Zeleno jezero** (green lake) with its fantastic backdrop of the Zelnarica crags (**4hr 55min**). Here a path heads left to Čez Hribarice but keep straight on for Koča pri Triglavskih jezerih. These upper reaches of the Triglav Lakes valley are the epitome of alpine wilderness – there are no trees and the ground is a turmoil of jumbled limestone interspersed with some grass and hardy colourful flowers.

The path continues easily down the valley and eventually some thickets of dwarf pine mark the point where you drop down to **Veliko jezero** (Ledvička), the largest and deepest of the lakes, named 'kidney lake' because of its shape. There are some similarities to a North American landscape in this part of the valley, with the rocky peaks and larches beyond the lake. The path passes above the water on the left-hand side, below the screes of Zelnarica, and continues down the valley, eventually meeting the first larches. As the trees begin to thicken, you reach the junction for Veliko Špičje and continue past it to regain the **Koča pri Triglavskih jezerih** (**6hr 30min**). It is about 3hr from here back down Komarča to Savica.

Triglav Lakes valley from the Veliko Špičje ridge

WALK 21

Triglav – the southern approach

Start/finish	Supermarket in Stara Fužina (551m)
Time	2 days
Distance	33.5km
Total ascent/descent	2560m
Grade	4
Maps	1:25,000 Bohinj, 1:25,000 Triglav
Accommodation	Dom Planika pod Triglavom
Access	Regular buses run from Bohinjska Bistrica via the Upper and Lower Bohinj valleys to Stara Fužina, and shuttle buses are usually added to regular services in high season. See www.bohinj.si for times or check at the bus stop. If you arrive by car, there are several car parks in Stara Fužina (parking fee)
Note	This route can be shortened by starting and finishing at Planinska koča na Vojah (toll road for private vehicles but there is also a transport service from Stara Fužina in summer), although this would leave out the walk alongside the Mostnica gorge
Warning	This is a true mountaineering route; via ferrata kit and helmet are strongly recommended

The landscape of the southern approach to Triglav (2864m), the highest point in Slovenia, offers a contrast to the stark faces of the northern side: the walk-in is longer, but the slopes are generally gentler, and the route is considered to be easier than those from the north. However, this is still a big mountain and not to be undertaken lightly. The approach here is through the Voje valley from Stara Fužina. The route then climbs up to Vodnikov dom (1817m) and then to Dom Planika (2401m), where you can spend the night. The hut is well positioned for making the final ascent of Triglav's summit rocks in the (hopefully!) clear morning air before you retrace the route to Stara Fužina.

DAY 1

Stara Fužina to Dom Planika

Start	Supermarket in Stara Fužina (551m)
Finish	Dom Planika pod Triglavom (2401m)
Distance	14.7km
Total ascent	1965m
Total descent	120m
Time	7hr–7hr 30min
Refreshments	Planinska koča na Vojah and Vodnikov dom na Velem polju (both also offer accommodation)

This is a long walk with a lot of height gain. It starts off quite gently, along the beautiful Mostnica valley, and then becomes a steady ascent that finishes at the foot of Triglav's steep southern rock wall.

From the supermarket in Stara Fužina, walk north and go straight ahead at the crossroads, following a sign to Korita Mostnice and Dolina Voje, with the river on your right and passing pretty houses on both sides. After crossing the river, turn left at a T-junction and walk up the lane. Soon after the large Rabič apartment building on your left, go through an iron gate, where the track is joined by another from the right, and continue round to the left across a small open pasture to reach **Hudičev most** (the Devil's bridge, **15min**).

From Hudičev most, walk up the track on the west bank of the Mostnica river for a short distance to a big orientation sign describing the gorge and take the path straight on, descending slightly into the woods, with the gorge falling away to your right. Walk pleasantly through the forest to the **pay kiosk** and turn right to cross a bridge, with more views down into the deep gorge. Further along from this bridge the gorge becomes much shallower and the path runs to the right of the extremely pretty river.

The path continues through beech woods, bending slightly away from the river, and the gorge gradually deepens again. Reach a viewpoint of a section of the gorge where the rocks are almost overhanging – the top ones are barely a metre apart. Further on, a stone bridge takes you back onto the west side, again with good views into the depths, where you take the right-hand path climbing

Glava 2426m
Kredarica
Rž
Triglav
2864m
Aljaž's tower
Mali
Triglav
2540m
2538m
Glava v
Zaplanji
2556m
2725m
Triglavski dom na Kredarici
2515m
Mali Pršivec
1996m
Map for days 1 and 2
Triglavska
škrbina
Dom Planika
2401m
N
Rjavec
2570m
SF
Konjsko sedlo
2019m
0
1
km
Koča na Doliču
2151m
Šmarjetna
glava
2355m
Mali
Draški vrh
2132m
VELSKA DOLINA
Vernar
2225m
Veliki
Draški vrh
2243m
Mišelj
vrh
2350m
Tosc
2275m
Velo
polje
Malo
polje
Vodnikov dom
na Velem polju
1817m
Ablanca
2005m
Prevalski
Stog
2079m
Mesnova
glava
1715m
Jezerski
Stog
2039m
Planina
Vrtača
Mali Stog
1879m
Planina Spodnja
Grintovica
1178m
Mostnica waterfall
773m

Ribnica
Rjavec
1161m
Planinska koča na Uskovnici
1154m
Studor v Bohinju
Studor
1002m
Kamen
1028m
Ribnica
Planinska koča na Vojah
690m
Stara Fužina
Okrepčevalnica Slap
VOJE VALLEY
pay kiosk
Mostnica
MOSTNICA GORGE
Hudičev most
Triglav National Park Information Centre
SF
N
0
1km
Kosijev Dom na Vogarju
1054m
Lake Bohinj
Planina Blato
Žagarjeva glava
1634m
Savica

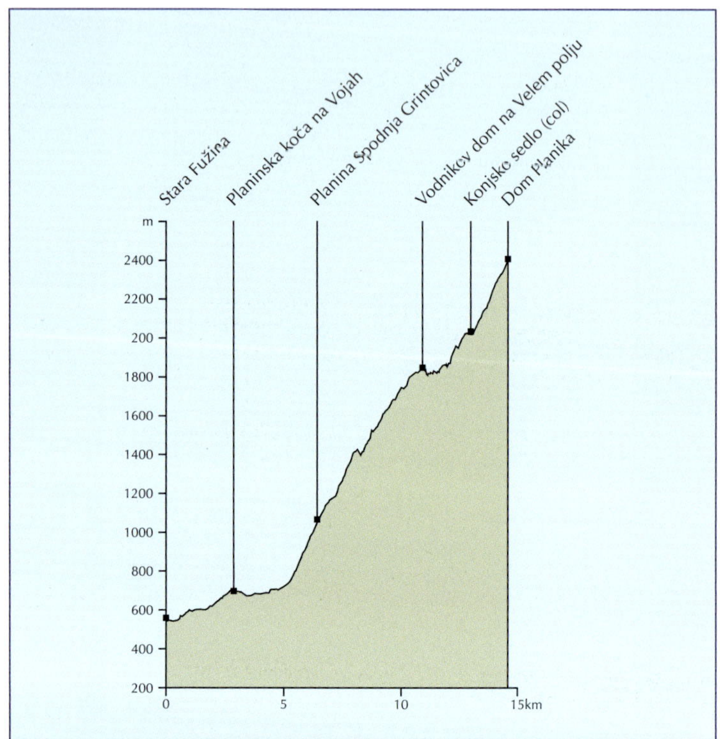

steeply away from the river into the forest, signed Dolina Voje. Follow the waymarks on a northward trail, with the noise of the river on your right.

About 15min from the bridge, the path joins a tarmac road coming up from Stara Fužina. Turn right and about 200m further on reach **Planinska koča na Vojah** (690m, **50min**), where you can get refreshments.

Continue past the hut on the unmade track for about 1km to a fork by a building. Take the left-hand track, signed Vodnikov dom and Triglav, and continue (ignoring the Slap Mostnica sign) to a wooden sign at a fork, where you bear left, signed Vodnikov dom and Triglav. The broad stony path immediately enters the woods and begins to ascend quite steeply in hairpins up the steep hillside at the head of the valley. After about 1hr the path reaches a little open alp, **Planina Spodnja Grintovica** (1178m, **2hr 40min**). Follow the waymarked path across it, passing a spring and water trough about 20m to the left. There are excellent views to the north of Tosc and Draški vrh.

Re-enter the woods and continue to wind up through the forest, quite steeply in places, for another 30min or so before the ground begins to level out. Pass some small outcrops to your left and then descend a little, with steep forested slopes down to your right where Planina Vrtača lies in the valley below, before beginning to ascend again. In the summer, the lush vegetation encroaches on the path, which is quite surprising considering this is one of the main paths to Triglav. Continue on, winding between boulders and karst hollows.

> Notice the subtle changes in the **alpine scenery** as you gain height. Spruce, larch and rowan trees give way to dwarf pine among tall larch trees, which gradually begin to thin out. The flowers, too, change with height, but all have the same rich range of colours.

Eventually, the path levels at a major junction signed Uskovnica to the right. Turn left, and the path immediately forks again; this time take the right fork, signed Vodnikov dom and Triglav. After another 20m or so you get an uninterrupted view of the classic three-headed profile of Triglav, which features on the Slovenia flag. The path traverses high above Malo polje (small pasture) and, in about 10min, reaches **Vodnikov dom na Velem polju** (1817m, **5hr**). There is a wonderful view of Mišelj vrh (2350m) to the west, a fine rocky peak that looks like it has been displaced from Yosemite!

The potholes and small waterfalls of the Mostnica river

The Vodnikov dom with Triglav in the background

Immediately after leaving the hut, the path forks; take the right-hand path, signed Planika on a rock, which you can see on a rocky shoulder (still a long way above!). The path traverses through dwarf pine and in less than 15min a handrail leads across the rocks of the lower slopes of **Vernar** (2225m). The route then climbs quite steeply across a scree slope to pass beneath the rocky summit. Soon reach the foot of rocks with steps cut into them and more steel cables for a handrail.

The path climbs on, skirting the foot of crags, over increasingly rocky terrain. About 40min from the hut, the path passes through a karst hollow, quite level and pretty with flowers, and then drops down a short gentle descent towards **Konjsko sedlo** (2019m). A number of paths head off from the saddle – take the signed path to Planika, heading north-west, following the waymarks carefully, especially in poor visibility, as a number of older worn paths criss-cross the quite featureless terrain.

The route climbs fairly steeply from the saddle and then begins a long rising traverse across the rocky hillside. About 40min from the saddle, reach the top of a shoulder and turn right. Continue up, heading north, again being careful to follow waymarks over increasingly barren ground. Another 15min brings you to a rocky scoop or bowl in the hillside. The hut is just above, and the main path leads to the right of the bowl to reach, in 10min or so, the overnight stop at **Dom Planika** (2401m).

DAY 2

Dom Planika to Stara Fužina

Start	Dom Planika pod Triglavom (2401m)
Finish	Supermarket in Stara Fužina (551m)
Distance	18.8km
Total ascent	595m
Total descent	2440m
Time	7–8hr
Refreshments	Dom Planika, Vodnikov dom na Velem polju, Okrepčevalnica Slap and Planinska koča na Vojah

From Dom Planika, the route soon becomes more serious as it is impossible to avoid the exposed scrambling that leads up to Triglav's airy ridge and summit. The descent to Stara Fužina involves huge height loss and requires stamina – walking poles recommended!

See Day 1 Stara Fužina to Dom Planika for map.

From Dom Planika take the waymarked route, signed Triglav (čez Mali Triglav). Head across fairly level scree, initially in a north-north-west direction, for about 200m, and then over steeper rocky ground as the route begins to ascend towards the south-east spur. Continue over scree and rubble, and more easy rocks, to reach the foot of steeper crags. The route turns right and passes through a cleft in the rock, where you meet the first steel cables (**20min**).

Reach the end of the cleft, which forms a notch with a gully dropping down the other side, and head straight up the fairly easy-angled rock, following steel cables and pegs. After a few metres the route trends left again for a short distance and then continues up to reach steeper rocks with more pegs. Shortly afterwards reach a shoulder, with Triglavski dom na Kredarici visible to the right below. Close by on the south side of the Mali Triglav buttress you can see the long rows of steel pegs that mark the bold traverse line on the route from Kredarica.

The path goes left and up again, with some exposure but no major difficulties, following steel cables all the while. After a final scramble over easy rock steps, join the ridge where the route comes up from Kredarica. The south-east spur joins the ridge a few metres below the summit of **Mali Triglav** (2725m), at a junction close

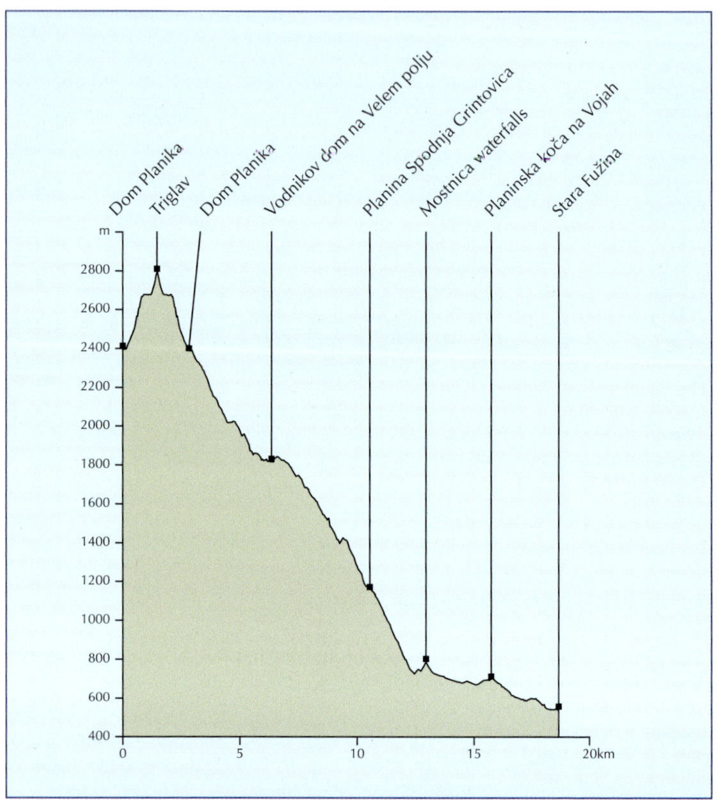

to a memorial plaque. The rocks of the summit ridge provide exciting scrambling with plenty of protection, but countless ascents have left the rocks quite polished. Continue quite easily at first, with big drops on both sides, for about 15min or so before the route steepens again. Another short, level section follows, just before the final steep rocks – which are well protected but have considerable exposure. Notice a sign that reads 'Staničevo zavetišče 30m', pointing left – this marks a small cave that can offer emergency shelter. Make the easy final short walk to the summit of **Triglav** (2864m, **1hr 30min**), marked by the metal Aljažev stolp (Aljaž's tower). The view is excellent if the air is clear. Triglav's considerable height difference is obvious as you survey, below you, all the other peaks of the Julian Alps.

The route along the ridge is well protected

The **tower** on the summit of Triglav was erected in 1895 on the order of a local pioneering priest from Dovje-Mojstrana, Jakob Aljaž, who had bought the summit area for a nominal sum. It was designed as a shelter and was once furnished with three round chairs, but as it is made of metal, it is advisable to make use of the Staničevo zavetišče cave instead if caught in a thunderstorm!

Return to Stara Fužina via the same route but, once you reach Voje valley, be sure to make the short detour (of about 10min) to the **Mostnica waterfalls** (773m). Once you reach the valley, ignore the first wooden sign, 'Slap 100m', indicating a path heading left; instead, continue for 5min on the main track to a second Slap Mostnica sign, where you turn left onto a narrower path. This path soon leads you to a bridge; cross it and continue for about 100m to come out opposite the restaurant **Okrepčevalnica Slap**. Turn left onto a broad path and walk for about 5min to the waterfalls. From here follow Walk 14 (Korita Mostnice) back to **Stara Fužina**.

Alternative endings

There are numerous alternatives to an immediate return to Stara Fužina once you have reached Triglav's summit. You could stay in one of the high-level huts, such as Dom Planika, Triglavski dom na Kredarici or Koča na Doliču, to ascend other peaks and/or return to a different valley: down the Triglav Lakes valley to Ukanc, down the Vrata to reach Kranjska Gora or down Zadnjica to Trenta.

Dom Planika

WALK 22

Kanjavec

Start	Dom Planika pod Triglavom (2401m)
Finish	Koča na Doliču (2151m)
Time	5hr
Distance	6.1km
Total ascent	475m
Total descent	710m
Grade	4
Maps	1:25,000 Kranjska Gora, 1:25,000 Bohinj, 1:25,000 Triglav
Accommodation	Dom Planika or Koča na Doliču
Access	Follow Walk 21 to Dom Planika from Stara Fužina
Warning	On this route, a helmet is recommended

The shapely peak of Kanjavec (2568m) stands in the heartland of the Julian Alps, high above the Triglav Lakes and the Trenta valleys. Its ascent makes a fine addition to any of the routes that venture into the Triglav area – the Triglav Lakes valley route (Walk 20) or Triglav itself (Walk 21).

The walk described here starts from Dom Planika and finishes at Koča na Doliču; if you don't wish to stay overnight at the hut, you can reverse the route to Planika or carry on down the Velska valley to Vodnikov dom (2hr of easy walking) from where, after an overnight stay, you can return to Stara Fužina. Alternatively, follow the path that ascends to the stony plateau of Čez Hribarice to reach the Triglav Lakes valley (1hr 30min from Koča na Doliču).

From Dom Planika take the waymarked path, signed Koča na Doliču 1hr 30min. The route descends diagonally over scree and stones before reaching the crags of Rjavec (2570m, **15min**). Steel cables and pegs protect the traverse of the rocky section, then the path levels for a while before descending again to reach the slopes of **Šmarjetna glava** (2355m).

Begin to ascend over steeper rocky ground and then continue traversing over scree and rubble on the left-hand side of the crags. After 20min or so reach a steeper section of rock fitted with steel cables and occasional pegs. The route

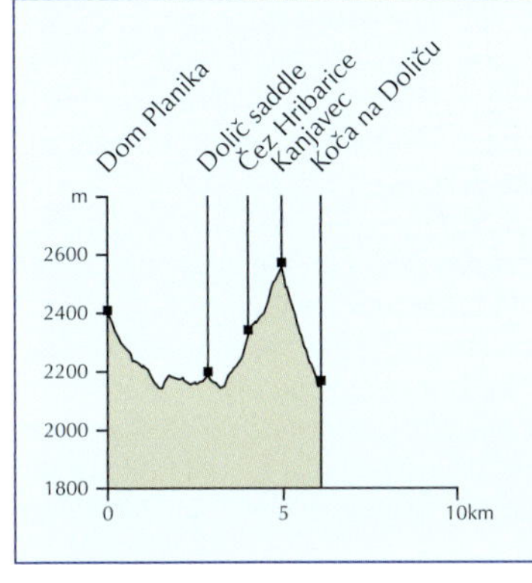

then continues on easier ground to eventually arrive at the **Dolič saddle** (2164m, **1hr 30min**) from which the hut takes its name.

From the saddle turn right if you wish to make the short detour to Koča na Doliču for refreshments, otherwise take the path to the left, signed Sedmera Jez (Triglav Lakes) on a stone. Descend a little on the stony path before beginning to gently climb through rocky karst scenery below the foot of the steep cliffs on the south-east side of Kanjavec. The route eventually begins to ascend more steeply, zigzagging up scree, following waymarks to the left of a boulder-filled hollow to reach the stony plateau of **Čez Hribarice** (2358m, **2hr 30min**).

Turn right, signed Kanjavec, and soon the path begins to ascend gently. After about 15min it steepens a little but is without difficulty. Ascend some easy rocky steps and join the crest of the east ridge; continue easily along here for about 100m to reach a notch. Descend into the notch via a short scramble, then continue up the easy rocks on the other side along the ridge to reach the summit of **Kanjavec** (2568m, **3hr 30min**). From here there are fabulous views of Triglav and beyond to Razor and Prisank. Further to the north-west you can see into Austria, with Grossglockner easily visible on a good day.

From the summit a waymarked path drops down on the north side of the mountain. Descend steeply over scree and loose rock for the first 100m or so, then traverse the top of a crag for a short distance before meeting steel cables that protect a steep scramble down of about 20m. Continue over slightly easier ground still covered with loose rock before beginning to traverse right across scree slopes. The path then heads down over typical karst landscape, with hollows and water-worn slabs, until you see the hut below. Continue winding down between rocks to arrive at **Koča na Doliču** (2151m).

Koča na Doliču

SECTION 3 BOVEC

High on the Slovene route up Mangart (Walk 31) (photo: Roy Clark)

The large village of Bovec (454m) lies in a wide flat basin called Bovška kotlina at the foot of Rombon, which forms, along with the rest of the Kanin range, a steep, impressive mountain backdrop. The valley sits at the confluence of two rivers, the Soča and the Koritnica; the former flows west from its source high in the Trenta valley, and the latter comes down from the north. Steep slopes rear up on every side, and Bovec even has its own 'Matterhorn' – Svinjak, a mountain of comparatively modest height but with an impressive profile, which guards the head of the valley between the two rivers. Routes to the high peaks of Krn, Mangart and Kanin are all described in this section.

Bovec has a plethora of companies offering guided outdoor activities, and it is easy to see why. As well as the mountaineering possibilities, Bovec sits on the banks of the river Soča, which flows through the valley, considered to be one of the finest in the whole of the Alps, with enormous potential for canoeing, rafting and canyoning. The ski resort of Kanin (2202m) is Slovenia's highest and only true alpine ski area – its height ensures a long season and it is justifiably popular. The gondola that lifts skiers to the heights in the winter is employed during the summer to spare walkers the grinding slog up nearly 1600m of slopes to reach the ridges and high hanging valleys of the Kanin peaks (Walk 26). In the autumn of 2023, inspectors shut down the gondola and, at the time of writing, a new operating licence has not yet been issued. Plans are underway to renovate the gondola, but there is currently no clear information on when the renovation work will begin and when the service will resume (for up-to-date information, check www.soca-valley.com). Caving is another popular sport; the area around Bovec is riddled with caves and potholes. There is also a small airfield that offers pleasure flights.

The Bovec area is steeped in history; this is the land that took the brunt of the fighting during World War 1 on the Soča (Isonzo) front. Many of the local settlements were evacuated (and at least partially destroyed) as soldiers from both the Italian and Austro-Hungarian armies took over the hillside and pass. Local walks are littered with old gun emplacements and fortifications.

Although Bovec is relatively small, it has a sporty, upbeat atmosphere and is used to visitors, with all the usual tourist requirements easily fulfilled. There are a number of hotels, hostels, restaurants and supermarkets, as well as a helpful tourist information centre in the village. Several campsites are located in the Bovec basin.

Bovec is comparatively remote; there are no trains, although there are regular buses. The main access by bus or car is from the south, on the 102 road which follows the Soča valley up from Tolmin and Nova Gorica. To the north the Vršič pass links Bovec to Kranjska Gora via Trenta, and several buses a day run during the summer season. In winter the pass is usually closed. Another pass, the Predel, also to the north, provides access to Italy and links to Tarvisio on the Austria–Italy border. The Predel pass is usually open all winter.

Additional bus services are provided in the area to reduce traffic congestion in the summer. The extensive list of connections includes bus shuttles for the entire Bovec area, an additional bus line to the Soča source and the Vršič Pass, and a cross-border bus line across the Predel pass (for more information, see www.soca-valley.com).

THE ROUTES

The nine routes described in this section offer a varied selection of possibilities for the Bovec area. Walk 25 visits water features in the area around Bovec and, with the peak of Svinjak (Walk 24), provides a good orientation of the area. Walks 23 and 24 visit World War 1 sites, and Walk 27, the Soča Trail, follows tracks alongside the river Soča to various points of interest. High-mountain walks, those of Kanin (Walk 26) and the Križ area above Trenta (Walks 28 and 29), are followed by routes up two mountains that stand alone – Krn (Walk 30) and Mangart (Walk 31).

MAPS

The 1:25,000 Bovec-Trenta map covers all the routes in this section. Walks 28 and 29 are also on the 1:25,000 Triglav and 1:25,000 Kranjska Gora maps. Walk 30 is also on the 1:25,000 Krnsko pogorje and 1;25,000 Bohinj maps.

The cross on the summit of Mangart (Walk 31)

WALK 23

Kluže

Start/finish	Tourist information office, Bovec (454m)
Time	4hr 30min
Distance	12.3km
Total ascent/descent	530m
Grade	2
Maps	1:25,000 Bovec-Trenta
Refreshments	None on the route

This walk climbs above Bovec and through the beautiful forests on the lower slopes of Rombon, visiting two military forts – Fort Hermann and Fort Kluže. The original wooden stronghold at Kluže was erected as early as 1420, and subsequent buildings have guarded the valley and the Koritnica bridge for centuries. The present fortress is a museum. The return walk to Bovec follows the valley of the Koritnica river through woodland and pastures.

Leaving the tourist information centre behind, take the slightly uphill road that leads to the church. Take the first right-hand fork, signed Plajerjeva skala. On your left is the new sports hall (under construction at the time of writing) and after about 50m take the small, slightly downhill road on the right, which goes around the back of the school. Shortly after, near a small chapel, the road becomes a track but soon returns to tarmac near a group of houses. Pass between the houses, cross a small stream and come to a T-junction, where you turn right onto a larger road. Almost immediately, turn left and walk along the road, which soon becomes a track, passing between small buildings and grazing animals. Near some small holiday cottages, the track becomes a path and begins to climb for about 500m. Pass through two gates and reach a junction, where you turn right up a tarmac road.

After 100m, at a bench, follow the sign for Plajerjeva skala and take the narrow path uphill to the left. Continue 300m to reach a house on the left (**50min**).

This is a good **viewpoint**, with Bovec and its airfield on the floor of the valley and Svinjak at its head. Straight across is Javorščcek, with a huge rock scar caused by a landslide in 1950, and higher up you begin to see into the complexity of the Krn massif.

The track becomes a narrow path with a stone wall on your right. In 50m, as you reach the corner of the wall, notice two rocks with markers directing you uphill to the left (follow the sign for Široki plaz). The path becomes a little indistinct as it doubles back just above the house and continues on over short grass with rocks and many varieties of small alpine flowers. After a short distance it turns sharply to the right as it ascends below the right-hand end of a small rocky outcrop, following waymarks. Within another 100m, enter a mixture of pine and oak woodland, where yellow signs for Široki plaz indicate the route on the now more distinct path.

After a winding ascent through the woods, arrive at the edge of a scree slope where a signpost at a T-junction points left to Bovec and right to Fort Hermann, heading across the scree slope. Turn right and beyond the scree slope the path traverses the hillside through attractive mixed woodland and, in another 10min, reaches a fork where you go right, signed Kluže. Occasional open sections of

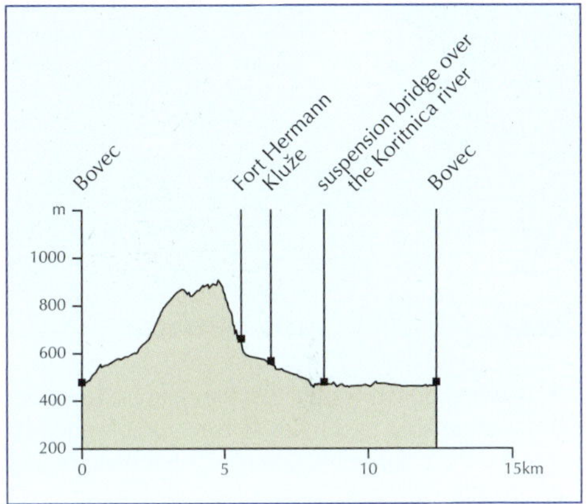

more scree and small outcrops offer views down the steep slopes to the right. After about 30min, the path begins to make a steady descent through beechwoods and very soon joins a track turning right and down, signposted Fort Hermann. After another 15min of descent come to **Fort Hermann** (645m, **2hr 20min**).

Turn left and head into the wood, away from the building, on a path signed Kluže. This was the supply line between the upper and lower fortifications. The route goes gently downhill, alongside crags which have additional strongholds hewn out of the cliff face. Continue to a right-hand hairpin and double back at a lower level to reach a **tunnel**, which is illuminated. Walk through for about 200m; when you emerge, you can see **Kluže** over the road not far away and the bridge over the Koritnica gorge. Walk a few hundred metres along the track to reach it (532m, **2hr 45min**).

The entrance to the tunnel on the path to the Fort Kluže

Inside the tunnel leading to Fort Kluže

To continue the walk, cross the road bridge over the surprisingly deep gorge. On the other side of the bridge turn right, signed Bavšica, and walk along this minor road for about 5min to take a track on the right, signed Šumnik. Ignore a track doubling back, which just leads to a house, and continue straight ahead, following the sign Bavšica, for about 200m to a right-hand hairpin.

A further 200m brings you to a fork. Both ways will continue the route; the left is a broader track favoured by mountain bikers, whereas the right is only suitable for walkers. The right-hand path, signed Kukč, goes alongside the northern bank of the Šumnik river, gradually descending and finally making a few steep zigzags to the river. However, the river, when you reach it, is actually the Koritnica, which is crossed via a **suspension bridge** about 50m upstream (**3hr 10min**). On the other side, pass a ruined stone building and continue on to meet a crossroads of paths. The route then carries straight on through the woods, signed Bovec, to emerge by a road bridge which goes to a house – this is where the left-hand path, which follows the southern bank, joins up again.

Continue on the rough vehicle track in the same direction, south-west, to eventually meet the main road (**3hr 40min**). About 50m ahead on the other side of the road, you can see the wooden signpost indicating the path continuation, signed Bovec. Continue along the narrow path through the woods to reach a diagonal crossroads with a vehicle track and go straight on, following a sign for Bovec. Continue through open hay meadows, passing a number of buildings. Cross a track, which serves some houses, and carry on across more meadows to reach a bench by a signpost where the main track swings left.

Continue straight ahead along another track signed Bovec. The main road and the industrial zone are visible on the left. Continue past more small buildings as the track becomes a narrow path passing through woodland to emerge at fields on the edge of Bovec (**Mala vas**) where you join a tarmac lane. At the next junction, just past house No. 47, turn left across a stream and walk down through the village towards the main road, then turn right to walk back to **Bovec**.

KLUŽE FORTRESS AND FORT HERMANN

Fort Hermann is the upper fortification at Kluže and is now very overgrown, but a suggestion of the part it played during World War 1 is still present in its eerie atmosphere. It was completed in 1900, but despite its heavy defences, including four cannons, four howitzers and eight heavy machine guns, it was badly damaged by the Italians during the very first attack in 1915. Excavation work has been carried out at the fort in recent years and information boards erected, but take care exploring the structure as some of the interior floors have now collapsed.

The present Kluže fortification was built in the early 1880s by the Austrians, in the same spot as previous defences, and was defended by 180 men with 3 cannons and 4 heavy machine guns. It played an important role as a command-and-control facility for the Austro-Hungarian forces in World War 1 and was also used in World War 2. Now a museum, it has an entrance fee (see www.kluze.net for more information).

The ruined Fort Hermann

WALK 24

Svinjak

Start/finish	Bus stop in Kal-Koritnica village (460m)
Time	5hr
Distance	7.3km
Total ascent/descent	1210m
Grade	3
Maps	1:25,000 Bovec-Trenta
Refreshments	None on the route; restaurant in Kal-Koritnica
Access	On foot: you can walk from Bovec by reversing Walk 27 as far as the campsites at Vodenca; cross the river Koritnica on the suspension bridge, follow the Soča Trail alongside the Soča to the Jablenca footbridge and turn up to reach Kal-Koritnica (about 1hr). By bus: during the summer season, shuttle buses from Bovec to the Lepena valley and the Vršič Pass all stop at Kal-Koritnica (see www.soca-valley.com for times or check at the bus stop). By car: there is a car park 200m past the bus stop, in front of the restaurant next to the main road
Note	Most of the trail is undemanding; only the last section takes in a steep ascent. This section can be slippery in wet weather and requires special care

Svinjak (1653m) is the shapely peak at the head of the valley as seen from Bovec; from this angle its magnificent pyramid form dominates the skyline. However, from other viewpoints its shape is not so satisfying and it becomes merely a point on the end of the long ridge of Bavški Grintavec. Although Svinjak is not as high as other mountains around Bovec, it offers a fine walk and an excellent airy viewpoint.

From the bus stop take the narrow street that leads into the village and continue straight ahead until it bends round to the left, heading to Bovec. At the bend is a water trough with a waymark, signed to Svinjak 3hr and Čelo 30min.

Leave the tarmac road here and start ascending gently on the grassy track, which crosses a stream and continues up a narrow field. At the top of the field, go

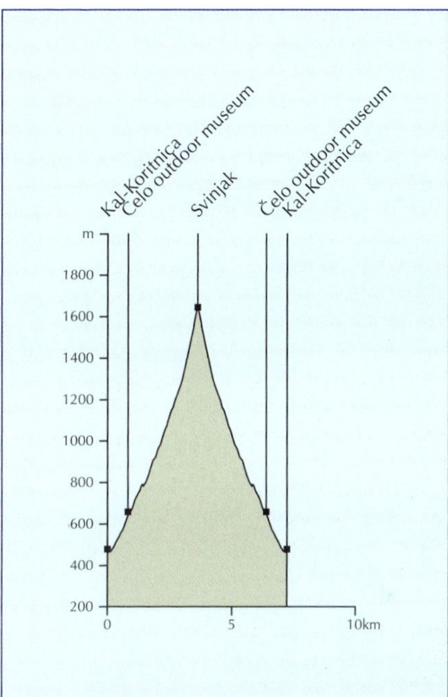

through a gate and walk on, with a dry-stone wall to the right and a steep wooded stream gully on the left, until you come to a signpost close to a concrete bunker with a metal door.

Svinjak and Čelo with the Pot miru peace dove motif are signed to the right. The path climbs pleasantly and after about 200m passes through a gate and continues for another 5min to the junction for Čelo (**20min**).

The path continues straight ahead, gently ascending at first and then making some zigzags and heading up left to join the crest of the ridge (**45min**). You can catch some good glimpses down into the Koritnica valley through the trees.

ČELO OUTDOOR MUSEUM

You could make a visit to the Čelo outdoor museum as a brief excursion (about 20min) on the descent, if you still have enough energy! These World War 1 defences are the remains of an important Austro-Hungarian fort that was part of the Bovec blockade (the Sperre Flitsch), which served as the defence against a possible Italian breakthrough. Two large gun emplacements were linked by almost 200m of stone and cement trenches, which included a kitchen and dormitories. A number of underground tunnels and bunkers were also cut into the hillside behind the fort. The view from here is truly spectacular, with the whole of the Bovec basin visible. The open-air museum is open all year round and there is no entrance fee. You'll need a torch to visit the bunkers.

Heading up the path towards Svinjak (photo: Roy Clark)

Turn right along the crest. Further on, the path leaves the crest and keeps to the right-hand side of the ridge, zigzagging up through the woods until it rejoins the crest at a short rocky step. Because the ridge is quite long, the gradient is not as steep as it appears from Bovec. Continue following waymarks, weaving up through the woods. The path always takes the right-hand side of the ridge when it is not on the crest. Pass through a recovered area of forest, which was devastated by fire that swept across the hillside in the summer of 2003, and not long after this a splendid view opens out quite suddenly to the right (**2hr 10min**). The turquoise Soča river can be seen on the valley floor, with the strange mound-like hill of Črni vrh just beyond and to the right of the hamlet of Podklanec. Javoršček and Krasji vrh lie to the south.

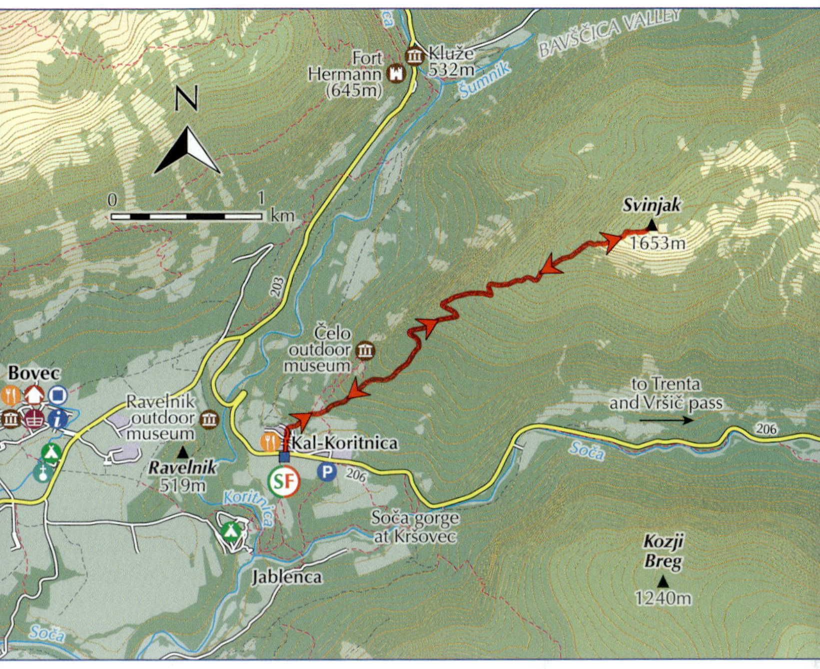

The path now skirts a small crag and continues ascending quite easily. Soon the trees begin to thin and an excellent view of the Bovec basin and the Kanin range opens up behind you. You are now on the final steep rise – there are no real difficulties but there is a feeling of airiness and space as the grassy slopes fall away steeply to the valley. By the dry stump of an old dead larch, there is a rocky step that requires an easy scramble. Quite suddenly, as you crest the last short rise, a rocky cairn confronts you and 100m beyond that, on the level ridge, is the summit of **Svinjak** (1653m, **3hr**).

On the **summit** there are blue gentians and many other alpine flowers, with a myriad of vibrantly coloured butterflies. The views are panoramic – along the ridge is Bavški Grintavec with its stratified precipices, and behind Jerebica and Rombon you can see the rocky, lofty heights of the Jôf Fuart group in Italy.

Retrace the route for descent.

WALK 25

Izvir Glijuna and Slap Virje

Start/finish	Ski gondola car park, Bovec (454m)
Time	2hr 15min
Distance	6.6km
Total ascent/descent	160m
Grade	1
Maps	1:25,000 Bovec-Trenta
Refreshments	None on the route
Access	From the centre of Bovec, follow the main road that leads west and take the right fork opposite a petrol station into the ski gondola car park

This is a short walk in terms of distance, but there is plenty of interest here to keep you out for a good 2–3hr. The route wanders pleasantly through woodland and pasture within 3km of Bovec to visit three water features: a reservoir and man-made water channels, the extraordinary source of the river Glijun and Slap Virje (Virje waterfall). The route continues through the charming village of Plužna before returning to Bovec through attractive woodland and pastures near the ski gondola.

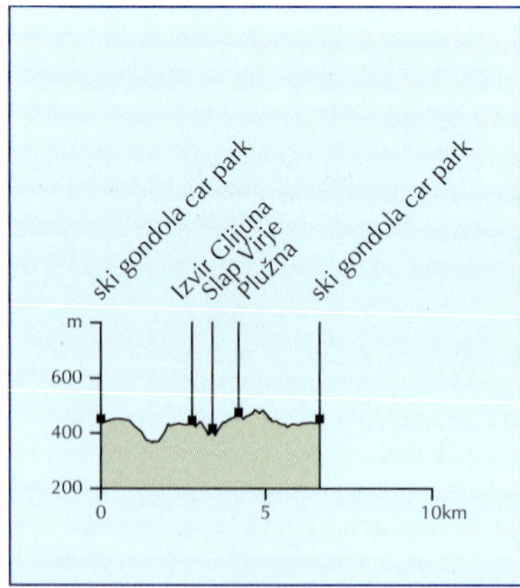

Cross the ski gondola car park to a track that leads west, signed Golf-slap Virje. Continue easily along the track for about 1km, with good views up towards the craggy peaks of the Kanin range; the top station of the gondola is also visible. The track enters some woodland and opposite a clearing you will reach a left-hand fork, again signed Golf-slap Virje. Follow this downhill for about 150m before reaching a second fork where you turn right, descending more steeply but still easily. After a few hundred metres the track joins a forest road; turn left onto it and continue to a T-junction with a vehicle road, opposite the second hole of Bovec golf course.

Turn right here, following a sign for Slap Virje-Plužna, and cross the little river Ročica, then immediately turn left, again signed Slap Virje-Plužna. After 50m cross the river Glijun on an attractive stone-built **humpbacked bridge** (**30min**). Pass a house and continue on a narrow path uphill, skirting the golf course, into more woodland. After about 500m the path emerges onto a level concrete walkway which is actually a covered water channel. Turn right and walk along it to a small man-made **reservoir**.

The **reservoir** forms part of a water-collection system that supplies a hydroelectric power station that was built when the area was under Italian rule; it is still working today. Although the reservoir is man-made, it is scenic, with two cottages to one side and wonderful views across the valley to Svinjak and the Polovnik ridge. Signs warn that fishing and bathing are forbidden.

Izvir Glijuna – the source of the river Glijun

The route skirts the western side of the lake and then continues along the concrete walkway to reach an adventure park and, shortly after, a dam and sluice gate complex just before Izvir Glijuna – the **source of the river Glijun** (430m, **55min**).

SOURCE OF THE GLIJUN

The unusual source of the river Glijun is one of those features that make limestone country so interesting. The river rushes along among attractive moss-covered boulders, but a few metres above it there is – nothing. The water gushes directly out of the rocks, and although the inclination is to go and look for the water descending from above, perhaps around a bend, it's just not there. The emerging water has a steady year-round temperature of 5.5°C, and changes in the level of the water table can be seen in the different types of mosses on the rocks and how wet they are. Unlike most of the other water sources nearby, it never dries out.

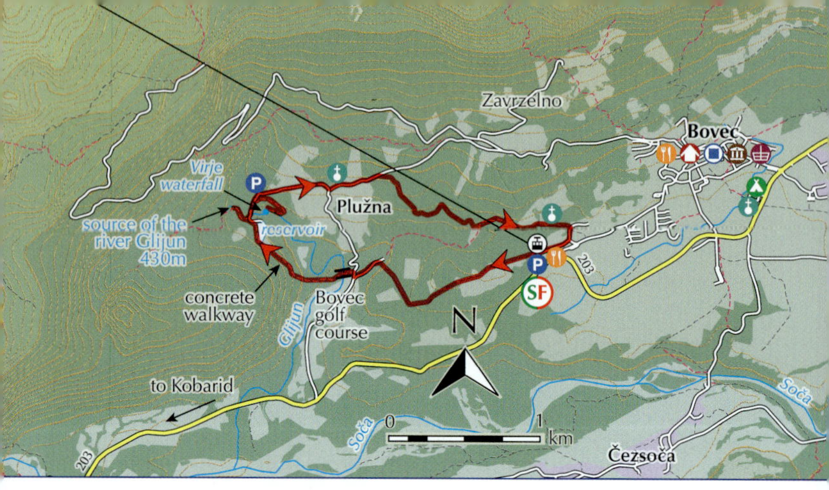

Retrace your steps a short distance to a path leading down left to a bridge over the river, then continue across the bridge and up the road on the other side. After about 100m a sign on the right indicates, Slap Virje 5min. Follow the broad track down and round to the water's edge in front of the beautiful **waterfall** (400m, **1hr 5min**). The pools below the waterfalls are 3.5m deep and the average water temperature is 8°C.

Return to the tarmac road and continue uphill, past a chalet on the left, and then on along the scenic lane, with excellent views up to Kanin, to reach the village of **Plužna**. Turn left past the war memorial and take the road leading up towards the church, signed Bovec. Just past the last houses, and before the sign saying you are leaving the village, take a track leading down to the right, signed Bovec (**1hr 35min**). After about 100m leave the track for a path on the right, again signed Bovec.

Cross a stream then continue through the woods, heading down quite steeply in places. About 5min after the stream the path makes a sharp right then bears left again, still descending, to reach a deep stream bed which it follows for a few metres before continuing on the other side. Cross a third stream and join another path on the far side, signed Bovec. This wider track eventually crosses a fourth stream on another little bridge.

Pass a cottage in an open pasture on the right before walking beneath the gondola cables. After yet another stream, turn right onto a vehicular track, signed Bovec, and continue to a tarmac road and houses; the road soon meets the main road at a T-junction. Turn right, following the signs to *Žičnica* (gondola) and walk 50m or so to the ski car park, or turn left to walk back along the main road to **Bovec**.

WALK 26

Visoki Kanin

Start/finish	Top station of Kanin ski gondola (2202m), near Bovec
Time	5hr
Distance	6.7km
Total ascent/descent	470m
Grade	4
Maps	1:25,000 Bovec-Trenta
Refreshments	Café at top station of gondola
Access	From the centre of Bovec, follow the main road that leads west and take the right fork opposite a petrol station into the ski gondola car park. The car park is at 454m, and the gondola ride takes about 30min
Note	In the autumn of 2023, inspectors shut down the gondola and, at the time of writing, a new operating licence has not yet been issued. Plans for its renovation are underway, but there is currently no clear information on when the renovation work will begin and when the service will resume (for up-to-date information, check www.soca-valley.com). Without the gondola, this walk involves a very long slog from the valley, with no huts available
Warning	Be sure to check the time of the last gondola ride (in 2023 it was 4pm) as there are no accommodation facilities at the Kanin ski resort. A helmet is also recommended on this route

The peak of Visoki Kanin (2587m) stands at the western end of a long ridge to the north of Bovec which marks the state boundary with Italy. The ridge is bounded on both sides by huge basins and plateaus of karst limestone, with their fissured surfaces reminiscent of a glacier. Access is made easy by the Kanin ski centre gondola, which lifts summer walkers up to 2202m – hence the short walking times.

At the top station of the gondola, just outside the building, several signs for local mountains are painted on a rock – follow the one for Kanin over rocky ground, heading north-west. Pass a small ski bar and follow waymarks a little further to

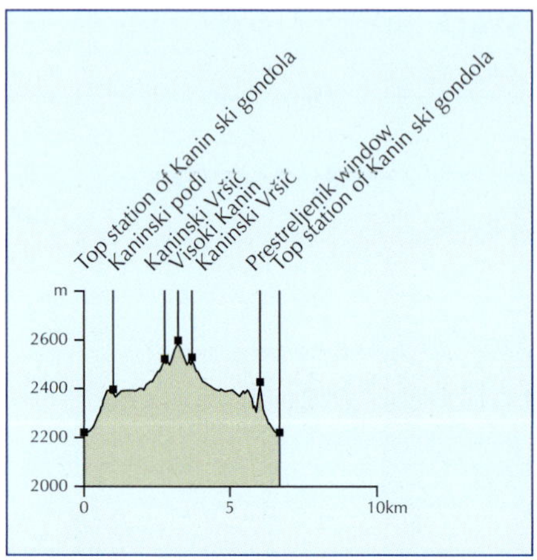

reach a junction where a path is signed left to Koča. The sign for Koča refers to Dom Petra Skalarja, which has been closed for several years. The Kanin path bears right, traversing a steep scree slope. Watch for the *okno* (window) on Prestreljenik, coming into view on the right.

Shortly after the turn for the path heading up to the window (**20min**), reach rocks and the first steel cable. After the cable the path bears right and climbs the rocky rib in an easy scramble, with another cable and occasional steel pegs. Continue over broken ground onto a rocky shoulder, where a short distance across scree and stone brings you to the edge of an enormous corrie, **Kaninski podi** (**40min**). From here the line of the path can be seen all the way to Kanin, following the foot of the crags along the rim of the corrie.

Kaninski podi is a distinctive example of high mountain karst. In recent decades, very deep potholes have been discovered. Four of these have been explored to depths greater than 1000m – the deepest is 1502m – and one of the largest vertical entrance shafts in the world, at 643m, has also been discovered here.

The landscape is bleak but extremely impressive. The distinct path follows waymarks across scree and rocks round the rim of the bowl for a good 30min. Towards the end, the route begins to ascend and arrives at the foot of crags (**1hr 15min**). Waymarks lead left and up the rocks to reach the ridge – some pegs and cables assist the easy scramble. At the crest turn left, with views down impressive drops to the equally bleak Italian side to the north.

The route continues along the broad ridge quite easily for a few minutes before descending to a notch, where a gully drops steeply away to the left. A steel cable and a few pegs protect the step across. Continue along the crest over slabs of broken rock to reach a minor top (**Kaninski Vršič**, 2514m) with a border post and cairn.

From here the route descends slightly across slabs for a short distance before rising again. Continue easily, then descend a little on the left-hand side. To the right is a curious karst feature in the form of a massive hole in the ridge. From here scramble down steeply to the left for about 20m (steel cables), then ascend again almost immediately to another notch below a big overhanging prow of rock. Continue up the ridge and look back for a view of the enormous chasm in the ridge. Reach a plaque that marks the top of a steep via ferrata on the Italian side and carry on along the crest of the ridge, following waymarks over shattered ground with occasional rock steps. Finally, the summit of **Visoki Kanin** (2587m, **2hr 30min**) comes into view.

Retrace your steps along the ridge to the scree path above Kaninski podi. At the end of the scree path, where it meets the rocky shoulder, be sure to follow waymarks and signs to *Žičnica* (gondola) – the right-hand path goes to the hut. Return across the rib to the junction of the Prestreljenik window path and turn left to visit the **okno** (**25min** detour).

Walking along the rim of Kaninski podi towards Kanin

The route climbs up the scree quite steeply to the rocks below the window, where waymarks direct you slightly left at first and then right, traversing the rocks. It is quite loose and not particularly pleasant. Bear left round a corner and then up the left-hand side of a small gully. At the head of it, turn right and scramble up a short distance to the window. This final section is secured with cables but there are no real difficulties. There is an exciting view through the window down into Italy.

Return the same way and continue down to the gondola station.

WALK 27

Soča Trail

Start	Trenta village (626m)
Finish	Bovec (454m)
Time	6hr 30min
Distance	21.7km
Total ascent	220m
Total descent	390m
Grade	2
Maps	1:25,000 Bovec-Trenta
Refreshments	Mini-markets can be found in Trenta and in the village of Soča, where there is also a restaurant. Camp Jelinc (by the Small Gorge) and Camp Klin also have restaurants. Outside the summer tourist season, it is advisable to bring refreshments with you, as these businesses may be closed
Access	During the summer season, several buses a day cross the Vršič pass between Bovec and Kranjska Gora and can drop passengers at Trenta (see www.soca-valley.com for times or check at the bus stop). If you arrive by car, there is a parking area at the Dom Trenta visitor centre
Note	It is quite a long walk, but the regular summer bus service between Bovec and Trenta allows you to shorten the walk as much as you like

The Soča river may be short, at 96km, but it is without doubt one of the most beautiful in the Alps. Its most notable characteristic is its incredible luminous green colour, which is difficult to credit from photos until you see it for yourself. The valley and the river have been an important trade and access route since early times and were of vital strategic importance during World War 1. As a result, there are many historical as well as natural sights to see along the way. The Soča Trail, which is well signposted with information boards, was created by linking several age-old routes through the valley. The section from Trenta to Bovec is the most spectacular, crossing a series of suspension bridges and following the emerald-green Soča river through waterfalls, rapids and narrow rocky gorges.

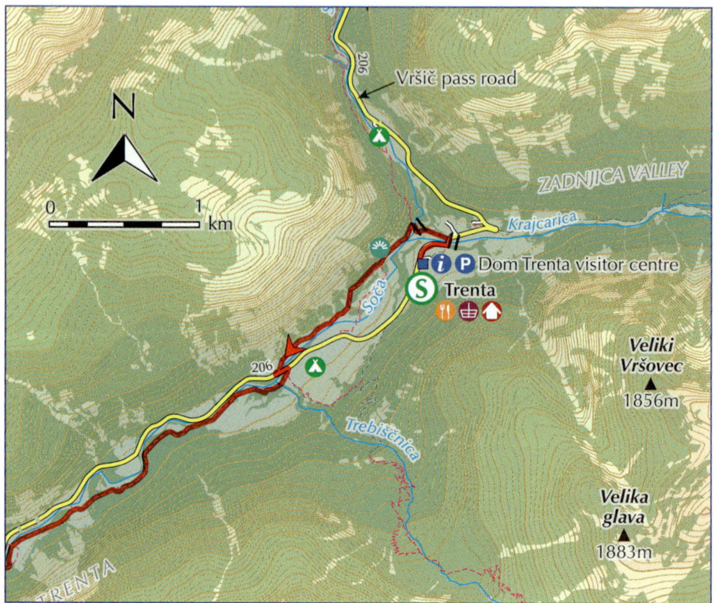

From the bus stop by the Dom Trenta visitor centre, turn right and walk along the main road through the village. Continue to the river Krajcarica, cross the bridge and then turn left on a track, signed Soška Pot (Soča Trail) and Alpe Adria Trail (these two markers will indicate the route all the way to Bovec). Almost immediately afterwards, at a fork, keep left and walk past a house. After 150m the path narrows and turns right, soon crossing the first footbridge over the Soča. Continue up the route, ignoring a signed path heading right to the source of the Soča (Izvir Soče), and in a few minutes arrive at an information board and a beautiful view of Triglav and Pihavec.

The path now enters the woods, bearing away from the river. After 5min, at the end of the woods, follow the sign for Soška Pot and meet the river again. In about 10min join the main road at a bridge; turn left, walk to the end of the bridge and turn right onto an unmade track opposite a **campsite**. Follow the track for a few metres and, as you pass the end of the campsite grounds, continue straight ahead on the signed narrow path along the fence line (**45min**).

The route now runs along the left side of the Soča and is very obvious all the way. It passes through the woods and meadows of the Spodnja Trenta valley, with

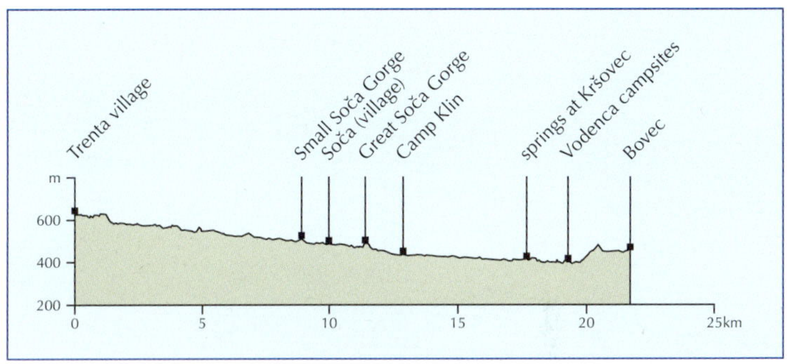

beautiful views of the river and the peaks above Zadnja Trenta (remember to look back!). After 45min on this pleasant path, come to a fork and take the left, climbing gently up some steps. Continue on a good path for another 10min to reach a suspension bridge and cross the river (**1hr 35min**). On the other side, turn left and follow the path parallel to the road for about 400m to cross the river again over a larger bridge. At the end of the bridge turn right, following signs, and walk for another 20min, keeping the river on your right. The route crosses the Soča again on another suspension bridge and then continues to the left, parallel to the road, to a crossroads. Turn left onto the stone bridge and admire the now turbulent river

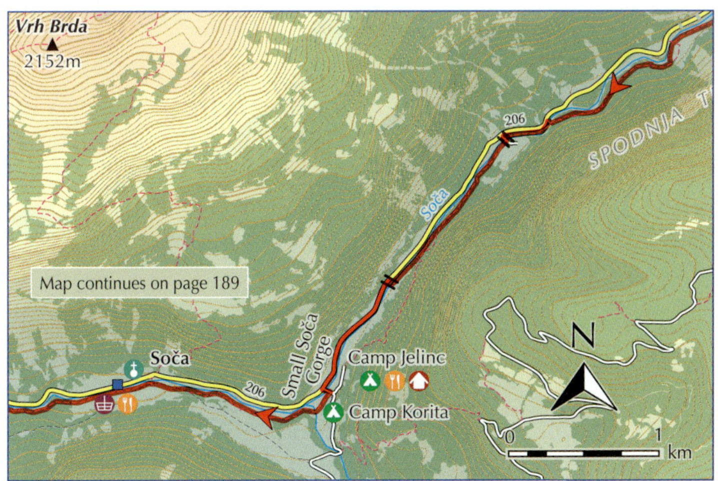

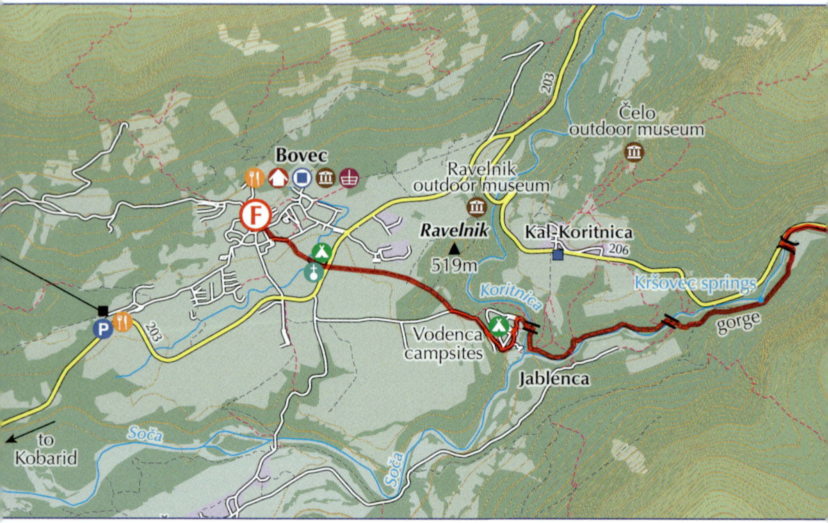

Suspension bridge over the Soča

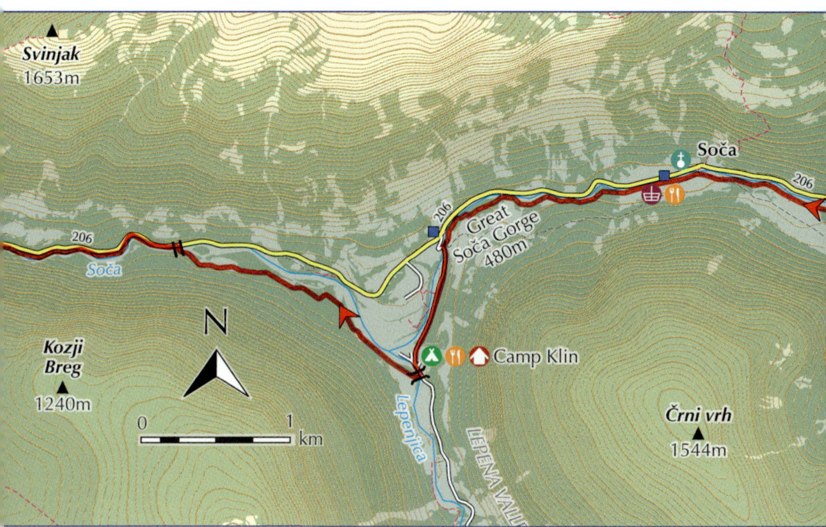

flowing through the **Small Soča Gorge** (Mala korita, **2hr 30min**). The gorge is up to 6m deep and only 1m wide at the narrowest part.

After crossing the bridge, turn right and take the broad track that passes under the wooden huts of Camp Korita to reach a house and a bench that makes a nice picnic stop with a beautiful view of the river. Continue on the signed path, past the right side of the house, and cross the tributary river Vrsnica on a footbridge. After about 15min the path joins the tarmac road near the iron bridge leading to the hamlet of **Soča**. In the village of Soča, near the church, there is a bar, a mini-market and a bus stop for Bovec or back to Trenta. Don't cross the river, go straight on and take the signed path to the right, which runs along the left side of the river. Initially, the route runs very close to the Soča, then once it reaches the **Great Soča Gorge** (Velika korita, 480m) it begins to bend slightly away from the river. The path soon comes out onto a tarmac road; turn right and walk down the road to a crossroads near a bridge (**3hr 30min**).

Turn left here, signed Lepena, but first take some time to admire a beautiful view of the gorge. If you don't want to go all the way to Bovec, turn right to reach the main road and the bus stop. Continue along the road to Lepena for almost 1km to reach the entrance to **Camp Klin**, near the confluence of the rivers Lepenjica and Soča. Cross the bridge over the Lepenjica, with a wonderful view of the Lepena valley, and continue along a good track with the river on your right.

Emerald pool near the Great Soča Gorge

After about 25min the route crosses the Soča again and continues on the other side towards Bovec, parallel to the main road (**4hr 15min**).

Continue on the path, which is quite rocky in places, for another 40min to reach a larger concrete bridge. Cross the river and turn right to reach the curious scenic springs at **Kršovec**, where the water emerges directly from the moss-covered boulders on the left-hand side of the track to flow across it and down into the river (**4hr 50min**). Further on, the route takes you to the edge of another impressive gorge and then to a fork where you take the right-hand path, which leads down to a scenic suspension bridge connected to a big rock.

After the bridge, at a fork, turn left and emerge onto a meadow bordered by a fence. Continue through the woods, parallel to the river, then follow the path round to the right at the confluence with the river Koritnica, turning away from the Soča. Keep the Koritnica on the left and continue for about 200m to another suspension bridge which you cross to the complex of campsites at **Vodenca** (**5hr 45min**). Walk across the campsites to reach the access road and turn right, walking gently uphill for a few minutes.

As the road levels out take a track to the right, signed Soška Pot, which enters woods after about 50m. The track passes between two small knolls then comes out into fields, with good views of Kanin and Bovec straight ahead. Follow cart tracks across the fields towards Bovec and reach the main bypass road, opposite a church. Cross over to a sign for the town centre and walk up the track, crossing a stream and passing through a small flower meadow to a parking area and bar. Turn right and follow a minor road to the centre of **Bovec**.

WALK 28

Pogačnikov dom and Kriški podi

Start/finish	Car park at bend 50 on the Vršič pass road (650m), about 700m from Trenta village centre and bus stop
Time	7hr 30min
Distance	16.8km
Total ascent/descent	1550m
Grade	3
Maps	1:25,000 Bovec-Trenta, 1:25,000 Kranjska Gora, 1:25,000 Triglav
Refreshments	Pogačnikov dom na Kriških podih
Warning	The route crosses several river canyons that can be dangerous after heavy rainfall
Access	During the summer season, several buses a day cross the Vršič pass between Bovec and Kranjska Gora and can drop passengers at Trenta (see www.soca-valley.com for times or check at the bus stop). If you arrive by car, turn off at bend 50 and drive a short distance to reach the car park (parking fee)

The ascent to Pogačnikov dom (2050m) makes a fine walk, and its spectacular position on the edge of the extensive karst plateau of Kriški podi, with its limestone pavements, three mountain lakes and magnificent cirque of craggy peaks, makes it well worth a day trip, even if you don't intend to go on and climb any of the surrounding summits (see Walk 29).

It is a fairly long day but it gives the walker an opportunity to reach a high-mountain environment without any major difficulties. The height gain is considerable and the path is steep at times, but the continuing interest of the forest vegetation and the spectacular, unfolding views make the effort worthwhile. This is a lovely walk for late spring and early autumn, as it is in the sun all the way when not under trees.

From the car park, follow the road to reach a **shrine** on the left (**20min**). Just before the shrine bear left and follow the forest track up the hill to arrive at the goods cableway that is used by the hut (**30min**). Follow a narrow path, which sets off steeply into the trees, signed for the hut.

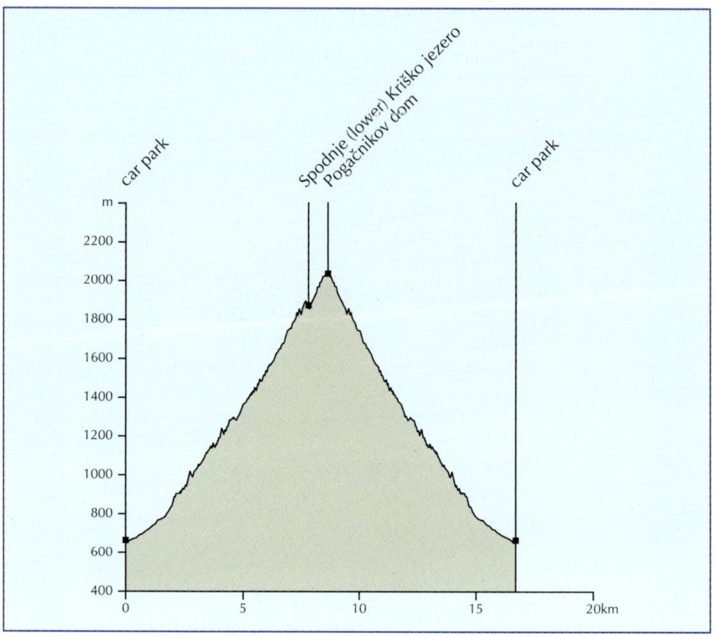

The path zigzags in hairpins high above the river, giving tremendous views of steep rock walls all around. The path is a well-engineered World War 1 mule track and although the hairpins make the gradient seem quite gentle, you gain height quickly. There are numerous shortcuts at the bends, but on the whole it is probably best to stick to the main path. Throughout the route there are several river canyons to cross and places where it can feel somewhat exposed, although the path is always wide enough for comfortable walking.

After about 1hr the path passes below rock outcrops where the hut can be seen far ahead, perched on the skyline. About 10min further on, pass a shrine on the left, and in 5min more reach the biggest of the river canyons (**1hr 45min**). Each crossing brings you further round to the right-hand side of the valley, where you eventually cross beneath the line of the **cableway**.

The path winds up steep hairpins beneath a crag and then continues above it as the vegetation gradually changes with the increased altitude. Eventually, you emerge from the dwarf pine onto an open slope with excellent views of the steep rock faces all around and the valley now far below. The track continues

Looking down into Trenta valley from Pogačnikov dom (photo: Roy Clark)

across steep scree and passes small rock outcrops up to a **spring** with a stone trough that lies a few metres to the right of the path. From here you can see the hut looking not too far away, but this last section can feel like hard work, especially on a hot day!

As you round the next bend, a sign points to the right, marking a short detour to visit the first of three mountain lakes along the route, **Spodnje (lower) Kriško jezero** (1880m, **3h 40min**). This is the lowest in altitude and largest of the lakes, 120m long and 9.5m deep.

Return to the track and continue over more open ground. Below the final crag you can go left or right to the **Pogačnikov dom** (**4hr**) – the right-hand route is waymarked and a little less steep than the left.

THE HIGH ALPINE PLATEAU OF KRIŠKI PODI

Pogačnikov dom (2050m) stands on the rim of the huge limestone corrie of Kriški podi, a paradise for geologists. It is surrounded by a ring of peaks – from left to right, Planja, Razor, Križ, Stenar, Bovški Gamsovec and Pihavec. Ibex can be seen here and a small herd often passes close to the hut.

From the hut it is about 30min to visit the middle lake, Srednje Kriško jezero, which, interestingly, was formed by water erosion not glacial action. Cold air collects in the hollow formed by the lake and snow can remain late into the season. The upper lake, Zgornje Kriško jezero, is over 200m higher up and is the highest lake in Slovenia. There is no path to it from here; it is best seen from the ridge that leads to Križ (Walk 29).

ROCKFALL

If you are planning to tackle any of the surrounding peaks from the hut, note that the peaks in this region appear to be more prone to rockfall and landslides than other mountains in the Julian Alps. Rockfalls near the summits of Razor, Križ and Pihavec have affected the normal ascent paths.

To descend from Pogačnikov dom, return the way you came.

WALK 29

Križ, Stenar and Bovški Gamsovec

Start/finish	Pogačnikov dom na Kriških podih (2050m)
Time	5hr 30min
Distance	6.6km
Total ascent/descent	815m
Grade	4
Maps	1:25,000 Bovec-Trenta, 1:25,000 Kranjska Gora, 1:25,000 Triglav
Accommodation	Pogačnikov dom na Kriških podih
Access	Follow Walk 28 up to the hut
Warning	This is a true mountaineering route, and via ferrata kit and helmet are strongly recommended

This route makes a fine high-level circuit of three peaks to the east of the Kriški podi plateau, starting and finishing at Pogačnikov dom. These mountains are in the heart of the northern Julian Alps and offer excellent views of the pillars of Triglav's north face and the surrounding mountains. There is only one walkers' route on Stenar (2501m), but its accessibility from Pogačnikov dom and the Vrata valley makes it one of the most visited peaks over 2500m. Križ (2410m) and Bovški Gamsovec (chamois mountain, 2392m) round out the tour for an especially satisfying mountain day, comfortably completed from the dom, and with time left to make the descent to Trenta if you wish (3hr 30min).

The path heads north from Pogačnikov dom, with views down to your right of Srednje Kriško jezero, the middle lake of Kriški podi. In less than 5min reach a signpost where you go straight on for Križ. For the first 15min the path climbs steadily, with occasional steel pegs for security. It then crosses limestone pavement with deep fissures and karst holes for another 5min before veering left and continuing on a leftward-rising traverse for a few minutes before waymarks lead you up through a notch in the rocks (**25min**). Continue up for another 10–15min, and Zgornje Kriško jezero, the upper Križ lake (2158m), comes into view. The path ascends quite steeply for a short while and then traverses above the lake on the slopes of **Kriški rob**. This brings you to a saddle on the west ridge of Križ at

Krnica 4h
Škrlatica 4h
Bivak IV 1h 15min
Aljažev dom 4h

A crossroads of routes on the saddle on the west ridge of Križ

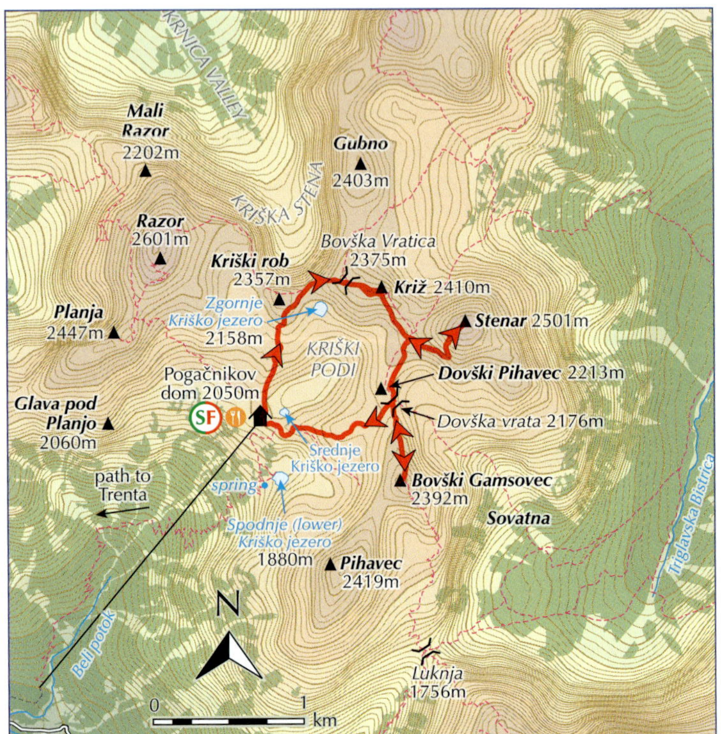

2275m. There are excellent views down into the Krnica valley below the wall of Kriška stena.

From here climb steeply towards Križ, heading immediately up the rocks via a pleasant scramble with occasional steel pegs and cables for security. After a few minutes' climbing the angle eases onto the broad grassy shoulder of Križ. Continue on over easy ground to reach a red sign, Križ 10min, at **Bovška Vratica** (2375m, **1hr 20min**). Ahead along the ridge you can see the rocky top of Križ, about 200m in distance and 40m higher. Just before you start to climb the final section, notice a sign painted on a rock pointing right to Stenar – this is the route to the next peak. The final section involves an easy scramble with protection and a short walk along to the rocky summit of **Križ** (2410m, **1hr 30min**). The next

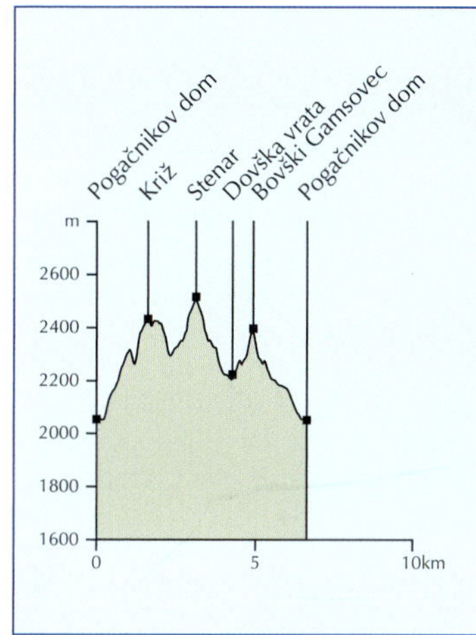

peak, Stenar, looks enticingly close, but there is a fair amount of descent and ascent to go yet!

The path that continues along the summit ridge is marked as closed due to a rockfall, so carefully retrace your steps from the summit to the sign for Stenar. Follow this path for a short distance to reach a sign, Vrata, painted on a rock. Beyond the sign the path continues down, at first over rock ledges covered with rubble and then across more scree in a leftward descending traverse, below crags. Reach a junction with Vrata signed down to the right and Stenar straight on (**1hr 50min**).

Young ibex on the Dovška Vrata saddle

The Stenar path begins to climb up a short scree slope and then joins a rocky rib, with views down to the col of Dovška vrata and the peak of Bovški Gamsovec to the right. After an easy ascending traverse across the rocky rib, reach another scree slope which you cross to reach a shoulder. Ascend this steadily for about 20min, with no difficulties, and then turn left to reach the skyline ridge. The last 20min or so climbs steadily but easily up to the summit of **Stenar** (2501m, **2hr 35min**), with its stunning views of Triglav.

Retrace your footsteps to the junction with the sign for Stenar and Vrata painted on a rock and take the Vrata path heading down to the left, following waymarks. This takes you down onto the plateau between Stenar and Bovški Gamsovec. Cross the plateau for 15min or so, passing a sign to the Vrata valley down to the left at the **Dovška vrata** saddle (2176m, **3hr 15min**). Continue straight on up a little rise to another sign – Pogačnikov dom to the right and Bovški Gamsovec straight ahead. The route ascends the easy rocky ridge for about 20min before it starts traversing on the right-hand side, with considerable drops into the corrie on the right. The path feels exposed but there are steel handrails for security along its length.

The route does a short zigzag and then continues up, with more steel cables and handrails, to pass between a narrow cleft in the rock. This brings you onto a sloping ramp, again quite exposed, which the route follows to its top, where it joins the crest of the ridge. It is now an easy scramble of 5min or so to the top of **Bovški Gamsovec** (2392m, **4hr**).

Triglav is the next peak to the south-east, and the huge bulk of its north face rears up before you. The Plemenice ridge, the most difficult of Triglav's waymarked paths, can be traced from just above the Luknja col right to the summit. The peak close by to the south is Pihavec.

Carefully retrace your steps from the summit to the sign for Pogačnikov dom (**4hr 45min**). The path heads due west, and the hut is visible from here in clear weather. The path skirts pleasantly around rocky hollows in the high mountain karst of the Kriški Podi plateau. The many crevices and holes of the limestone pavement require careful footwork in places, so ensure you keep sight of the waymarks while choosing the best line. Lovely alpine flowers brighten the cracks and there is a good chance you will see ibex and chamois. The path joins the main route from Trenta just below **Pogačnikov dom** – bear right here to return to the hut or left to walk down to Trenta.

WALK 30

Krn

Start/finish	Dom dr. Klementa Juga at the head of the Lepena valley (700m)
Time	9–10hr
Distance	19.8km
Total ascent/descent	1710m
Grade	3
Maps	1:25,000 Krnsko pogorje, 1:25,000 Bovec-Trenta, 1:25,000 Bohinj
Refreshments	Dom dr. Klementa Juga, Dom pri Krnskih jezerih and Gomiščkovo zavetišče na Krnu (all also offer accommodation)
Access	During the summer season, shuttle buses run from Bovec to Dom dr. Klementa Juga. See www.soca-valley.com for times or check at the bus stop. If you arrive by car, there are parking areas at the dom and near the lower cableway station (but please keep access to the station clear)

The distinctive profile of the summit of Krn (2244m) can be seen from many viewpoints in the Julian Alps, and it is one of the stalwarts of the range in spite of its comparatively modest altitude. Krn is not so much a single mountain as a great massif thrusting ridges and shoulders in all directions. Krn offers three main walking routes: the western approach is the most difficult and the southern the shortest (with transport). The northern approach, described here, goes past the largest high-mountain lake in Slovenia and is the most practical approach for those dependent on public transport. It is a long walk, but you can stay overnight at either Dom dr. Klementa Juga, Dom pri Krnskih jezerih (1385m) or Gomiščkovo zavetišče na Krnu (2182m).

From the dom follow the signs for K. Jezero and Planinski dom pri Krnskih jezerih. The route heads into the forest on a well-marked stony track and, after just 50m, it turns left and ascends gently through spruce and beech trees. Continue up the broad main track as it makes a series of zigzags through the wood, passing under the cableway line. In about 30min it bears right below a line of crags and soon

to Bovec
Lepena Valley
Lepenjica
Dom dr. Klementa Juga 700m
SF
N
0
1
km
Kaluder 1980m
top cableway station
Velika Bab 2013m
Veliki Lemež 2043m
Planinski dom pri Krnskih jezerih 1385m
Dupeljsko jezero 1260m
Lopatnik 2012m
Planina Duplje
Krnsko jezero 1395m
Veliki Šmohor 1939m
Planina Na Polju
Srednji Vrh 2134m
Mali Šmohor 1944m
Krn 2244m
Vrh nad Peski 2176m
Gomiščkovo zavetišče na Krnu 2182m
Krnska škrbina 2058m
Batognica 2164m
Škofič 2013m
Planina Zaslap
Planina Slapnik

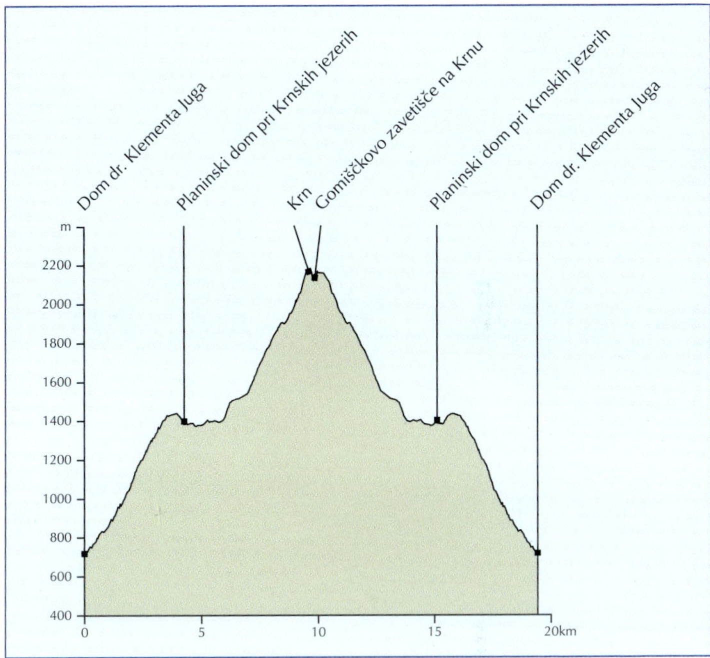

after this the terrain of the hillside changes somewhat – still forested, but with small outcrops of limestone with random boulders and rocks.

The route continues steadily up, passing under the cableway supply line several times. Eventually, it levels as it passes between the **top cableway station** and another small stone building (**1hr 40min**). Continue along the level track for about 100m, with a crag to the right, before beginning to gently ascend again.

At the brow of the rise, a sign marks the annual snow depths and temperatures. After a further 250m, the track starts to descend a little and passes a narrow path heading left, signed Velika Baba. Soon reach another junction where you turn left, signed Pl. dom pri Krnskih jezerih 10min, and follow the path through the woods, passing through small open glades to reach **Planinski dom pri Krnskih jezerih** (1385m, **2hr**).

Leave the dom on a broad waymarked track, following a sign for Krnsko jezero and Krn, and in 100m arrive at a junction close to the pasture buildings of **Planina Duplje**. Cheese and other dairy products are made and sold here in the

Planinski dom pri Krnskih jezerih

summer season. Continue straight ahead, passing to the left of the buildings, to reach a signpost; Dom na Komni is signed to the left but continue straight on for Krn. The path continues across open level ground for another 300m to arrive at the lake of **Krnsko jezero** in its idyllic alpine setting (**2hr 15min**).

Every year in November a **memorial hike** is held in memory of fallen soldiers on the Isonzo Front during World War 1. The main ceremony takes place at the shore of Lake Krn, and the event is usually attended by hundreds of people, numerous diplomats and military representatives.

The level path continues just above the shore on the left-hand side of the lake, with Krn directly ahead on the skyline. Another path traverses the loose rock and hillside above the lake but is not recommended due to the risk of rockfall. At the end of the lake, the path bears left and begins to ascend gently then steepens as it climbs to the left of a rocky outcrop. The terrain has become more alpine and rocky, with sparse trees.

After a more level section the path crosses a dry watercourse and reaches the open grassy **Planina Na Polju** (1530m, **2hr 50min**), surrounded by wild and rocky slopes. There are two small buildings over to the right, one of which is used as a hunting lodge. Cross the *planina* (alp) and on the other side the path begins to climb again. After about 10min notice *'voda'* painted on a rock to the left, indicating a spring about 100m away. The terrain becomes increasingly rocky and barren, although there are still many flowers to catch the eye.

After ascending between boulders and rocks reach a fork, with the left path heading to Vrh nad Peski. The path to Krn bears right and continues, waymarked and signed on a boulder a few metres ahead. Begin to zigzag up the hillside, with views to the north opening up as you climb. Pass another small spring at a level area and continue to ascend the last rocky, grassy slopes to the col **Krnska škrbina** (2058m, **4hr 30min**). Signs indicate left to Komna and Vrh nad Peski and right to the hut below the summit of Krn. At the col, there is a 149mm shell case from World War 1 mounted on a pole and a partisan memorial plaque.

Turn right at the col, passing lots of rusted barbed wire and twisted metal, a sad reminder of terrible times. After about 10min the path forks, and a waymark and sign on a rock indicate *'vrh'* (summit), pointing right. Follow these waymarks and, shortly after, follow another sign on a rock for Krn pointing right. A grassy path, which is a little indistinct at first, leads up to the crest of the ridge and continues on the left-hand side for another 15min or so to the summit of **Krn** (2244m, **5hr**).

On the top there is an orientation plate and signs of defences; the front line ran directly over the **summit** here. Uninterrupted views of the Julian Alps to the north and east, to the Adriatic down to the south and to the Dolomites to the west entice you to linger.

From the summit follow waymarks, dropping down to the south-west, to reach **Gomiščkovo zavetišče na Krnu** (2182m), within 5min or so.

At the hut the **views** to the south dominate the horizon, dropping down the uniformly steep grassy slope to the valley below with its tiny herders' buildings at Planina Zaslap and Planina Slapnik. The Soča river can be seen flowing along the floor of the valley, with Kobarid and Matajur to the west and, beyond them, the Adriatic Sea.

From the hut head east, following signs for the Planinski dom pri Krnskih jezerih, and continue traversing along the hillside to reach the junction just above the col. Then retrace the outward route to the **Dom dr. Klementa Juga**.

WALK 31

Mangart

Start/finish	Shuttle bus stop on the Mangart road at Mangartsko sedlo (Mangart saddle) (1830m)
Time	5hr
Distance	7km
Total ascent/descent	840m
Grade	4
Maps	1:25,000 Bovec-Trenta
Refreshments	Koča na Mangrtskem sedlu
Access	During the summer season, shuttle buses run from Bovec via Log pod Mangartom to Mangartsko sedlo (see www.soca-valley.com for times or check at the bus stop). The bus stops at the car park before the last tunnel on the Mangart road. By car: due to rockfall, the Mangart road (toll) is only driveable up to the ninth kilometre or to the car park 400m from the turn-off to the hut
Warning	This is a true mountaineering route – a helmet, self-belaying equipment and possibly an ice axe are all strongly advised

At 2679m Mangart (also known as Mangrt) is the third highest peak in Slovenia, and its mighty bulk dominates the skyline of the northern Julian Alps. A former Italian military road climbs from the Predel pass and is open for public use as far as the ninth kilometre, well above 1800m. It is worth the trip up just to witness the incredible engineering of the road, which has been damaged and repaired several times because of earthquakes and landslides, and for the excellent views from the saddle.

The route described here takes the Slovene side in ascent and descends the easier Italian route; however, note that snow can lie very late on the Italian, northern, slopes. The difficult, steep and exposed parts of the route are well protected; in fact, most of the danger is on the easier-angled unprotected sections that cross loose scree over rock, a combination requiring great caution. An easier option would be to take the Italian route in ascent and descent.

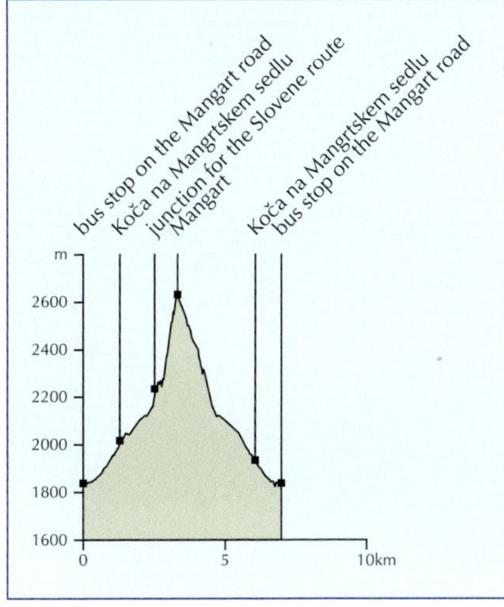

From the shuttle bus stop, walk up the road through the tunnel and after about 300m turn left onto the service road leading to **Koča na Mangrtskem sedlu** (1906m). Continue up to the hut, where a sign for Mangart directs you onto a path to the left. The path climbs up the grassy plateau for 15min until it reaches the tarmac road. Turn left here and continue along the road for about 50m, then take another path to the left, following signs for Mangart (**30min**).

Reach the top of the Mangart road and head east over short grass towards the rocky top of **Mali Mangart** (2262m). The route traverses its foot, eventually bearing left and up easy rocks to reach a small saddle between Mali Mangart and Mangart itself. There are precipitous drops on the north side and views to the two small lakes lying in Mangartska dolina (the Mangart valley) at the foot of the mountain.

Just beyond the col the easier Italian route, signed 'Ital.smer' – here used for the descent – continues straight on, while the Slovene route, signed 'Slov.smer!' (the exclamation mark warning that this is a difficult route) now heads right. Its destination is obvious – a huge gash ascending from left to right across the west face. The path leads across boulders and scree and then descends slightly to the foot of the route (**1hr 30min**).

Begin to ascend, scrambling steeply up on good rock (steel cables). On closer inspection the line of the route immediately begins to show the varied rock architecture within the enormous cleft in the mountain. After 150m, the cleft has become a steep gully and the route continues up its left side for about 50m before traversing right and ascending a ramp of good clean rock to reach an easier-angled rock spur.

The way ahead continues for another 40min or so with a mixture of easier ground, albeit topped with loose stones and scree, interspersed with steeper equipped sections, to eventually arrive at an exposed little crest where a steep spur of rock abuts the west face. More cables lead steeply up from here, but the

Steep descent on the Italian route

angle quickly relents and easier ground leads to a boulder-choked gully that is climbed until waymarks direct you again to the right. Like the previous gully, this one is also part of the structure of the great cleft.

Soon arrive at a level area from where the route turns left and climbs over a jumble of rocky steps and boulders as it heads up into a cleft. Climb easily through the cleft then step down through a notch in the rocks and turn right. A few more paces bring you to more steel cables, but the real difficulties of the route are over. Continue to ascend over rock steps and ledges covered with loose stones for another 20min or so before the angle finally relents at the summit of **Mangart** (2679m, **2hr 45min**).

The **summit** is marked by a large wooden cross. There are superb views of nearby Jalovec and Ponca, as well as Triglav, Bavški Grintavec, Rombon, the Kanin group, the Jôf Fuart range in Italy, and on into Austria. Mangart is also an area of great interest to botanists; due to its geographical position, plants from both the Julian Alps and the Central Alps are found here.

From the summit, turn east and begin to descend to the right, just below the ridge. The path soon drops down more steeply to a point about 100m below the summit ridge before levelling out and starting to traverse. Within a short distance the path bears left, heading down towards a grassy ridge line that leads east, signed Kotovo sedlo. Before you reach this grassy ridge, the path soon turns left again, crossing the border into Italy. In a few more minutes it begins a surprisingly easy traverse that cuts across the upper section of Mangart's steep northern side (**3hr 15min**). Straight ahead and far below, you can see the two lakes in the Italian corrie. The traverse is quite level, and a steel cable handrail along the way provides security should the rock be wet.

After about 15min the route makes a slight rise then drops down more steeply with cables, occasional pegs and even steps cut into the rock. The path, which has no real difficulties, continues over easy-angled, water-worn slabs and grooves, but it is a little polished in places. It steepens a little more in the final section and then reaches the scree and boulders at the junction with the Slovene route (**4hr**). From here reverse the ascent route to return to the start.

Traversing across the upper section of Mangart's steep northern side on the Italian route

SECTION 4 BLED

Lake Bled and its island from the viewpoint on Osojnica, with the Karavanke range behind (Walk 32) (photo: Roy Clark)

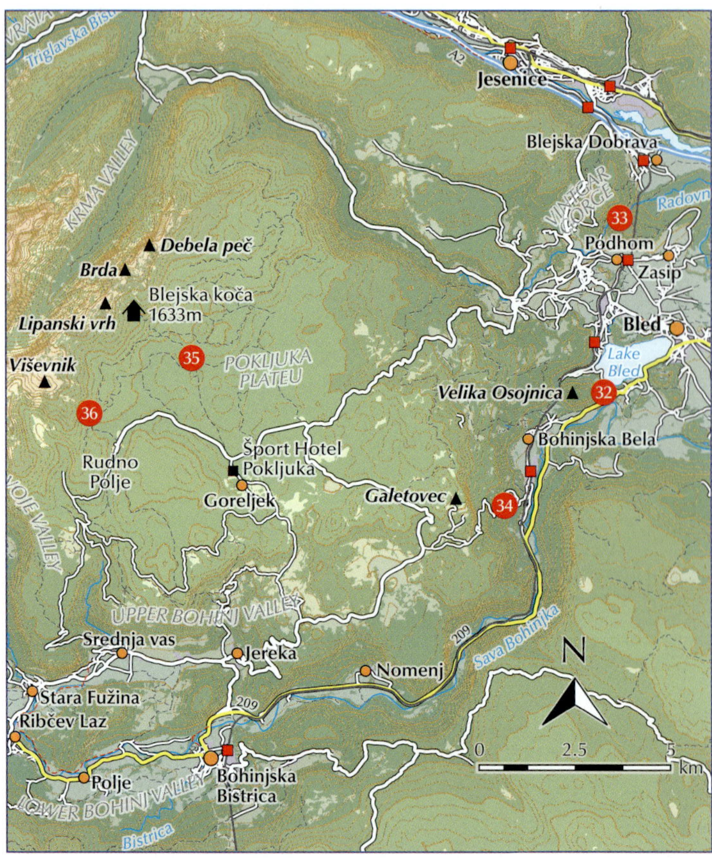

Bled (508m) is arguably Slovenia's best-known tourist resort, both within and outside the country, and has probably the most developed tourist infrastructure of any of the bases described in this book. The fairy-tale combination of church, island, castle and lake against the mountain backdrop has brought people to Bled for hundreds of years (Bled celebrated its 1000th anniversary in 2004), and somehow it has still managed to retain its charm in spite of thousands of visitors each year. Buildings line the eastern shore, competing for the view, but there are places where the hotels and casinos do not intrude, where you can be almost alone with the scenery.

Bled is about 10min or so from the Ljubljana–Jesenice motorway. It has train connections to Ljubljana and to Jesenice, where there are international links to Austria and North-West Europe, as well as south to Nova Gorica with its links to Italy. Brnik, Ljubljana's international airport, is about 30min by car. Bus links are also excellent and during the summer season, shuttle buses run around Bled and to the Pokljuka plateau with the aim of taking as many cars off the roads as possible and providing transport for everyone.

The main street rises from the lakeshore at the eastern end. Major hotels, the tourist information centre and a pedestrianised area with shops and cafés are located in this area. More hotels, pensions and shops are located on the road leading off from the main street. Hostels are mainly concentrated in the area below the castle. The bus station is within the town, while Bled Jezero train station is above the north-west side of the lake on the Bohinj railway line, which links Jesenice with Nova Gorica. The other train station, Lesce-Bled, has train links to Ljubljana and is found on the Radovljica road 4km to the south-east. Camping Bled is at the western end of the lake, while other campsites are located to the south-east, a couple of kilometres away by the Sava river.

A pletna boat on idyllic Lake Bled (photo: Roy Clark)

Looking down on Bohinjska Bela from the top of the crags (Walk 34)

The name Bled refers to the lake, the town and the surrounding area. There are a number of interesting places to visit, including the castle (which dates from the 11th century and is now a museum) and the ninth-century church on Slovenia's only true island, reached by the unique pletna boats from various places around the shore. The Triglav National Park Information Centre with its permanent exhibition 'Paradise under Triglav' is located on Ljubljanska cesta 27, a 5min walk from the centre. The centre has a shop selling local products, souvenirs and hiking literature.

THE ROUTES

Walk 32 explores the lake and its immediate vicinity. Slightly further afield lies the river-carved Vintgar gorge (Walk 33), while Galetovec (Walk 34) is a stunning viewpoint well worth the rather greater effort needed to get there. The main Julian Alps are not within easy walking distance of Bled, with the exception of the delightful Debela peč and Viševnik (Walks 35 and 36); however, it is possible to stay in the Bled area and use a car or public transport to reach the big mountains.

MAPS

Walks 35 and 36 are on the 1:25,000 Bohinj map and Walk 36 is also on the 1:25,000 Triglav map. Walks 32–34 are not on a large-scale map; these can be found on the Julijske Alpe 1:50,000 map.

WALK 32

Tour of Lake Bled and Osojnica

Start/finish	Grand Hotel Toplice by the lakeshore, Bled (508m)
Time	3hr 30min
Distance	9.1km
Total ascent/descent	390m
Grade	2
Maps	1:50,000 Julijske Alpe
Refreshments	Plenty of bars and restaurants along the way

It is a universal law that people want to walk around a body of water, if it is practical to do so, and Lake Bled is no exception. The tour of the lake is an easy stroll and a good introduction to the area. It is described here in a clockwise direction from the town end of the lake, but it can be walked in either direction and started from any point – there is no navigational difficulty here!

This walk also climbs three small tops to the south-west of the lake. Each has a different character and each offers a different view, including the best lake viewpoint of all, from Mala Osojnica (691m), which gives a bird's-eye view of the island and the church with the massif of Stol behind. This part of the route is mostly well waymarked on a good path, although it is steep at times.

Keeping the lake on your right, walk past the Grand Hotel Toplice, along the shore path. The main road to Bohinj is on the left and a little further on, it passes through a short tunnel cut in the rock, while the shore path continues along the edge of the lake.

Continuing round, the path comes to the little hamlet of **Mlino**, a popular place for swimming (**25min**).

Pletna boats, unique to Bled, can be taken from here, and other points on the lakeshore, to the **island**. There has been a church on the island since the ninth century. It is traditional to ring the church bell and make a wish; visitors to the island ensure that the 'wishing bell' tolls almost constantly during high season!

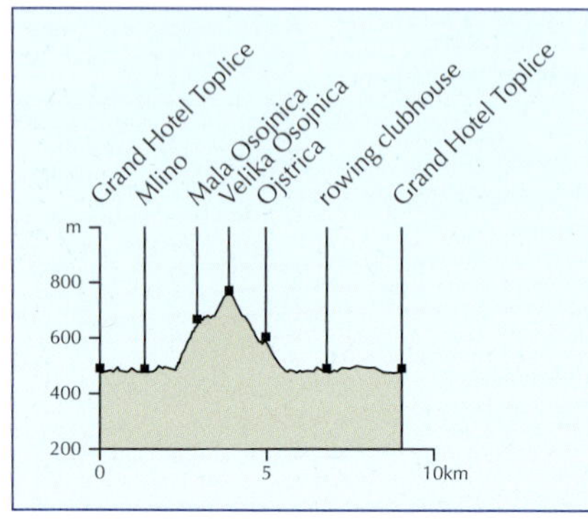

At Mlino the road moves away from the lake, and the path passes the grounds of Vila Bled, now a top-class hotel. This is where President Tito used to stay when he visited Bled.

After passing below some crags, the route comes out of the woods and continues across a small grassy area to run close to the road again. After 100m or so take the path on the other side of the road, signed Mala Osojnica (**35min**). The path climbs steeply up from the road on a rough track with some wooden steps. Continue around the back of a chalet and begin to climb steeply up through attractive beech forest.

The path winds up through the woodland in a series of swinging hairpins that bring you to the foot of some steep crags. At one point a section of steel cable provides a handrail as the path follows a narrow ledge. After a couple more hairpins the path arrives at the bottom of a **steel staircase**, which climbs about 20m up a narrow cleft in the crag. The 88 steps are steep but not difficult, and there

The excellent view from Mala Osojnica

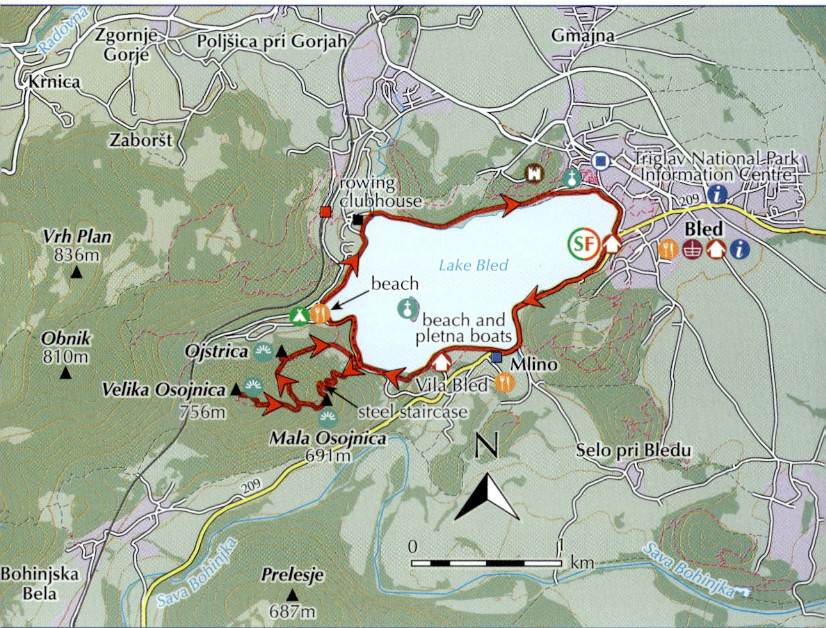

is a handrail if required. You emerge at the top of the steps at a viewpoint with a bench, and from here you can look directly down on to the lake, with the island, the castle and the Karavanke range.

The path continues up behind the bench, turns left and traverses above the cliffs. It then descends a little before climbing again to reach, after about 5min, an even better viewpoint on the flat top of **Mala Osojnica** (691m, **1hr 10min**), which is clear of trees. The path then turns away from the view, back into the wood. Follow the well-waymarked path through the forest for some minutes to a junction with a more obvious track, where there are signs and a bench. Velika Osojnica is signed to the left and Ojstrica to the right.

Turn left, ascending again, and in 10min or so reach a fork where the left track goes down to the village of Bohinjska Bela. Here turn right and continue for around 300m to the summit of **Velika Osojnica** (756m, **1hr 35min**). This is completely covered in trees, but if you follow the path to the left (west) from the top for about 30m there is a pleasant bench and viewpoint looking out over forested hills and ridges towards the north and the Karavanke range.

To continue, retrace your steps to the junction with the bench. Take the route towards Ojstrica, descending on a broad track that is very water-eroded near the top. Arrive at a signpost that points left to **Ojstrica**; you can see its craggy top close by through the trees. A few minutes' climb brings you to yet another summit, quite different in character from the other two, but with one more wonderful view of the lake (**2hr**).

Return to the main path and continue down towards Bled. Come to a small open pasture and follow the track down along the edge of the pasture to the road and the lakeside near where you started climbing into the woods (**2hr 20min**).

Now the walk around the lake follows a boardwalk section, a good place for fish-spotting and another nice viewpoint. The peak of Stol (2236m), highest in the Karavanke range, makes a perfect backdrop to the combination of island, church and castle. After the boardwalk, continue for a short distance on a wooden pier at the edge of the lake and then on a path by the side of the road towards the western end of the lake, another popular place for swimming, close to the **campsite**.

The **concrete stands** were erected for rowing spectators, and the lanes of Slovenia's oldest rowing club are marked with buoys.

Cross the swimming 'beach' and continue round to the right on a pedestrian-only road, in and out of trees, past a restaurant and the **rowing clubhouse** (**2hr 45min**). In the next section there are a number of springs close to the lakeshore; Lake Bled is fed by the springs at 23°C. From this side of the lake the stern face of Babji zob (old woman's tooth) makes a dramatic backdrop to the island. The path continues beneath the crags of **Bled Castle** before returning to the grassy park area below the town.

WALK 33

Vintgar gorge

Start/finish	Bled bus station (508m)
Time	3hr (alternative return route 3hr 45min)
Distance	9.7km (with alternative return route 12km)
Total ascent/descent	300m (alternative return route 320m)
Grade	1/2
Maps	1:50,000 Julijske Alpe
Refreshments	Gostilna Vintgar, Vintgar Visitor Centre, café at the end of the gorge and pizzeria near Sveta Katerina
Access	If you do not want to walk the 4km or so from Bled, free shuttle buses run from Bled bus station to the entrance of the gorge. The parking area at the entrance to the gorge is reserved for motorcycles and bicycles only, so if you come by car, there are two car parks in Bled and Blejska Dobrava (parking fee), which are also served by shuttle buses (see www.vintgar.si)
Note	Access to the gorge is only possible from Podhom, and the route through the Vintgar gorge to the Šum waterfall is one way. The gorge is open from spring to autumn and there is an entrance fee. You can buy tickets on site but keep in mind that the number of visitors is limited daily and a certain number are admitted each hour, so it is advisable to buy tickets online in advance (www.vintgar.si)

This spectacular gorge lies within easy walking distance of Bled. It was formed by the Radovna river as it flows east towards its confluence with the Sava Dolinka. The gorge is about 1200m long and is traversed by a series of wooden walkways and bridges that were originally constructed in 1893 – but which of course have been repaired since! Afterwards the walk continues up to the pilgrimage church of Sveta Katerina, with its excellent views of the surrounding countryside, and there is an alternative route for the return to Bled.

From Bled bus station, follow Grajska cesta up the hill, passing the youth hostel on the left just on the brow. The road goes downhill for a short distance to reach a T-junction. Turn right here and continue for a few hundred metres before turning

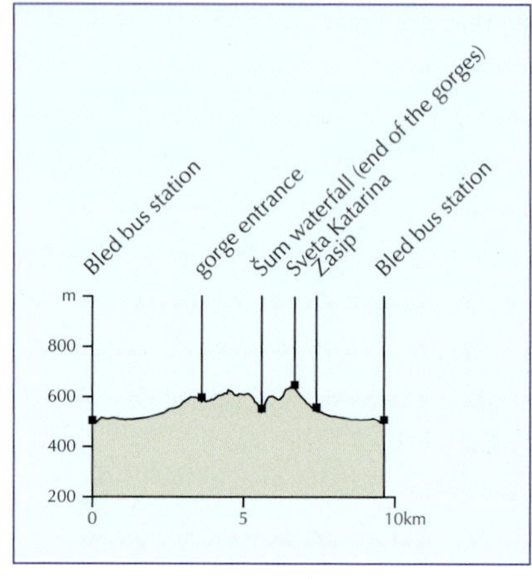

left onto a minor road, signed Soteska Vintgar (Vintgar gorge), and heading towards Hom, the small hill you can see in the distance – the gorge is on the far side of this. After about 300m cross the main road, just before the village of **Gmajna**, and turn left on a quiet side road, signed for cyclists, towards Podhom (**20min**). Stol, the highest peak of the Karavanke range, dominates the skyline to the right.

The road passes underneath the railway line just before **Podhom**. Continue along the narrow twisting lane, following signs for Vintgar, through the delightful village for almost another kilometre until you reach the Radovna river. Cross the river and pass **Gostilna Vintgar** on the left, about 250m before the gorge entrance and the Vintgar Visitor Centre (**1hr 10min**).

The wooden walkways of the Vintgar gorge

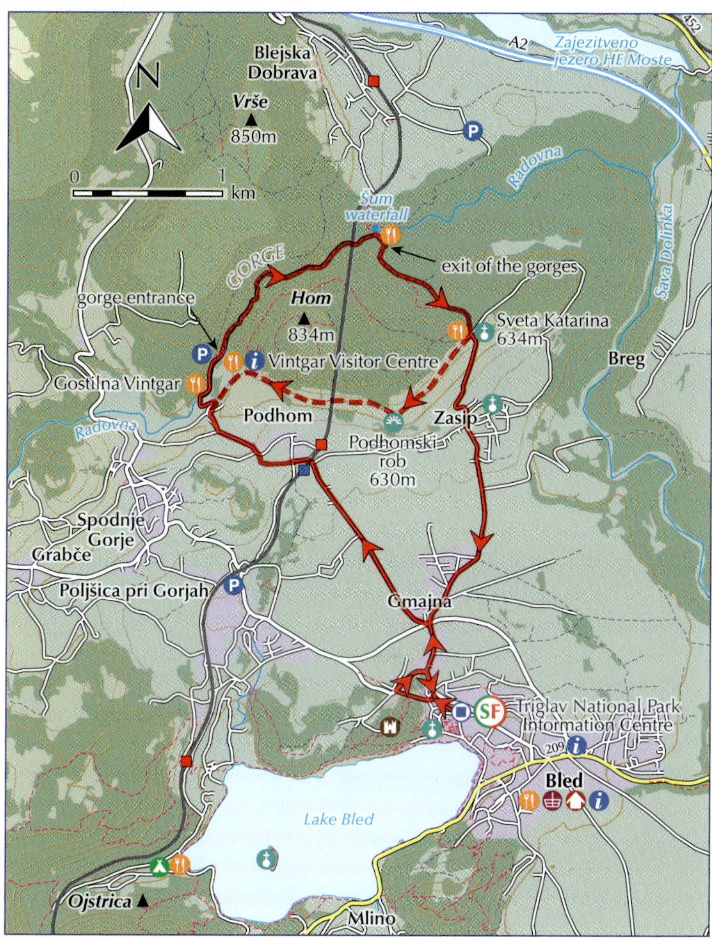

The route follows the wooden walkways and bridges for just over 1km, with impressive views of the walls of the narrow gorge and the rushing river below. Further on, the gorge opens out a little and continues to reach a wooden bridge over the 13m-high **Šum waterfall**, where a small café marks the end of the gorge walk (**1hr 40min**).

From the café take the waymarked track signed Katarina and Bled. After about 100m the track bears right, signed SV Katarina, and continues pleasantly up through the beautiful beech wood for another 300m to arrive at a fork. You can go either way; the right fork continues on the broader track, passing through a forest plantation, while the left fork continues on a narrower path that bears right to cross a grassy *planina* (alp) and then joins the broader track again.

After another 300m, reach the small medieval church of **Sveta Katarina** (634m, **2hr 5min**) with its squat shingle-roofed tower. There is a pizzeria just to the right for refreshments. From here there is a magnificent view across the Radovljica plain towards the Karavanke range. You cannot see the lake, but the castle marks its position.

To return, take the narrow tarmac road leading down the hill. This passes through the pretty village of **Zasip** with its old church and then continues through the hamlet of Gmajna and back to **Bled**.

Alternative return route

In the corner of the pizzeria car park, go through a small metal gate, signed Vintgar. Walk along the charming grassy balcony path with wonderful views over the plain, where you can see the line of the river Sava Dolinka and Bled Castle. The path contours the hillside, passing through more gates on the way, and arrives after about 1km at the pretty viewpoint of **Podhomski rob** (630m). The view has opened out to the right giving a vista of the Julian Alps and mighty Triglav himself. The path bears right and continues to traverse the hillside before eventually passing through a larger gate to join a broader track. In another 200m the path makes a slight descent to arrive at a small field where cattle graze and continues along its left edge. At the end of the field reach the road, turn left towards Podhom and retrace your outward route to **Bled**.

The grassy balcony path on the alternative return route

WALK 34

Galetovec

Start/finish	Square in Bohinjska Bela (478m)
Time	4hr 45min
Distance	12.7km
Total ascent/descent	845m
Grade	3
Maps	1:50,000 Julijske Alpe
Refreshments	Take refreshments with you as there are no mountain huts on this walk
Access	Bohinjska Bela lies on the road between Bled and Bohinj, so all the regular buses on this route stop here; see www.arriva.si for times or check at the bus stop. If you arrive by car, there is a small parking area outside the Mercator supermarket
Note	The steel staircases at the waterfall are steep but not difficult, and there is a handrail if required. If you prefer to avoid them, you can use an alternative start and join the route beyond the waterfall

This route leads through forest and alp to the wonderful viewpoint of Galetovec (1265m), high above Bohinjska Bela. The 180-degree panorama, from the Karavanke in the north, across the Radovljica plain and south to the Vogel hills, is nothing short of stupendous. This walk is not as well frequented as others in the Julian Alps and is therefore less well signed and rather overgrown in places. Long trousers are recommended for protection against the encroaching vegetation.

From the main square in Bohinjska Bela, ignore the sign to Galetovec and turn left and walk along the main road through the village, passing a school and a partisan memorial, to a railway bridge. Go under the bridge and follow a track on the right, signed for pedestrians and cyclists, which immediately passes in front of a house and continues up a minor road. In 50m bear right up another minor road, signed Iglica, as it climbs steeply between the attractive houses, coming to an end at house No. 95. Continue up the now grassy track, heading right to reach the foot of the crags. Walk past **Iglica waterfall** (Slap pod Iglico), which is seen at the back of a dark gash in the cliffs (**15min**).

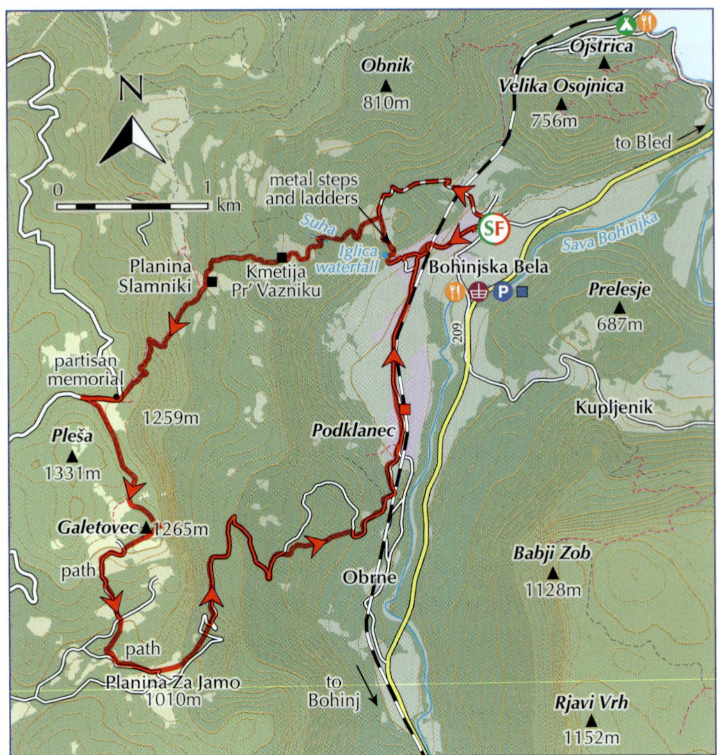

This is a popular rock-climbing area and there are a number of bolted routes on the crags. Tucked in a corner to the right of the waterfall, two sections of **metal steps and ladders** lead up a cleft in the cliffs, giving access to the top. Climb the ladders and steps in the rock cleft to reach the top of the crag and walk a few metres to the left to an excellent viewpoint above Bohinjska Bela. There's a fine view of Babji zob opposite, with the river, railway line, terraced pastures and the road up to Kupljenik laid out as if on a map.

The path continues on, away from the viewpoint, into a meadow. Skirt the left edge of the meadow for about 50m and take a grassy track which heads right towards some houses, where you reach a tarmac road by a wooden *toplar* (hayrack) – the alternative start joins the main route here – and a sign indicating Galetovec and Slamniki. Admire the attractive *planina* (alp) with its hay meadows,

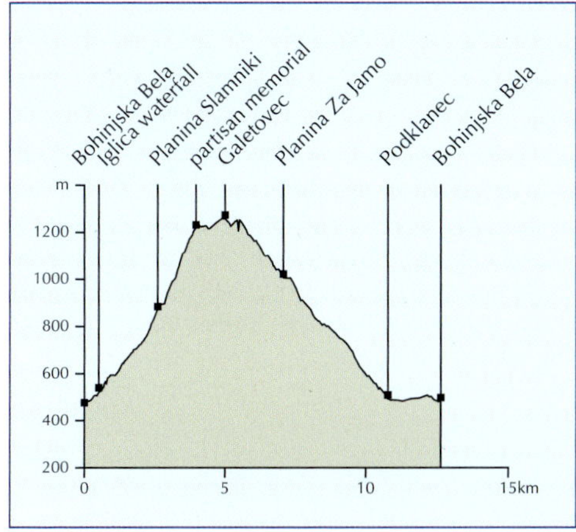

buildings and good view of Stol in the Karavanke chain before taking the tarmac road, which soon heads off into the forest.

Ascend gently through the forest to reach a T-junction about 5min after leaving the meadow and houses. Take the left-hand turn, signed Galetovec, which crosses the little Suha stream that forms the waterfall lower down. Within 100m, notice a narrow waymarked path that leads right, ascending into the wood – this just cuts off a bend in the road which it soon joins again.

Continue up the road, ignoring another gravel road that heads right, and arrive at a small attractive farm called **Kmetija Pr' Vazniku** (**55min**). Already, good views are beginning to open up to the north and east, with the Karavanke mountains rising above the flat Radovljica plain. As you pass between the farm and its holiday apartments, the road swings sharply right but take the rougher track, signed Galetovec, which leads left from the bend. In another 50m arrive at a fork and take a rough stony track that leads steeply uphill to the right, again signed Galetovec.

In less than 10min this track forks; take the right and continue steeply up. In another 150m, leave this stony track, following waymarks on a tree for a narrower path that leads off to the right, still ascending steeply into the wood. The path brings you to a forest road where you turn left. Within a short distance, reach a junction with another gravel road and continue on in the same direction, signed Galetovec. You will soon see more wooden buildings to the left of this road, which has now become a grassy cart track, and a meadow opens out to the left – this is **Planina Slamniki** (**1hr 25min**).

Just past the last of the buildings, an overgrown path heads up into trees on the right, with a sign to Galetovec and Rčitno and a waymark painted on a boulder. Walk into this green tunnel and almost immediately reach a fork; the right path is signed to Rčitno, and the other goes to Galetovec. Within another 50m the path passes to the left of an old alpine wooden building. Climb steeply up this path through the trees, and in another 150m climb past a waymarked tree stump to the right and continue up this overgrown section of path.

Soon the way clears somewhat, and in another 100m reach a broad track. Cross it, following waymarks, on a path that bears left as it crosses a small wooden footbridge across a tiny stream flowing from a spring and water pipe a few metres away, where a sign for '*voda*' (water) indicates it is drinkable.

Pass another sign for Galetovec just before another pasture (Rižišče), seen to the left with its wooden weekend cottages. About 30m further on cross a forest road and continue up on the waymarked path, which becomes more distinct and open as you gain height. The way crosses another rough logging track after about 5min and continues straight up, signed Galetovec.

The path now winds its way steeply up through the wood. After about 45min of steady climbing from Slamniki, the route finally eases and after a few more minutes you emerge onto an unmade vehicle road, where you turn left and within a few paces reach a **partisan memorial**, which lies just to the left (**2hr 15min**).

Continue past the memorial, due west, for 250m, then turn sharply left onto another gravel track heading south, signed Galetovec. Stay on this track, which is fairly level, as it passes on the right-hand side of a meadow which has a small water-catchment area for the cattle that graze here in the summer months.

After about 15min, as you round a bend, ignore a track going uphill on the right. Pass through a cattle gate and descend a little and in about 200m notice a small sign pointing left to Galetovec (**2hr 35min**). The path dips to cross the lower end of the pasture, close to the edge of the trees, then re-enters woods by a waymark. Climb easily through the woods, following waymarks, to reach a fence line and go through a dogleg gate to arrive at the summit of **Galetovec** (1265m, **2hr 45min**).

On the summit of Galetovec

Picnic tables and benches, as well as an information board with its panoramic picture, mark the summit. The **view** is sensational: straight across are the crags of Babji zob, and on the plain the towns of Radovljica and Lesce, Lake Bled like a blue jewel with the castle standing guard above it, mighty Stol and the Karavanke, and the Kamnik-Savinja Alps in the distance. Bohinjska Bela lies below, huddled against the cliffs.

From the summit take the path signed for Boh. Bela čez Pl. Za Jamo and follow the waymarks for 5min until you reach a track. Turn left here and follow the track down through the fields. Shortly afterwards walk between two wooden buildings and follow the track as it bends to the left.

At the end of the pasture the route enters the wood for a few minutes and then skirts the left edge of another meadow with a wooden building. Reach a forest road and continue straight, following a waymark on a tree. The path runs along the right side of a pasture and then soon re-enters the wood. The marked path now becomes steeper until it reaches another grassy meadow with a nice cottage. Cross the pasture and continue into the trees again for 5min to reach **Planina Za Jamo** (1010m, **3hr 20min**).

Here the path joins a broad track which leads to a house on the left. Cross the track and continue straight on, walking on the left-hand side of the meadow. At the end of the pasture follow the sign, Boh. Bela, and enter the wood.

The path now meets and crosses a forest road twice. At the third time, turn left and continue on the forest road for about 50m to a junction, signed Boh. Bela (*zimska pot*, winter route) to the right, but also Boh. Bela along the road straight ahead. Continue straight on along the forest road for 10min to another fork, where you bear right. Continue down the road for another 10min until you see a path to the right, with a sign to Boh. Bela on a tree (**4hr**).

Take this path and soon reach a broad track. Cross it and continue straight ahead, following waymarks, to join the road again. Turn right here and continue for another 5min. The gravel road then becomes tarmacked, leading down to the hamlet of **Podklanec**. When you reach the main road, turn left and walk through the hamlet, past the railway station. Continue on for about 1.5km to **Bohinjska Bela**, back to the start.

Alternative start avoiding ladders

If you want to avoid the steep ladders by the waterfall, follow the Galetovec sign from the square and bear right past a water trough. Cross a stream and walk up the tarmac road for about 1km, under the railway line and up left to the planina to meet the main route at the hayrack, at the edge of the small meadow close to the top of the crags.

WALK 35

Debela peč, Brda and Lipanski vrh

Start/finish	Šport Hotel Pokljuka on the Pokljuka plateau (1280m)
Time	6hr 15min
Distance	18.4km
Total ascent/descent	1145m
Grade	3
Maps	1:25,000 Bohinj
Refreshments	Blejska koča na Lipanci
Access	During the summer season, the Pokljuka plateau is served by a shuttle bus service from both Bled and Bohinj: once on the plateau, get off the bus at the Pokljuka-Goreljek stop. See www.bled.si and www.bohinj.si for times or check at the bus stop. If you arrive by car, limited parking is available at the turning for the Šport Hotel or near the hotel

This superb walk is a must-do from Bled. The route runs through some of the most beautiful forest on the Pokljuka plateau to a mountain hut on a little alp and then sets off through wonderful natural gardens to Debela peč (2014m), the highest summit on the Lipanca ridge. The views are thrilling, with dizzying drops to the Krma valley before the vista of the northern Julian Alps and equally panoramic views to the south. The path then runs along the ridge to Brda (2009m) and Lipanski vrh (1975m) before dropping easily back down to Blejska koča.

There are no difficulties except for one short steep descent in a narrow gully, but the route can be cut short a little to avoid this if necessary. It is a perfect introduction to alpine walking, giving you the sense of being in the high mountains but without the technical difficulties or extreme exposure.

From the Šport Hotel walk to the main road (where the Pokljuka-Goreljek bus stop is located), turn left and after 200m take the forest road on the right, signed Blejska koča-Lipanca. After 2km on an excellent forest road through beautiful woodland with tall straight spruce, arrive at the delightful open pasture of **Planina Javornik** with its wooden buildings (1282m, **40min**). Here the first view of the

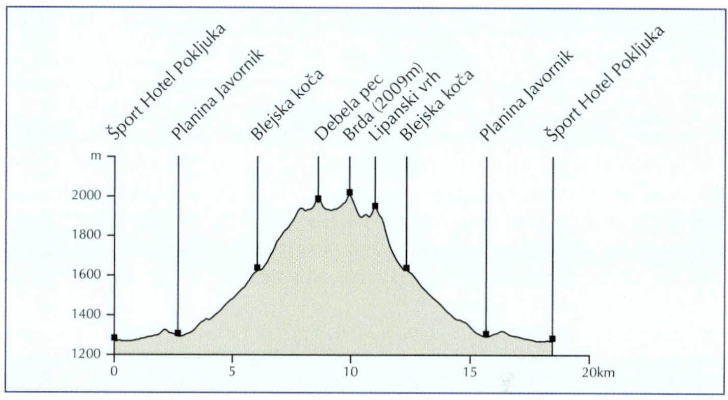

ridge is laid out before you: Debela peč is the summit to the right, with Brda and Lipanski vrh straight ahead.

Cross the alp on a grassy track towards the buildings to reach the forest road at the northern edge of the *planina* (alp) and continue straight ahead in the same direction. After 100m or so cross a cattle grid and re-enter the forest. In a short distance come to a crossroads with another forest road, where cars are often parked. Cross it and follow the sign for Lipanca, taking a rougher but still broad track, continuing north.

The track is generally good but some sections can be very boggy after rain. After about 20min cross another forest road and begin to climb a little more steadily. In another 10min reach a junction; turn right, signed Blejska Koča. Continue on the good track, which ascends steadily as it traverses up through the forest, and soon make a sharp left turn where another track heads right, signed Medvedova konta. In another 5min the path bears right at a sign indicating Planina Lipanca and asking that dogs are kept on leads as this is a grazed pasture. Rounding a

The idyllic Planina Javornik

right-hand corner gives a view up the planina, and the roofs of the hut buildings can be seen with the ridge towering above.

The path turns left again, crossing the planina, and passes a partisan memorial plaque to take a final right turn up to **Blejska koča** (1633m, **1hr 45min**).

Beside the hut, an elaborate signpost gives numerous directions, including to Debela peč. Take this path, heading across the planina. From the first little rise on the right-hand side there is a good view back to Planina Javornik. About 20m past the viewpoint the path divides; take the left fork to Debela peč and Brda. The path climbs pleasantly away from the alp through sparser stands of larches and dwarf pine. About 10min from the hut, pass a sign on a tree pointing left to Lipanski vrh – this is the main descent route.

Continue straight on, zigzagging up through rocks and trees to emerge above the alp at a signpost. Continue straight on for Debela peč, with a waymarked rock a few paces ahead. Some 25m further on, the path forks, and the Debela peč path bears round to the left and ascends again to reach a level section of grassy hillside with clumps of dwarf pine and small larch trees. This area is like walking through a carefully designed rockery, with flowers in every crevice. Watch out for waymarks painted on the rocks directing you left, up onto the steeper hillside again, and continue ascending, with views to the right of the Karavanke range.

About 1hr from the hut you reach the summit ridge, with the first magnificent views to the north. Turn right, passing a signed boulder to Debela peč, and notice after a few paces another sign painted on a rock to the left to Brda and Lipanski vrh. You will take this path on the return from Debela peč.

Walk across a balcony section on the easy path, with wonderfully precipitous drops to the north into the Krma valley, and watch Triglav come into view to the left. The northern view disappears behind the ridge for a while as you cross an area of karst hollows and rocks, among dwarf pine and clusters of flowers, that leads you onto the right-hand side of the ridge. Another 10min brings you to the final steep pull up to the summit of **Debela peč** (2014m, **3hr 15min**).

The **panorama** from the top starts at Triglav, very obviously the biggest of them all. Looking right from Triglav, you can see the whole of the northern Julian Alps, the Krma valley almost vertically below and to the right the flat valley floor of Zgornja Radovna, with the village of Mojstrana in the Upper Sava valley behind. Beyond is Kepa in the Karavanke range, with the hills of Austria behind. The Karavanke continue to Stol, their highest summit, and further right are the high peaks of the Kamnik-Savinja Alps. Lake Bled can be seen on the edge of the Radovljica plain, the whole of the Pokljuka plateau is visible to the left of Planina Javornik, and on the southern skyline are the Lower Bohinj mountains, with Črna prst to the left and Vogel to the right.

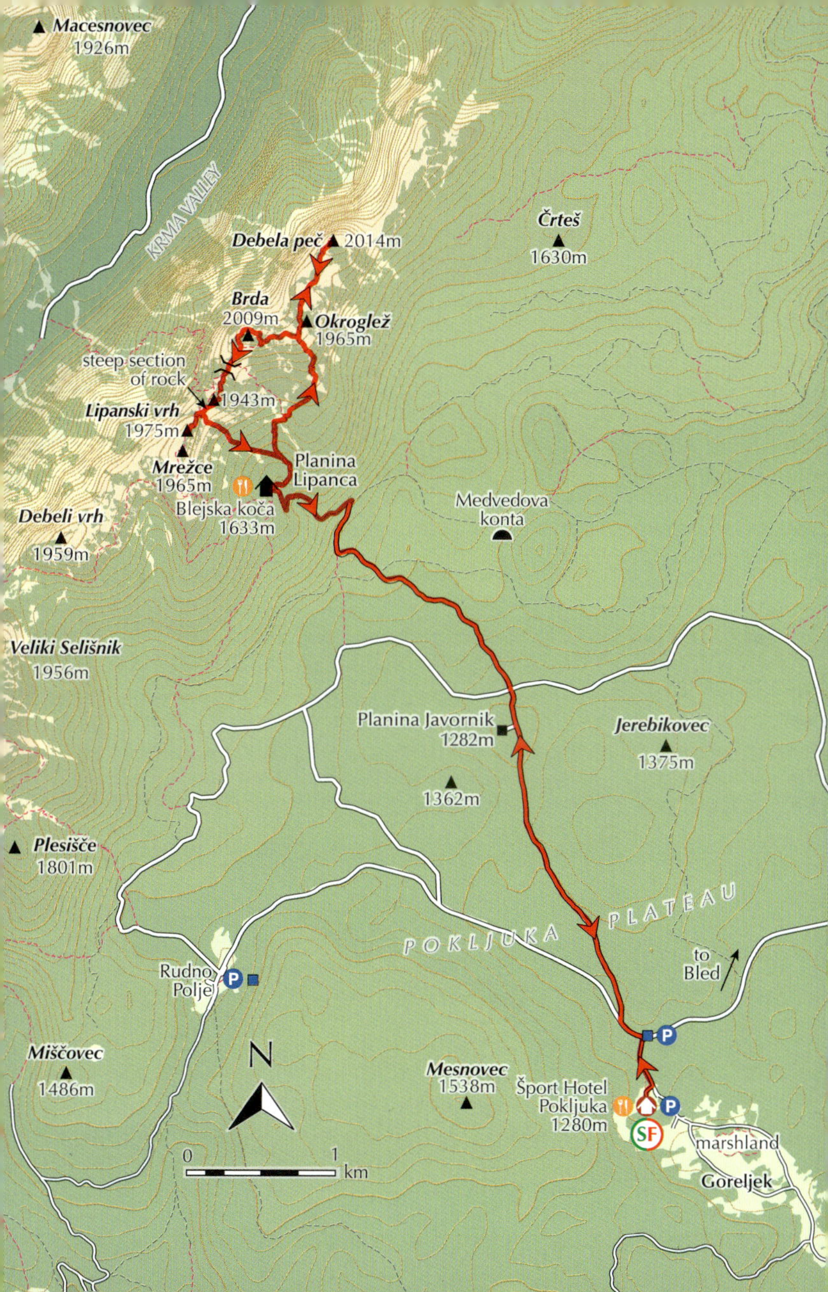

Macesnovec
1926m
KRMA VALLEY
Debela peč 2014m
Črteš
1630m
Brda
2009m
Okrogléž
1965m
steep section
of rock
1943m
Lipanski vrh
1975m
Mrežce
1965m
Planina
Lipanca
Blejska koča
1633m
Debeli vrh
1959m
Medvedova
konta
Veliki Selišnik
1956m
Planina Javornik
1282m
Jerebikovec
1375m
1362m
Plesišče
1801m
POKLJUKA PLATEAU
to
Bled
Rudno
Polje
Miščovec
1486m
N
Mesnovec
1538m
Šport Hotel
Pokljuka
1280m
SF
marshland
Goreljek
0
1
km

Enjoying sunshine and magnificent views from the summit of Debela Peč

Retrace your steps from the summit to where you joined the ridge and the sign for Brda and Lipanski vrh. Take this path which passes close to two sinkholes before climbing more steeply over the rocky terrain. The path then bears right, following waymarks and a sign for Brda painted on a rock. At this point, notice the path descending straight ahead; you will join this path a little further along the ridge on the descent. In another 5min arrive at the summit of **Brda** (2009m, **4hr**).

Leave the summit of Brda, still heading south-west along the ridge – in just a few metres the grassy path begins to descend, passing a direction marker on a rock. The route bears left and descends more steeply, but within 10min it levels as it merges with the path mentioned earlier that traverses below the summit of Brda.

Continue along easily and, within 150m, pass a path that descends left, signed Blejska koča. **There is a steep section of rock on the path ahead to Lipanski vrh. If you want to avoid it, you must take this path back to the hut.**

Within another 50m reach another junction – a route to the right leads down to the Krma valley, so continue straight on, signed Lipanski vrh. The dwarf pine encroaches on the path as the route passes below the left-hand side of the ridge.

Begin to climb again, and soon afterwards enter a short, easy-angled rocky gully that you exit on the left just before the top. The route then picks its way through the limestone, following waymarks and paint slashes, to reach a subsidiary top at 1943m.

From here there is a particularly good view over to **Triglav** – the metal *stolp* (tower) on the summit is visible, glinting in the sun, and two of the huts can be seen: to the left is Dom Planika and you can just make out the Kredarica hut directly below the summit.

The path now immediately descends an unexpectedly steep gully for about 30m, which is protected with steel cable and pegs – it's an easy scramble but you might want to put away your walking poles so you can use both hands. At the bottom, turn right and traverse some quite steep ground on a good path for a little longer before continuing more easily. In another 100m, and just before reaching the col below Lipanski vrh, a path goes down to the left – this is the main descent route. Continue to the right and ascend the last 25m up to the col and turn left. It is not far to the top of **Lipanski vrh** (1975m, **4hr 25min**).

Retrace your steps to the path descending from the col. Follow the path down towards Blejska koča, visible directly below. Soon the path divides, with the right-hand fork traversing the hillside and the left continuing down, at first quite steeply and then less so, through the woods to rejoin the main path from the hut, where you turn right to follow the outward route back to the **Šport Hotel Pokljuka**.

WALK 36

Viševnik

Start/finish	Rudno polje on the Pokljuka plateau (1347m)
Time	3hr 45min
Distance	6.3km
Total ascent/descent	695m
Grade	3
Maps	1:25,000 Triglav, 1:25,000 Bohinj
Refreshments	Take refreshments with you as there are no mountain huts on this walk
Access	During the summer season, the Pokljuka plateau is served by a shuttle bus service from both Bled and Bohinj: once on the plateau, get off the bus at the Rudno polje stop. See www.bled.si and www.bohinj.si for times or check at the bus stop. If you arrive by car, there is a large car park in Rudno polje (parking fee)

This shapely mountain is justifiably popular due to its ease of access from the road head at Rudno polje, which means it can be completed in half a day. At 2050m, the summit of Viševnik offers spectacular views of Triglav. It is one of the easier 2000m peaks to do in winter, as the road to Rudno polje is kept open for the excellent cross-country skiing on Pokljuka – one of the biathlon World Cup events is held there each year.

Just past the large military building at Rudno polje, turn right onto a forest road, following a sign for Viševnik. Walk up here and reach the foot of a ski lift (**10min**). Continue towards a **small hut** where a sign, Viševnik 2hr, directs you onto a path just to the left of the ski slope and lift towers along the edge of the wood. The ski slope is grassy and cattle graze here in the summer months, so keep to the waymarked path near the forest edge to avoid disturbing the livestock and trampling the alpine flowers.

In a few minutes meet and cross the forest road and, just past a sign for Viševnik, continue up the steep path, crossing a stile. Follow the line of the ski lift and then, at the top of it, cross another stile to enter woods. Soon afterwards the path passes under the ski lift cable as it nears the top of the piste. Continue climbing steeply as the path runs through small trees and shrubs, lined with an

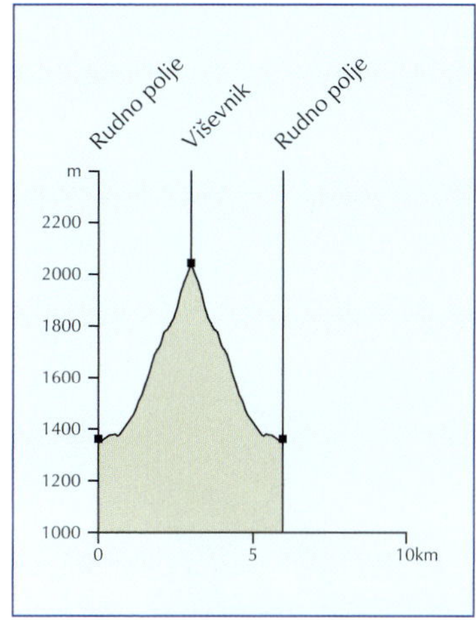

abundance of flowers, including thistles, cow parsley, red campion and even Triglav rose.

The route follows a broad gully that forms a natural grassy break in the trees, and as you gain more height, views of the vast tree-covered Pokljuka plateau and beyond begin to open up behind you. In another 10min arrive at a level area where a sign on a tree directs you on to Viševnik. Bear left and continue level for almost 100m before climbing steeply again, passing a junction signed to the right for Blejska koča na Lipanci and to the left for Viševnik (**1hr**).

Hikers on the summit of Viševnik with Triglav high in the background

Eventually reach a small grassy col on a tree-covered shoulder, where a wonderful panorama of the Lower Bohinj mountains can be seen on the horizon straight ahead. Turn right and continue up, initially through larch then through dense thickets of dwarf pine. Finally, the dwarf pine relents and the path emerges onto open slopes, with the summit seen up ahead to the left. Bear left along the grassy edge of a rocky escarpment to reach the summit of **Viševnik** (2050m, **2hr**).

Triglav dominates the **view**, with both the Planika and Kredarica huts clearly visible. To the right of Triglav, Rž and the long alpine ridge of Rjavina lead the eye all the way down to the distant Sava valley, where the village of Dojve can be seen below Kepa. Directly below to the south, you can see the wooden huts of Planina Uskovnica.

Return by reversing the route.

Looking towards Triglav from the summit of Viševnik (photo: Roy Clark)

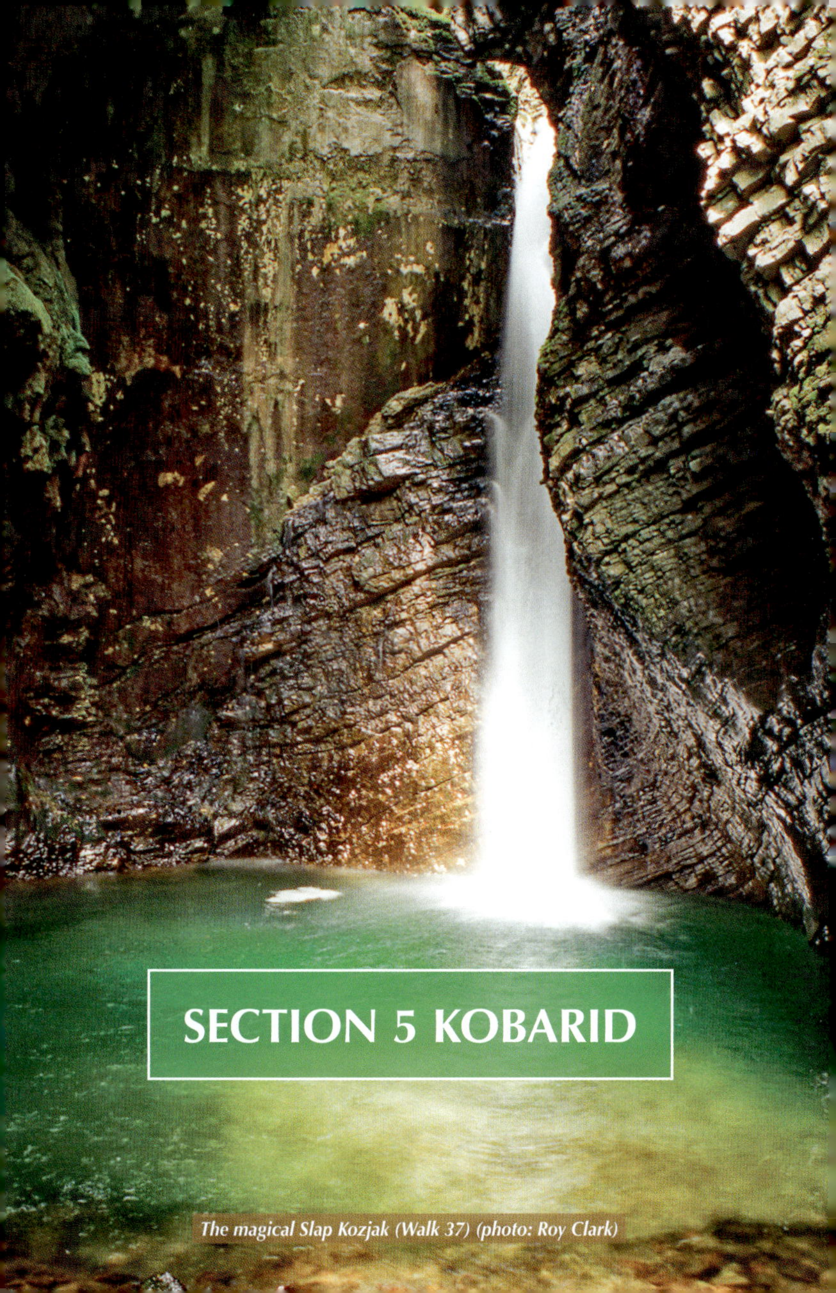

SECTION 5 KOBARID

The magical Slap Kozjak (Walk 37) (photo: Roy Clark)

Compared to the other bases in this book, Kobarid is tiny and its Italian feel provides a stark contrast to the alpine atmosphere of the others. The village lies in the Soča valley, and although it is surrounded by peaks of around 2000m, its own more modest altitude of 235m gives it a Mediterranean climate and atmosphere, accentuated by the white houses and terracotta-tiled roofs. The little backstreets and courtyards are choked with flowerpots in the summer, not only the inevitable window boxes of geraniums but also huge pots of oleanders in bright pinks and purples. Kobarid has a timeless sleepiness that not even the many visitors of July and August can dispel. Ernest Hemingway immortalised the village in his novel about the Isonzo (Soča) Front, *A Farewell to Arms*, and it is easy to imagine that he is about to walk around the corner.

The area is of significant historical interest, as the Soča river was at the centre of the greatest mountain battle in history when the fighting on the Isonzo Front, between the Italians and the Austrians, raged between 1915 and 1917. In October 1917, the 12th offensive, by the weaker Austrian army, surprised the Italians and pushed the fighting back towards Italy with a massive loss of life on both sides. It is impossible to walk any distance here without seeing evidence of those turbulent times, whether it be fortifications or rusting shell cartridges.

In terms of access, Kobarid lies to the west of the main Julian Alps, only 9km from the Italian border. It is 21km from Bovec by road (although only around 10km south as the crow flies) as the road must travel round the great ridge of Polovnik. Buses run between the two bases, going on to Tolmin and Nova Gorica. The nearest train station is at Most na Soči, on the Bohinj railway line. In summer, shuttle buses are provided to make the walks more accessible. During the rest of the year, the limited service means that some routes are out of reach for those without their own transport. A local taxi service can also provide transport to the start of some of the walks if required.

There is limited accommodation in Kobarid, but there is one hotel, three hostels and a number of houses offering private rooms and apartments. The Soča valley has some excellent campsites, reflecting the fact that many visitors come here to canoe and

Winter panorama from the top of the Stol (Walk 39)

The village and church of Drežnica below Krn (Walk 37) (photo: Roy Clark)

kayak the river. A number of supermarkets and eating places are also available. The tourist information centre is located in the town centre, as is the Kobarid Museum, which has fascinating exhibits on World War 1. Next to the museum is the visitor centre of the Walk of Peace Foundation, an organisation founded in 2000 to protect and preserve the historical and cultural heritage of the Isonzo Front. Here you can find all kinds of information, maps and guides to the Walk of Peace Trail as well as a nice souvenir shop.

The high alpine valley of Drežniški kot offers rooms, apartments and tourist farmhouses in its several villages. Surrounded by high peaks, it has a stunning setting and would be a wonderful place to stay for a few days (for more information, visit www.dreznica.si).

THE ROUTES

Walk 37 visits the high valley of Drežniški kot, which is surrounded by wonderful mountain scenery, and Walks 38–40 climb local peaks that offer stunning views of the Julian Alps to the north and all the way to the Adriatic Sea to the south.

MAPS

The Krnsko pogorje 1:25,000 map covers Walks 37, 38 and 40, as well as a large part of Walk 39, while the full length of Walk 39 is on the 1:50,000 Julijske Alpe.

WALK 37

Drežniški kot

Start/finish	Square in Kobarid (234m)
Time	4hr
Distance	13.7km
Total ascent/descent	545m
Grade	2
Maps	1:25,000 Krnsko pogorje
Refreshments	Restaurant in Drežnica (only open in summer in good weather)

This easy walk explores the beautiful valley of Drežniški kot, which opens out high above the Soča valley. The scenery is spectacular, with the villages and churches set against a backdrop of towering crags, dominated by the distinctive summit profile of Krn (Walk 30).

The route initially visits Slap Kozjak, one of the most beautiful waterfalls in Slovenia (entrance fee), then climbs on a good track to the hamlet of Magozd and wanders along a quiet road to visit the larger village of Drežnica before heading back down a forest path above the gorge of the river Ročica to the Soča valley.

From the square in Kobarid, take Gregorčičeva ulica and walk through the village. About 200m past Kobarid Museum, the road bears left; keep straight ahead on a side road signed Drežnica. Follow the road down to **Napoleon Bridge**, cross the river and turn left on the other side. Continue up this road, and 100m past Camp Koren turn left onto a track signed Slap Kozjak. Follow the track for about 10min, crossing fields at first with the Soča to your left. Pass the World War 1 trenches and a suspension bridge and shortly afterwards, at a beautiful **viewpoint** on the emerald-green Soča river, follow the main track signed Slap Kozjak to reach, after 300m, the bridge above the lower Kozjak waterfall (**35min**).

After the bridge follow another sign for Slap Kozjak, branching right at a fork, and continue on the forest path to the pay kiosk, with the pretty Kozjak river on your right. After 300m cross the river on a plank bridge and walk a short distance on the far bank, then cross back again on another plank bridge as the walls of the gorge begin to close in. Rocks lead down to the water's edge, where you continue round a corner to reach a wooden walkway leading to the **Slap Kozjak viewpoint**

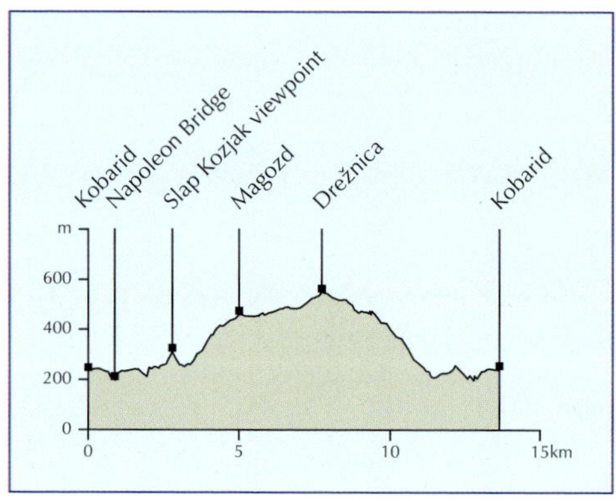

(**45min**). The waterfall drops 15m into a cavern, and as the sun shines through the narrow cleft at the top onto the pool below, the light is reflected back onto the side walls, creating an enchanting fairy grotto.

Retrace your steps to the stone bridge over the lower Kozjak waterfall and at the fork turn right, following signs for Magozd and Drežnica. Shortly afterwards the track emerges in a meadow with an old stone building. Cross the meadow before curving round to the left behind the building and begin to climb gently into the forest. Continue up the path, rising steadily round several hairpins to skirt the knoll to your left. After about 15min come out into an open meadow to a stunning view of Krn to the right.

Cross the pasture and follow the track round to the left beneath some crags. Pass through a belt of trees with crags on both sides to reach a junction. Turn right, past a building on the right, and then bear left, and as you come round the corner you can see the roofs of the village of **Magozd** beneath the steep slopes of Krasji vrh. Walk along the track to enter the village on a tarmac road, where you turn right (**1hr 25min**).

Walk through the village and continue on the quiet road between pasture and woodland. After about 1.2km reach the turning for the village of Jezerca and continue straight on, following the sign for Drežnica. Shortly after the junction cross the **river Kozjak**. The view is now dominated by the big church of the Sacred Heart of Jesus at Drežnica on its small knoll, with stunning views of Krn behind. Come to a junction (about 2km from Magozd) and turn left into **Drežnica**; the gravel track almost immediately on the left leads up into the village (**2hr**).

The huge Italianesque church with its 52m-high church tower is the most striking feature of **Drežnica**. Amazingly, it wasn't damaged during World War 1. Walk up to the knoll by the church for superb views of the whole of Drežniški kot, with the villages of Magozd and Jezerca below the long ridge of Krasji vrh to the north-west, while in the distance are the rocky peaks of Kanin. To the west is the enormously long ridge of Stol, and to the east the

N
0
1
km
Soča
Dolenji Hrib
482m
Jezerski vrh
670m
to Bovec
203
Baba
772m
Magozd
Drežniške Ravne
Drežniški kot
Jezerca
Slap Kozjak
Kozjak waterfall viewpoint
Kozjak
lower Kozjak waterfall
Drežnica
Camp Lazar
WW1 trenches
Camp Koren
Ročica
Italian Charnel House
Napoleon Bridge
Koseč
Idrija
SF
Kobarid
GORGE
102
Mlinsko
Ladra
Soča
Smast
Idrsko

A beautiful view of the Soča along the trail

craggy face of Krn, which was greatly changed by the devastating earthquake of 1998.

The route continues down the road from Drežnica to Kobarid, heading west out of the village. About 50m past the '*Nasvidenje*' (goodbye) sign, take an old stone-laid track on the left and cross a field for about 100m to a T-junction. Take the left-hand trail which goes slightly downhill, ignoring sidetracks giving access to fields – if in doubt, head downhill (this part of the route is also marked by the red-and-black waymarks of the Walk of Peace). Pass a little waterfall and continue down with the stream on your right. Reach a short level section at a fork and bear right, following waymarks. Pass an old building on the left and follow a small stream until you reach a T-junction, where you turn right.

The path now becomes more distinct again, with the sound of the **river Ročica** to the left. Cross a stream and continue on the path, which is now obvious all the way. At first it traverses close above the gorge, gaining height above the water, and then bears away from the river a little, although you can still hear the rushing water to the left. Cross a small stream and continue on, traversing steep ground on the level track, which has been broadened for logging activity. Descend a little and then traverse again before beginning a gradual descent.

Pass an open field on the left with a building; a grassy track leading from it merges with the route. The river gorge is on the left, a good 100m below, appearing almost bottomless as you peer over the edge. Shortly afterwards follow a right-hand bend with a good view of the village of Smast on the floor of the Soča valley. Head down on the broad rocky track in the direction of Kobarid. As you descend, the atmosphere seems to change quite suddenly, becoming more Mediterranean, with clouds of butterflies in the warm dry air.

After about 1km bear left by a small quarry to emerge on a tarmac road, where you turn right (**3hr 30min**); you can walk along here for about 1km to Napoleon Bridge. However, for a nicer route take the track on the right a few metres further on. Follow this between the fields for about 500m, then bear right, slightly uphill, and left again to reach a house. Take a track on the right between stone walls and then leave it to bear left on a narrow path following the outside edge of the left-hand field. Begin to descend and pass another house and then join the concrete road that serves the house, heading down to rejoin the main road about 250m short of Napoleon Bridge. Cross the bridge and walk back up the road into **Kobarid**. From the square, a short 30min round-trip detour, along the Way of the Cross, leads to the Italian Charnel House, which is worth a visit for its symbolic significance and for the view of Kobarid and the lower Soča valley.

The wonderful valley of Drežniški kot

WALK 38

Krasji vrh

Start/finish	Spring above Drežniške Ravne (753m)
Time	5hr
Distance	11.4km
Total ascent/descent	1120m
Grade	3
Maps	1:25,000 Krnsko pogorje, 1:25,000 Bovec-Trenta
Refreshments	Take refreshments with you as there are no mountain huts on this walk
Access	During the summer season, shuttle buses run from Kobarid to Drežniške Ravne. See www.soca-valley.com for times or check at the bus stop. By car: drive through Drežnica, following the road sign 'Drež. Ravne', and continue for about 1km to cross the river Kozjak on a bend. Follow the road around to the left and at the top of the slope turn right at a 90-degree bend by a house. Take the first right, which comes almost immediately, and drive up for about 500m to a right turn signed Planina Zaplеč and Planina Zaprikraj. Continue up here for about 1km. Just past the end of the tarmac there is a parking area with a water trough and spring signed Krasji vrh

Krasji vrh (1773m) is the highest point on the Polovnik ridge, which runs roughly east from the massif of Krn, forcing the Soča river into a wide curve between Bovec and Kobarid. Its position allows for spectacular views of the Julian Alps to the north and east and of Italy and the Adriatic Sea to the south and west. Many remains of World War 1 can still be seen near the summit: at the beginning of the conflict, Italian soldiers occupied the mountain, setting up numerous firing positions in order to control the nearby battlefields.

Continue along the gravel road, ignoring a path to the right signed for Krn after about 100m. In another 40m, take a narrow path heading right, signed and waymarked Krasji vrh and Pot miru Zaprikaj. Soon join the road again and continue up it for almost 200m before turning left onto another path that is not well marked.

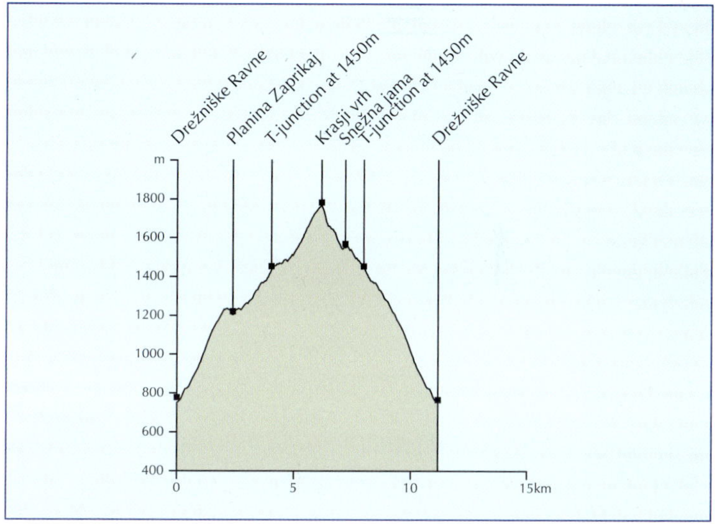

The path meets and crosses the road several more times before emerging at a hairpin bend where a track immediately heads right, signed Slap Curk and Drežnica; don't take this but stay on the road for a few more metres to see waymarks and the continuation of the path heading steeply up to the right (**30min**). Reach and cross the road again, following waymarks, and within 5min arrive at a junction where the path forks; a sign for Pot miru points right to the road, but continue following the waymarked route that climbs up into the woods, signed Zaprikaj on a wooden table. Carry on for a few minutes to where the track swings sharply right. Here continue straight on, where direction waymarks on rocks soon confirm the way. The path climbs pleasantly in the shade of the trees, with the forest floor littered with limestone boulders.

After 20min or so arrive at a broader track where Krasji vrh is signed left along it and Planina Zaprikraj is signed straight ahead (**1hr 5min**).

Detour to Planina Zaprikraj

For a pleasant detour of about 30min to Planina Zaprikraj (1208m, **1hr 20min**), follow the narrow path up through the wood for about 5min and cross a fence by a stile. Head across a somewhat more open area on an indistinct narrow path with occasional waymarks. Soon the trail drops down a little to reach the working *planina* (alp) with its numerous buildings. One of the largest in the Soča valley,

this planina is set in a pretty valley below the Krnica ridge, with many paths leading off onto the surrounding hills. During the summer season, it is possible to buy cheese and albumin curd here. Retrace your steps to the stile and now follow the path that heads right along the fence line. The path passes close to a *lovska koča* (hunting lodge) before bearing left to reach the signed junction in the description below.

Main route continues

Turn left along the broad track and in another 7–8min arrive at a junction where a sign for Krasji vrh points left on a good broad track, with Planina Zaprikraj signed to the right. Continue on for Krasji vrh, where after 10min the path forks; an older track heads left but continue following the waymarked route that climbs up to the right. In just over another 5min the track narrows briefly as it crosses a small grassy glade then re-enters the woods by a waymark on a tree, immediately becoming broader again.

Soon the path begins to zigzag steeply up through the woods to arrive at a T-junction at **1450m** (**2hr 5min**). Krasji vrh is signed both left and right; the path to the right is also signed *snežna jama* (snow cave) – this will be the descent route. Turn left and begin to traverse the wooded hillside where in another 10min the trees abruptly cease and wonderful views open to the south. The Soča winds along the floor of the valley as it passes Kobarid, while in the distance is the Adriatic Sea.

The path curves round onto the open hillside, becoming narrow and grassy. Continue, rising gently on the left-hand side of the hill, with the grassy summit visible up to the right – it looks deceptively close but is still over 30min away. Soon the path turns sharply right and in another 10min you arrive at a junction. Straight ahead is signed to the viewpoint of Koluji, but turn right, signed Krasji vrh. The way continues up the hillside in a series of zigzags over the tussocky grass to the crest of the summit ridge. Turn left to reach the summit of **Krasji vrh** (1773m, **2hr 50min**).

On the grassy top, which has a summit book and stamp, take a moment to linger over the **wonderful view**. Clockwise from Krn, you can see the villages of Drežniški kot below then Kobarid with Matajur behind and beyond to the sea. Further round is the long ridge of Stol leading into Italy, with the

Looking towards Krn from the summit of Krasji vrh (photo: Roy Clark)

Dolomites sometimes visible in the distance. Next is the Kanin ridge, and the view continues uninterrupted, taking in all the giants of the Julian Alps, including Triglav.

Either retrace your steps for the descent or continue; from the summit cairn take the waymarked path on the north side that almost immediately bears right and drops down steeply over fissured limestone rocks to reach the dwarf pine. As you lose height, the path levels and becomes more distinct as you pass the entrance to a World War 1 bunker built into the rock. Large sinkholes and other karst rock formations make up the wild terrain and soon the route passes more ruined buildings – one with an ornate stone pillar. These Italian anti-aircraft gun emplacements were used to deter Austrian surveillance missions during the battles on the Isonzo Front.

About 25min after leaving the summit of Krasji vrh, reach a junction where a narrow path heads right to **Snežna jama** (**3hr 15min**).

The **snow cave** is an interesting geological feature. To visit it, follow the vague path, which within a short distance descends past a sinkhole and then rises a few metres to a small level area. The snow-filled shaft of the cave can be seen below, and the path drops down closer to it – but the last few metres of path leading to it are extremely steep and slippery, and it is recommended you go no closer.

From the junction follow the path through dwarf pine and conifers and soon notice a World War 1 mule track over to the left. Continue straight on down the path, which soon broadens as it reaches beech woods once again. In a few more minutes arrive back at the T-junction passed on the ascent and retrace your steps to the start of the route.

WALK 39

Stol

Start/finish	Square in Kobarid (234m)
Time	9–10hr
Distance	23.9km
Total ascent/descent	1505m
Grade	3
Maps	1:50,000 Julijske Alpe
Refreshments	Take plenty of refreshments with you as there are no mountain huts on this walk
Warning	This walk is long and mostly over open ground, so you will need good protection from the sun. At the time of writing, the timings suggested on the signposts were shorter than the actual time required to complete the walk, so it is essential you build in more time than that stated

This long, long whaleback is only part of an even longer ridge that continues into Italy, and Stol (the chair, 1673m) is its highest point within Slovenia. The ridge can be seen to the south of Bovec as a high wall marking the southern extent of the Julian Alps. Its sub-alpine feel makes for an excellent day out, with the initial steep ascent through the forest giving way to a gently rising ridge. The views to both sides are superb, and the vista of the Kanin range above Bovec is particularly spectacular.

A sign in the northern corner of the square in Kobarid, opposite the church, indicates, Stol 4hr, pointing up a narrow road. Fork right within a few paces and follow the pretty cobbled street up the hill. Once you pass the last house, the route enters trees and becomes a broad stony track up through the forest, well waymarked and signed. After 10–15min, a path to the right is signed to **Veliki rob**.

It is worth making the **15min detour to Veliki rob** for a good aerial view of Kobarid. Follow the sign off the main route and in less than 100m another one directs you right. Waymarks lead you to a little glade in the woods before you drop down 20m or so in height to the viewpoint, atop a rocky outcrop. Retrace your steps to the main path.

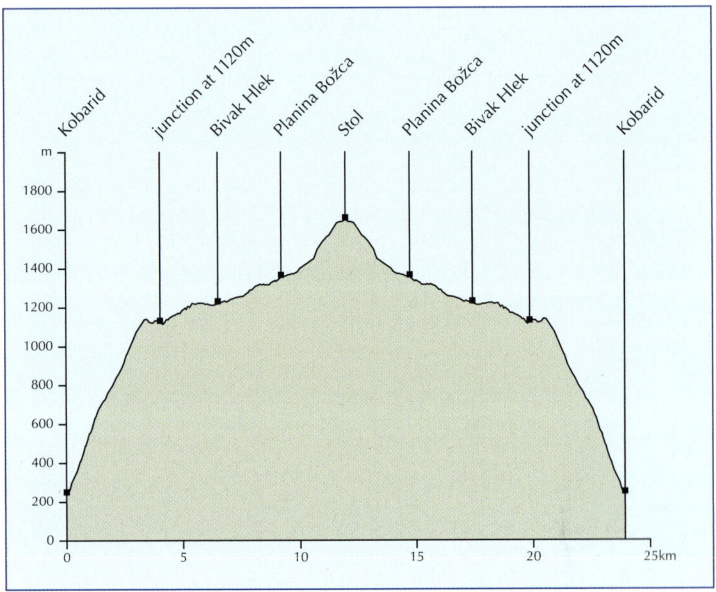

The excellent mule track continues winding up through the trees and then traverses the hillside on the left of the ridge (**50min**). After another 10min come to a small clearing, with views to the left of Matajur, where the track narrows a little and becomes grassy. Pass a weekend cottage on your left and then continue up through the woods, now on the right-hand side of the hill. Join a broad track at a bend and continue; the going is easy, although in parts the trees encroach a little on the track.

About 20min from the weekend cottage, waymarks direct you onto a path heading left, leaving the broader track (**1hr 20min**). This narrower path ascends more steeply and soon bears more to the left. In another 100m skirt a small clearing in the trees, bearing right. Re-enter the wood and continue ascending steadily, quickly joining the crest of the ridge, which is still forested, although with smaller trees. This section is surprisingly narrow, with steep wooded slopes on both sides, but the path is easy. The path levels out at an open grassy area, with the first good views to the right (**2hr**). The TV mast on top of Stol can be seen ahead, still looking a long way away!

The path continues along the broad grassy ridge and then begins to descend slightly. The walking now is really pleasant among beautiful flowers. Look around. Here it is quite common to see chamois. Reach a junction at a saddle (**1120m**), where a broad track comes up from the left (**2hr 20min**). A sign indicates Stol straight on, Staro Selo to the left and Trnovo to the right. Go straight ahead on the now broad track and up some zigzags before continuing on the left of the ridge. The track now continues on a fairly level route, passing through several cattle gates.

There are good views down into the valley on the left, with the curve of the **river Nadiža** clearly visible at the foot of Matajur; it rises in Italy and enters Slovenia for only about 11km before crossing the border again. Out in the distance you can see the Adriatic Sea.

Pass a *lovska koča* (hunting lodge) and further on reach **Bivak Hlek** (1225m, **3hr**), an unmanned hut with tables outside and running water for picnics. The

The ridge with the Stol antenna in the distance

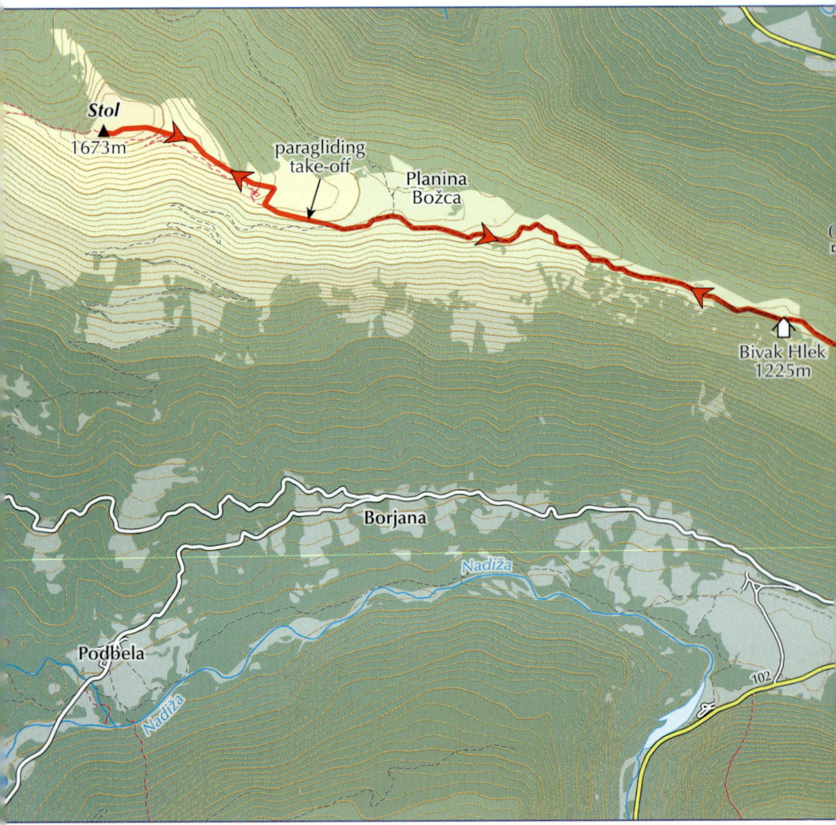

broad track continues almost level for about 3km past the hut, until it meets the driveable track that comes up from Sedlo to the south and from the village of Učja to the north, just above **Planina Božca** (**3hr 45min**).

The track divides 200m further on; take the right-hand fork signed Stol and continue up, passing the **paragliding take-off point**. As the highest take-off point in the Soča valley, Stol is often the only launch site above the inversion layer, providing opportunities for thermal flying. After about 500m follow the waymarks through a gap in the fence to the right and cross the hillside for about 150m to a small marker post. The path now heads quite steeply to the left up the ridge,

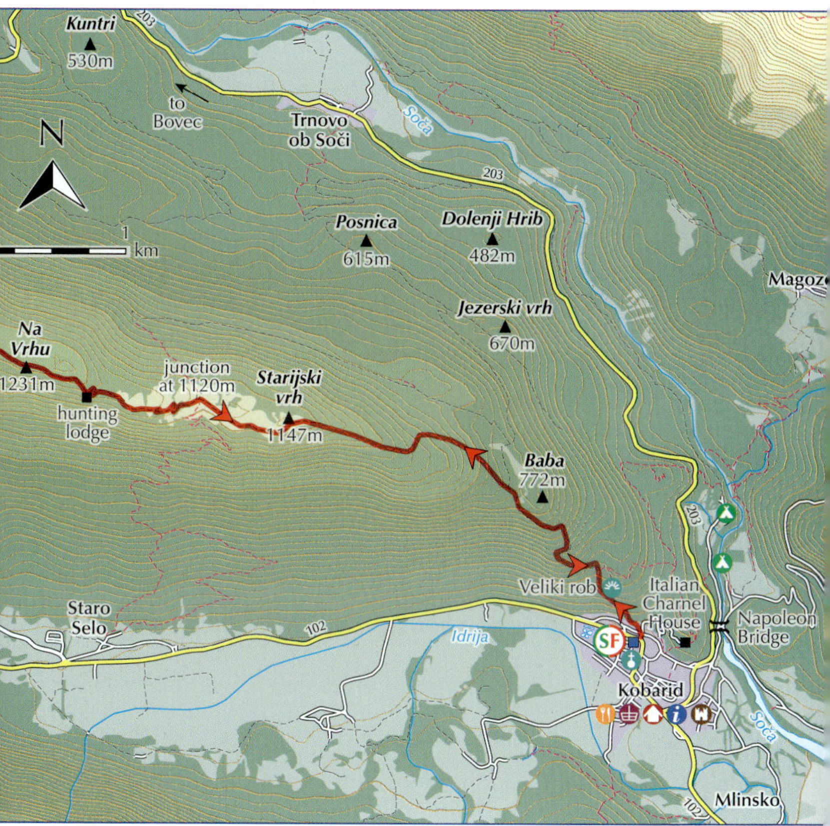

following waymarks, then levels out and continues for about 20min more to the summit of **Stol** (1673m, **4hr 45min**).

From **Stol** there are excellent views north and back along the broad crest, but it is to the right, and the Julian Alps, that the eye is constantly drawn. At the summit you can see the continuation of the ridge, with its steep bare slopes to the south and the trees reaching to the crest on the north side.

Return the same way.

WALK 40

Matajur

Start/finish	Avsa village (896m), above Livek, south of Kobarid
Time	5hr
Distance	12.4km
Total ascent/descent	845m
Grade	3
Maps	1:25,000 Krnsko pogorje
Refreshments	Dom na Matajure (1545m) 10min from the summit – open Sundays only
Access	During the summer season, shuttle buses run from Kobarid to Avsa. See www.soca-valley.com for times or check at the bus stop. If you arrive by car, there is a parking area just near the start of the path; when you reach the hamlet of Avsa, take the right fork, signed Matajur and parking 300m

Matajur (1641m) is the forested mountain to the south of Kobarid, and its bare summit, right on the Italian border, gives particularly extensive views, from Austria down to Venice and the Adriatic Sea. The mountain can be climbed from Kobarid, but the route can be overgrown in places and difficult to follow. The walk described here starts from the village of Avsa and mostly follows the *stara pot* (old path) then ascends the broad eastern ridge of Matajur for the final section.

At the parking area the waymarked path heads into the woods to the right of the road. The path bears right and within 50m joins a broad stony track. Turn left onto it; the track soon forks but keep left and in just 40m leave the track for a narrower path on the right, following painted waymarks on the trees.

The path continues up through the wood, soon passing a small grassy *planina* (alp) on its right side. At the top of the planina a good view of Krn across the valley opens out to the right. Carry on straight ahead, heading steeply up, with the tangled knots of exposed tree roots covering the path. Shortly after you will come across a well-preserved **trench** from World War 1 (**20min**). The path now enters a section of beautiful mature beech wood and passes directly between the moss-covered walls

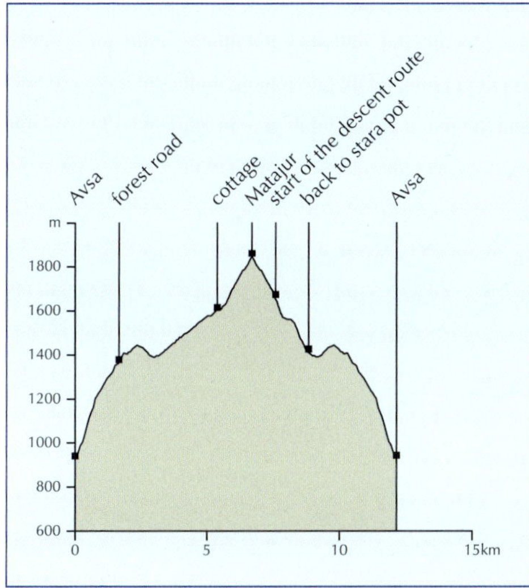

of two small, ruined crofts. The woodland scene is enchanting: boulders and small outcrops lie draped in lush green moss while an almost mystical silence pervades the air.

After walking through this enchanted wood, go through a gate and turn right up a broad rough track signed Matajur (**45min**). After 100m, as the track levels, follow waymarks to the left at the edge of the wood to emerge onto open pasture. Continue up the meadow and bear left at the top between stands of trees where straight ahead the summit of Matajur can be seen on the skyline, marked by a small chapel.

Continue straight ahead across the open grassy hillside, noting a forest road close by, below and to your left. In another 100m the path merges with the road opposite a **small cottage** (**1hr 5min**). Walk up this gravel road, soon rounding a hairpin bend. Beyond the bend, the road reaches a rise then begins a gentle descent to reach a fork.

Take the left fork, signed Matajur, and continue down the road, passing through a gate after a further 100m. In another 400m or so reach a junction where a narrower path leads off the main track to the right, signed Matajur. This path stays inside Slovene territory until the final summit section and is slightly more direct; it will be used for the descent. Stay on the broad track, bearing left and signed for Dom na Matajure.

The track gently ascends and a wonderful view of Krn and some of the Lower Bohinj mountains further to the right opens out briefly to the north-west. Arrive at another junction at a gate where the main track appears to fork right, but go through the gate, still following signs for Matajur. This track is grassier and seemingly less frequented than the track you have just left as it begins to traverse the hillside, now on the Italian side of the mountain. Pass a path heading down to the

left to Bivio Masseris – notice the Italian signs and waymarks (**1hr 50min**). Matajur is signed straight ahead.

In another 100m a view opens out to the left and the large Rifugio Pelizzo (1325m) can be seen on the southern flank of Matajur, with the flat plains beyond the Friuli hills stretching all the way to the sea. Dom na Matajure (1545m) is located higher up the hillside, slightly to the west.

The broad grassy track is now fairly level; pass the door of a neatly maintained **cottage** and make a sharp left-hand bend past its open well (**2hr 10min**). In another 5min reach a sign that points left along a narrow path for the Pelizzo refuge but continue straight ahead for Matajur.

In about 100m the track swings left past rocks painted with both Italian and Slovene waymarks. Leave the track at this bend and follow the narrower path straight ahead, which soon leads to a junction of paths on the skyline ridge. Here the view opens out to the north: the long mountain – Stol – lies below to the left in the mid-ground, while Krn, with the Julian Alps in the background, is to the right. Note the path that leads right at this junction for Livek and Avsa; this will be used for the descent. Turn left along the ridge. White border stones can occasionally be seen a few metres to the right, marking the Slovene (northern) side of Matajur.

The **border on Matajur** was very bloody during World War 1. The young Lieutenant Erwin Rommel, the hero of the battle of Kobarid, passed over this mountain when he broke through the front with his troops. This allowed the Austro-Hungarian army to enter Italy and reach as far as the Piave river, where it was eventually stopped. It is said that when Rommel arrived at the Matajur crest, some of his soldiers saw the sea for the first time.

Continue up the final section of the ridge to reach the little chapel and orientation plate on the summit of **Matajur** (1641m, **2hr 40min**). The extent of the view will depend on how hazy it is – an early morning ascent in the clear air following a previous night's storm can reveal views as far afield as Austria, Venice and the Adriatic Sea.

Retrace your steps to the junction where you joined the ridge and follow the path for Livek and Avsa (**3hr**). The path turns left and drops down on the northern side to reach another junction in about 100m. The path bears right here, signed Avsa and Livek, and soon crosses shale-covered slabs of rock that lie in an area of clay-like soil. Just beyond, the Kobarid Svino path descends to the left; continue straight ahead, quite level, following signs for Avsa and Livek, then make a short descent and cross another slab of rock before arriving at a gravel track.

Continue straight ahead on the narrow path that descends over grass and yet more exposed slabby rock, barely covered by the thin topsoil. Ten minutes of descent brings you back to the junction on the broad track and the old path (**3hr 40min**). Turn left and retrace your steps to **Avsa**.

Winter panorama on the way to Matajur

Mountain bikers on the descent

APPENDIX A

Useful contacts

If ringing Slovenia from overseas, use the dialling code +386, then dial the Slovene number as listed here, omitting the initial 0.

Local tourist offices

Kranjska Gora
Kolodvorska 1c
4280 Kranjska Gora
tel +386 (0)4 580 94 43
info@kranjska-gora.eu
www.kranjska-gora.si

Bohinj
Ribčev Laz 48
4265 Bohinjsko jezero
tel +386 (0)4 574 60 10
info@tdbohinj.si
www.bohinj.si
(offices also in Stara Fužina and Bohinjska Bistrica)

Bovec
Trg golobarskih žrtev 47
5230 Bovec
tel +386 (0)5 302 96 47
info.bovec@dolina-soce.si
www.soca-valley.com

Bled
Cesta svobode 10
4260 Bled
tel +386 (0)4 574 11 22
info@td-bled.si
www.bled.si

Kobarid
Trg Svobode 16
5222 Kobarid
Tel +386 (0)5 380 04 90
info.kobarid@dolina-soce.si
www.soca-valley.com

Tourist information

TNP Information Centre Bohinj
Stara Fužina 37
4265 Bohinjsko jezero
tel +386 (0)4 578 02 40
info.bohinjka@tnp.gov.si
www.tnp.si

TNP Information Centre Dom Trenta
Na Logu v Trenti 31
5232 Soča
tel +386 (0)5 388 93 30
dom-tnp.trenta@tnp.gov.si
www.tnp.si

TNP Information Centre Bled
Ljubljanska cesta 27
4260 Bled
tel +386 (0)4 578 02 05
info@visitbled.si
www.tnp.si

The Walk of Peace Visitor Centre
Gregorčičeva ulica 8
5222 Kobarid
tel +386 (0)5 389 01 67
info@thewalkofpeace.com
www.thewalkofpeace.com

Slovenian Tourist Board
www.slovenia.info

Alpine Association of Slovenia
www.pzs.si

Mountain huts

Up-to-date information on all listed huts can be found at www.pzs.si

Kranjska Gora

Dom v Tamarju
tel +386 (0)4 137 80 77

Erjačeva koča (at Vršič pass)
tel +386 (0)5 139 92 26
www.erjavcevakoca.com

Poštarski dom (at Vršič pass)
tel +386 (0)4 133 59 19
www.postarskidom.com

Tičarjev dom (at Vršič pass)
tel +386 (0)7 070 90 93
www.ticarjev-dom.si

Aljažev dom
tel +386 (0)5 166 57 38

Zavetišče pod Špičkom
tel +386 (0)7 011 29 75
www.zavetiscepodspickom.si

Koča v Krnici
tel +386 (0)4 045 79 48

Bohinj

Koča pri Savici
tel +386 (0)4 069 57 87

Planinska koča na Vojah
tel +386 (0)4 123 46 25

Kosijev Dom na Vogarju (Vogar dom)
tel +386 (0)5 161 33 67
www.vogar.si

Bregarjevo zavetišče na planini Viševnik
tel +386 (0)3 127 08 84

Koča na Planini pri Jezeru
tel +386 (0)5 163 27 38

Orožnova koča
tel +386 (0)4 164 51 18

Dom Zorka Jelinčiča na Črni prsti
tel +386 (0)3 126 04 00

Dom na Komni
tel +386 (0)4 062 07 84
www.nakomni.si

Koča pod Bogatinom
tel +386 (0)5 123 58 66

Koča pri Triglavskih jezerih
tel +386 (0)4 062 07 83

Zasavska koča na Prehodavcih
tel +386 (0)5 161 47 81

Dom Planika
tel +386 (0)5 161 47 73

Vodnikov dom
tel +386 (0)4 133 83 74

Koča na Doliču
tel +386 (0)5 161 47 80

Bovec

Pogačnikov dom
tel +386 (0)4 828 13 00

Dom dr. Klementa Juga
tel +386 (0)5 996 95 04

Dom pri Krnskih jezerih
tel +386 (0)5 828 03 00

Gomiščkovo zavetišče na Krnu
tel +386 (0)6 861 33 92

Koča na Mangrtskem sedlu
tel +386 (0)5 163 08 63

Bled

Blejska koča na Lipanci
tel +386 (0)5 162 10 21

Kobarid

Dom na Matajure
tel +39 335 1445734

Map suppliers

Stanfords
tel 020 7836 1321
www.stanfords.co.uk

The Map Shop
tel 01684 593146
0800 085 40 80 (UK only)
www.themapshop.co.uk

Sidarta
www.sidarta.si

APPENDIX B

Language notes

There is no doubt that Slovene is one of the harder European languages for English speakers to learn. The six cases, three genders and extra 'dual' form, used whenever there are two of something (and unique now in European languages), give a dizzying array of 54 possible word endings, and that's just the nouns! These different case endings can make references to place names confusing, as their endings depend on their relationship to other words; for example, the Slovene for 'castle' is 'grad', but 'Castle Road' becomes Grajska cesta. However, when in a foreign country, it is always polite to try to use some words and phrases, and while you will find that the majority of Slovenes speak English, they will be delighted if you attempt to say something in their language.

Pronunciation

The pronunciation of the different letter sounds does not present a big problem in Slovene; more difficult are the varied stress patterns that can completely change the sound of a word. Listed below are the sounds in Slovene. Once you have mastered them, the sound always correlates to the written spelling (unlike in English).

c – always pronounced ts like zz in pizza, even at the beginning of words
č – as ch in church
j – as y in yacht
h – as ch in loch
r – always rolled as in Scottish English
š – sh as in ship
v – this sound is not pronounced at the end of words; this means, for example, that the final three letters in Triglav rhyme with 'cow'
ž – the sound in the middle of the English 'leisure', or at the beginning of the French 'gîte'

Glossary of useful words and phrases

English	Slovene
Being sociable	
hello	dober dan
goodbye	nasvidenje
goodnight	lahko noč
no	ne
yes	ja
please	prosim
thank you	hvala
I don't speak Slovene	ne govorim slovensko
Food and drink	
tea	čaj
coffee	kava
water	voda
milk	mleko
beer	pivo
wine	vino
cheese	sir
meat	meso
sausage	klobasa

English	Slovene
potato	krompir
soup	juha
salad	solata
ice cream	sladoled
Home-made	domača kuhinja
enjoy your meal!	dober tek!
drinking water	pitna voda
non-potable water	voda ni pitna
Accommodation	
mountain hut	dom, koča
log cabin	brunarica
room	soba
apartment	apartma
dormitory	skupno ležišče
winter room	zimska soba
eating house	gostilna, gostišče, okrepčevalnica
Weather	
forecast	napoved
sun	sonce
wind	veter
rain	dež
snow	sneg
cloudy	oblačno
thunderstorm	nevihta
hot	vroče
cold	mrzlo

English	Slovene
good/bad weather	lepo/slabo vreme
Landscape	
mountain	gora
summit	vrh
face, wall	stena
ridge	greben
edge	rob
hill	hrib
river	reka
mountain stream	potok
source, spring	izvir
lake	jezero
forest	gozd
waterfall	slap
open pasture, alp	planina
path	pot, pešpot
col, saddle	sedlo
valley	dolina
bridge	most
church	cerkev
limestone formation	karst
double hayrack	toplar

English	Slovene
Miscellaneous	
Help!	na pomoč!
day, today	dan, danes
night	noč
evening	večer
tomorrow	jutri
yesterday	včeraj
week	teden
month	mesec
year	leto
one hour	ena ura
monday	ponedeljek
tuesday	torek
wednesday	sreda
thursday	četrtek
friday	petek
saturday	sobota
sunday	nedelja
man	moški*
woman	ženska*
child	otrok

*Useful in toilets, which are often labelled 'M' and 'Z'

DOWNLOAD THE GPX FILES

All the routes in this guide are available for download from:

www.cicerone.co.uk/1215/GPX

as standard format GPX files. You should be able to load them into most online GPX systems and mobile devices, whether GPS or smartphone. You may need to convert the file into your preferred format using a conversion programme such as gpsvisualizer.com or one of the many other such websites and programmes.

When you follow this link, you will be asked for your email address and where you purchased the guidebook, and have the option to subscribe to the Cicerone e-newsletter.

www.cicerone.co.uk

LISTING OF CICERONE GUIDES

BRITISH ISLES CHALLENGES, COLLECTIONS AND ACTIVITIES

Great Walks on the England Coast Path
Map and Compass
The Big Rounds
The Book of the Bivvy
The Book of the Bothy
The Mountains of England and Wales:
  Vol 1 Wales
  Vol 2 England
The National Trails
Walking the End to End Trail
Cycling Land's End to John o' Groats

SHORT WALKS SERIES

15 Short Walks Hadrian's Wall
15 Short Walks in the Lake District: Keswick, Borrowdale and Buttermere
15 Short Walks in the Lake District: Windermere Ambleside and Grasmere
15 Short Walks Lake District: Coniston and Langdale
15 Short Walks in Arnside and Silverdale
15 Short Walks in the Ribble Valley
15 Short Walks in Nidderdale
15 Short Walks in Northumberland: Wooler, Rothbury, Alnwick and the coast
15 Short Walks in the Yorkshire Dales: Grassington, Skipton, Malham and Ilkley
15 Short Walks in the Peak District: Bakewell and the White Peak
15 Short Walks on the Malvern Hills
15 Short Walks in Cornwall: Falmouth and the Lizard
15 Short Walks in Cornwall: Land's End and Penzance
15 Short Walks in the South Downs: Brighton, Eastbourne and Arundel
15 Short Walks in the Surrey Hills
15 Short Walks on Dartmoor North: Okehampton and Chagford
15 Short Walks on Dartmoor South: Ivybridge and Princetown
15 Short Walks on Exmoor
15 Short Walks Winchester
15 Short Walks in Bannau Brycheiniog: Brecon Beacons
15 Short Walks in Pembrokeshire: Tenby and the south
15 Short Walks in Dumfries and Galloway
15 Short Walks in the Trossachs: Callander and Aberfoyle
15 Short Walks on the Isle of Mull
15 Short Walks on the Orkney Islands
15 Short Walks on the Shetland Islands

SCOTLAND

Ben Nevis and Glen Coe
Cycling in the Hebrides
Cycling the North Coast 500
Great Mountain Days in Scotland
Mountain Biking in Southern and Central Scotland
Mountain Biking in West and North West Scotland
Not the West Highland Way: A Mountain High Way
Scotland
Scotland's Best Small Mountains
Scotland's Mountain Ridges
Scottish Wild Country Backpacking
Skye's Cuillin Ridge Traverse
The Borders Abbeys Way
The Great Glen Way
The Great Glen Way Map Booklet
The Hebridean Way
The Hebrides
The Isle of Mull
The Isle of Skye
The Skye Trail
The Southern Upland Way
The West Highland Way
The West Highland Way Map Booklet
Walking Ben Lawers, Rannoch and Atholl
Walking in the Cairngorms
Walking in the Pentland Hills
Walking in the Scottish Borders
Walking in the Southern Uplands
Walking in Torridon, Fisherfield, Fannichs and An Teallach
Walking Loch Lomond and the Trossachs
Walking on Arran
Walking on Harris and Lewis
Walking on Jura, Islay and Colonsay
Walking on Mull, Coll and Tiree
Walking on Rum and the Small Isles
Walking on the Orkney and Shetland Isles
Walking on Uist and Barra
Walking the Cape Wrath Trail
Walking the Corbetts
  Vol 1 South of the Great Glen
  Vol 2 North of the Great Glen
Walking the Fife Pilgrim Way
Walking the Galloway Hills
Walking the John o' Groats Trail
Walking the Munros
  Vol 1 Southern, Central and Western Highlands
  Vol 2 Northern Highlands and the Cairngorms
Winter Climbs in the Cairngorms
Winter Climbs: Ben Nevis and Glen Coe

NORTHERN ENGLAND ROUTES

Cycling the Reivers Route
Cycling the Way of the Roses
Hadrian's Cycleway
Hadrian's Wall Path
Hadrian's Wall Path Map Booklet
The Coast to Coast Cycle Route
The Coast to Coast Map Booklet
The Coast to Coast Walk
Walking the Dales Way
The Dales Way Map Booklet
Walking the Pennine Way
Pennine Way Map Booklet

LAKE DISTRICT

Bikepacking in the Lake District
Cycling in the Lake District
Great Mountain Days in the Lake District
Joss Naylor's Lakes, Meres and Waters of the Lake District
Lake District Winter Climbs
Lake District:
  High Level and Fell Walks
  Low Level and Lake Walks
Mountain Biking in the Lake District
Outdoor Adventures with Children — Lake District
Scrambles in the Lake District —
  North
  South
Trail and Fell Running in the Lake District
Walking The Cumbria Way
Walking the Lake District Fells —
  Borrowdale
  Buttermere
  Coniston
  Keswick
  Langdale
  Mardale and the Far East
  Patterdale
  Wasdale
Walking the Tour of the Lake District

NORTH-WEST ENGLAND AND THE ISLE OF MAN

Cycling the Pennine Bridleway
Isle of Man Coastal Path
The Lancashire Cycleway
The Lune Valley and Howgills
Walking in Cumbria's Eden Valley
Walking in Lancashire
Walking in the Forest of Bowland and Pendle
Walking on the Isle of Man
Walking on the West Pennine Moors
Walking the Ribble Way
Walks in Silverdale and Arnside

NORTH-EAST ENGLAND, YORKSHIRE DALES AND PENNINES

Cycling in the Yorkshire Dales
Great Mountain Days in the Pennines
Mountain Biking in the Yorkshire Dales
The Cleveland Way and the
  Yorkshire Wolds Way
The Cleveland Way Map Booklet
The North York Moors
Trail and Fell Running in the
  Yorkshire Dales
Walking in County Durham
Walking in Northumberland
Walking in the North Pennines
Walking in the Yorkshire Dales:
  North and East
  South and West
Walking St Cuthbert's Way
Walking St Oswald's Way and
  Northumberland Coast Path

DERBYSHIRE, PEAK DISTRICT AND MIDLANDS

Cycling in the Peak District
Dark Peak Walks
Scrambles in the Dark Peak
Walking in Derbyshire
Walking in the Peak District -
  White Peak East
  White Peak West

WALES AND WELSH BORDERS

Cycle Touring in Wales
Cycling Lon Las Cymru
Great Mountain Days in Snowdonia
Hillwalking in Shropshire
Mountain Walking in Snowdonia
Offa's Dyke Path
Offa's Dyke Map Booklet
Scrambles in Snowdonia
Snowdonia: 30 Low-level and Easy
  Walks — North, South
The Cambrian Way
The Pembrokeshire Coast Path
The Pembrokeshire Coast Path Map
  Booklet
The Snowdonia Way
The Wye Valley Walk
Walking Glyndwr's Way
Walking in Carmarthenshire
Walking in Pembrokeshire
Walking in the Brecon Beacons
Walking in the Wye Valley
Walking on Gower
Walking the Severn Way
Walking the Shropshire Way
Walking the Wales Coast Path

SOUTHERN ENGLAND

20 Classic Sportive Rides
  in South East England
  in South West England
Cycling in the Cotswolds
Mountain Biking on the North Downs
Mountain Biking on the South Downs
The North Downs Way
The North Downs Way Map Booklet
The South Downs Way
The South Downs Way Map Booklet
The Cotswold Way
The Cotswold Way Map Booklet
The Ridgeway National Trail
The Ridgeway Map Booklet
The Thames Path
The Thames Path Map Booklet
The Two Moors Way
Two Moors Way Map Booklet
Walking the South West Coast Path
South West Coast Path Map Booklet
  Vol 1: Minehead to St Ives
  Vol 2: St Ives to Plymouth
  Vol 2: St Ives to Plymouth
  Vol 3: Plymouth to Poole
Suffolk Coast and Heath Walks
The Kennet and Avon Canal
The Lea Valley Walk
The Peddars Way and Norfolk
  Coast Path
The Pilgrims' Way
Walking Hampshire's Test Way
Walking in Essex
Walking in Kent
Walking in London
Walking in Norfolk
Walking in the Chilterns
Walking in the Cotswolds
Walking in the Isles of Scilly
Walking in the New Forest
Walking in the North Wessex Downs
Walking on Dartmoor
Walking on Guernsey
Walking on Jersey
Walking on the Isle of Wight
Walking the Dartmoor Way
Walking the Jurassic Coast
Walking the Sarsen Way
Walks in the South Downs National
  Park

ALPS CROSS-BORDER ROUTES

100 Hut Walks in the Alps
Alpine Ski Mountaineering Vol 1 —
  Western Alps
The Karnischer Hohenweg
The Tour of the Bernina
Trail Running — Chamonix and the
  Mont Blanc region
Trekking Chamonix to Zermatt
Trekking in the Alps
Trekking in the Silvretta and Ratikon
  Alps
Trekking Munich to Venice
Trekking the Tour du Mont Blanc
Tour du Mont Blanc Map Booklet
Walking in the Alps

FRANCE, BELGIUM, AND LUXEMBOURG

Camino de Santiago — Via Podiensis
Chamonix Mountain Adventures
Cycling London to Paris
Cycling the Canal de la Garonne
Cycling the Canal du Midi
Mont Blanc Walks
Mountain Adventures in the
  Maurienne
Short Treks on Corsica
The GR5 Trail
The GR5 Trail —
  Vosges and Jura
  Benelux and Lorraine
The Moselle Cycle Route
Trekking in the Vanoise
Trekking the Cathar Way
Trekking the GR10
Trekking the GR20 Corsica
Trekking the Robert Louis Stevenson
  Trail
Via Ferratas of the French Alps
Walking in Provence — East
Walking in Provence — West
Walking in the Auvergne
Walking in the Brianconnais
Walking in the Dordogne
Walking in the Haute Savoie: North
Walking in the Haute Savoie: South
Walking on Corsica
Walking the Brittany Coast Path
Walking in the Ardennes

PYRENEES AND FRANCE/SPAIN CROSS-BORDER ROUTES

Shorter Treks in the Pyrenees
The Pyrenean Haute Route
The Pyrenees
Trekking the Cami dels Bons Homes
Trekking the GR11 Trail
Walks and Climbs in the Pyrenees

SPAIN AND PORTUGAL

Camino de Santiago: Camino Frances
Coastal Walks in Andalucia
Costa Blanca Mountain Adventures
Cycling the Camino de Santiago
Mountain Walking in Mallorca
Mountain Walking in Southern
  Catalunya
Spain's Sendero Historico: The GR1
The Andalucian Coast to Coast Walk
The Camino del Norte and Camino
  Primitivo
The Camino Ingles and Ruta do Mar
The Mountains Around Nerja
The Mountains of Ronda and
  Grazalema
The Sierras of Extremadura
Trekking in Mallorca
Trekking in the Canary Islands
Trekking the GR7 in Andalucia
Walking and Trekking in the Sierra
  Nevada
Walking in Andalucia
Walking in Catalunya —
  Barcelona
  Girona Pyrenees
Walking in the Picos de Europa
Walking La Via de la Plata and
  Camino Sanabres
Walking on Gran Canaria
Walking on La Gomera and El Hierro

Walking on La Palma
Walking on Lanzarote and Fuerteventura
Walking on Tenerife
Walking on the Costa Blanca
Walking the Camino dos Faros
Portugal's Rota Vicentina
The Camino Portugues
Walking in Portugal
Walking in the Algarve
Walking on Madeira
Walking on the Azores

SWITZERLAND

Switzerland's Jura Crest Trail
The Swiss Alps
Tour of the Jungfrau Region
Trekking the Swiss Via Alpina
Walking in Arolla and Zinal
Walking in the Bernese Oberland — Jungfrau region
Walking in the Engadine — Switzerland
Walking in Ticino
Walking in Zermatt and Saas-Fee

GERMANY

Hiking and Cycling in the Black Forest
The Danube Cycleway Vol 1
The Rhine Cycle Route
The Westweg
Walking in the Bavarian Alps

POLAND, SLOVAKIA, ROMANIA, HUNGARY AND BULGARIA

The Danube Cycleway Vol 2
The High Tatras
The Mountains of Romania

SCANDINAVIA, ICELAND AND GREENLAND

Hiking in Norway —
North
South
Trekking the Kungsleden
Trekking in Greenland — The Arctic Circle Trail
Walking and Trekking in Iceland

SLOVENIA, CROATIA, SERBIA, MONTENEGRO AND ALBANIA

Hiking Slovenia's Juliana Trail
Mountain Biking in Slovenia
The Islands of Croatia
The Julian Alps of Slovenia
The Mountains of Montenegro
The Peaks of the Balkans Trail
The Peaks of the Balkans Trail
The Slovene Mountain Trail
Walking in Slovenia: The Karavanke
Walks and Treks in Croatia

ITALY

Alta Via
1 — Trekking in the Dolomites
2 — Trekking in the Dolomites
Day Walks in the Dolomites
Italy's Grande Traversata delle Alpi
Italy's Sibillini National Park
Ski Touring and Snowshoeing in the Dolomites
The Way of St Francis: Via di Francesco
Trekking Gran Paradiso: Alta Via 2
Trekking in the Apennines
Trekking the Giants' Trail: Alta Via 1 through the Italian Pennine Alps
Via Ferratas of the Italian Dolomites:
Vol 1
Vol 2
Walking in Abruzzo
Walking in Italy's Cinque Terre
Walking in Italy's Stelvio National Park
Walking in Sicily
Walking in the Aosta Valley
Walking in the Dolomites
Walking in Tuscany
Walking in Umbria
Walking Lake Como and Maggiore
Walking Lake Garda and Iseo
Walking on the Amalfi Coast
Walking the Via Francigena Pilgrim Route
Part 1
Part 2
Part 3
Part 4
Walks and Treks in the Maritime Alps

IRELAND

The Wild Atlantic Way and Western Ireland
Walking the Kerry Way
Walking the Wicklow Way

EUROPEAN CYCLING

Cycling the Route des Grandes Alpes
Cycling the Ruta Via de la Plata
The Elbe Cycle Route
The River Loire Cycle Route
The River Rhone Cycle Route

INTERNATIONAL CHALLENGES, COLLECTIONS AND ACTIVITIES

Europe's High Points
Pocket First Aid and Wilderness Medicine

AUSTRIA

Innsbruck Mountain Adventures
Trekking Austria's Adlerweg
Trekking in Austria's Hohe Tauern
Trekking in Austria's Stubai Alps
Trekking in Austria's Zillertal Alps
Walking in Austria
Walking in the Salzkammergut: the Austrian Lake District

MEDITERRANEAN

The High Mountains of Crete
Trekking in Greece
Walking and Trekking in Zagori
Walking and Trekking on Corfu
Walking on the Greek Islands — the Cyclades
Walking in Cyprus
Walking on Malta

HIMALAYA

8000 metres
Everest: A Trekker's Guide
Trekking in the Karakoram

NORTH AMERICA

Hiking and Cycling the California Missions Trail
Hiking the Pacific Crest Trail
The John Muir Trail

SOUTH AMERICA

Aconcagua and the Southern Andes
Hiking and Biking Peru's Inca Trails
Trekking in Torres del Paine

AFRICA

Climbing Toubkal
Kilimanjaro
Walking in the Drakensberg
Walks and Scrambles in the Moroccan Anti-Atlas

NEW ZEALANDAND AND AUSTRALIA

Hiking the Overland Track

CHINA, JAPAN AND ASIA

Annapurna
Hiking and Trekking in the Japan Alps and Mount Fuji
Hiking in Hong Kong
Japan's Kumano Kodo Pilgrimage
Japan's Kumano Kodo Pilgrimage
Trekking in Bhutan
Trekking in Ladakh
Trekking in Tajikistan
Trekking in the Himalaya

TECHNIQUES

Fastpacking
The Mountain Hut Book

MINI GUIDES

Alpine Flowers
Navigation

MOUNTAIN LITERATURE

A Walk in the Clouds
Abode of the Gods
Fifty Years of Adventure
The Pennine Way — the Path, the People, the Journey
Unjustifiable Risk?